C000181112

DOMESDAY BOOK

Northamptonshire

History from the Sources

DOMESDAY BOOK

A Survey of the Counties of England

LIBER DE WINTONIA

Compiled by direction of

KING WILLIAM I

Winchester
1086

DOMESDAY BOOK

general editor

JOHN MORRIS

21

Northamptonshire

edited by

Frank and Caroline Thorn

from a draft translation prepared by

Margaret Jones, Philip Morgan and Judith Plaister

PHILLIMORE
Chichester
1979

1979
Published by
PHILLIMORE & CO. LTD.,
London and Chichester
Head Office: Shopwyke Hall,
Chichester, Sussex, England

ISBN 0 85033 163 3 (case)
ISBN 0 85033 164 1 (limp)

Printed in Great Britain by
Titus Wilson & Son Ltd.,
Kendal

NORTHAMPTONSHIRE

Introduction

The Domesday Survey of Northamptonshire

Notes on Text and Translation

Index of Persons

Index of Places

Maps and Map Keys

Systems of Reference

Technical Terms

History from the Sources
General Editor: John Morris

The series aims to publish history written directly from the sources for all interested readers, both specialists and others. The first priority is to publish important texts which should be widely available, but are not.

DOMESDAY BOOK

The contents, with the folio on which each county begins, are:

Domesday Book is termed *Liber de Wintonia* (The Book of Winchester) in column 332c

INTRODUCTION

The Domesday Survey

In 1066 Duke William of Normandy conquered England. He was crowned King, and most of the lands of the English nobility were soon granted to his followers. Domesday Book was compiled 20 years later. The Saxon Chronicle records that in 1085

> at Gloucester at midwinter ... the King had deep speech with his counsellors ... and sent men all over England to each shire ... to find out ... what or how much each landholder held ... in land and livestock, and what it was worth ... The returns were brought to him.[1]

William was thorough. One of his Counsellors reports that he also sent a second set of Commissioners 'to shires they did not know, where they were themselves unknown, to check their predecessors' survey, and report culprits to the King.'[2]

The information was collected at Winchester, corrected, abridged, chiefly by omission of livestock and the 1066 population, and fair-copied by one writer into a single volume. Norfolk, Suffolk and Essex were copied, by several writers, into a second volume, unabridged, which states that 'the Survey was made in 1086'. The surveys of Durham and Northumberland, and of several towns, including London, were not transcribed, and most of Cumberland and Westmorland, not yet in England, was not surveyed. The whole undertaking was completed at speed, in less than 12 months, though the fair-copying of the main volume may have taken a little longer. Both volumes are now preserved at the Public Record Office. Some versions of regional returns also survive. One of them, from Ely Abbey,[3] copies out the Commissioners' brief. They were to ask

> The name of the place. Who held it, before 1066, and now?
> How many *hides*?[4] How many ploughs, both those in lordship and the men's?
> How many villagers, cottagers and slaves, how many free men and Freemen?[5]
> How much woodland, meadow and pasture? How many mills and fishponds?
> How much has been added or taken away? What the total value was and is?
> How much each free man or Freeman had or has? All threefold, before 1066, when King William gave it, and now; and if more can be had than at present?

The Ely volume also describes the procedure. The Commissioners took evidence on oath 'from the Sheriff; from all the barons and their Frenchmen; and from the whole Hundred, the priests, the reeves and six villagers from each village'. It also names four Frenchmen and four Englishmen from each Hundred, who were sworn to verify the detail.

The King wanted to know what he had, and who held it. The Commissioners therefore listed lands in dispute, for Domesday Book was not only a tax-assessment. To the King's grandson, Bishop Henry of Winchester, its purpose was that every 'man should know his right and not usurp another's'; and because it was the final authoritative register of rightful possession 'the natives called it Domesday Book, by analogy

[1] Before he left England for the last time, late in 1086. [2] Robert Losinga, Bishop of Hereford 1079-1095 (see *E.H.R.* 22, 1907, 74). [3] *Inquisitio Eliensis,* first paragraph. [4] A land unit, reckoned as 120 acres. [5] *Quot Sochemani.*

from the Day of Judgement'; that was why it was carefully arranged by Counties, and by landholders within Counties, 'numbered consecutively ... for easy reference'.[6]

Domesday Book describes Old English society under new management, in minute statistical detail. Foreign lords had taken over, but little else had yet changed. The chief landholders and those who held from them are named, and the rest of the population was counted. Most of them lived in villages, whose houses might be clustered together, or dispersed among their fields. Villages were grouped in administrative districts called Hundreds, which formed regions within Shires, or Counties, which survive today with minor boundary changes; the recent deformation of some ancient county identities is here disregarded, as are various short-lived modern changes. The local assemblies, though overshadowed by lords great and small, gave men a voice, which the Commissioners heeded. Very many holdings were described by the Norman term *manerium* (manor), greatly varied in size and structure, from tiny farmsteads to vast holdings; and many lords exercised their own jurisdiction and other rights, termed *soca*, whose meaning still eludes exact definition.

The Survey was unmatched in Europe for many centuries, the product of a sophisticated and experienced English administration, fully exploited by the Conqueror's commanding energy. But its unique assemblage of facts and figures has been hard to study, because the text has not been easily available, and abounds in technicalities. Investigation has therefore been chiefly confined to specialists; many questions cannot be tackled adequately without a cheap text and uniform translation available to a wider range of students, including local historians.

Previous Editions

The text has been printed once, in 1783, in an edition by Abraham Farley, probably of 1250 copies, at Government expense, said to have been £38,000; its preparation took 16 years. It was set in a specially designed type, here reproduced photographically, which was destroyed by fire in 1808. In 1811 and 1816 the Records Commissioners added an introduction, indices, and associated texts, edited by Sir Henry Ellis; and in 1861-1863 the Ordnance Survey issued zincograph facsimiles of the whole. Texts of individual counties have appeared since 1673, separate translations in the Victoria County Histories and elsewhere.

This Edition

Farley's text is used, because of its excellence, and because any worthy alternative would prove astronomically expensive. His text has been checked against the facsimile, and discrepancies observed have been verified against the manuscript, by the kindness of Miss Daphne Gifford of the Public Record Office. Farley's few errors are indicated in the notes.

6 *Dialogus de Scaccario* 1,16.

The editor is responsible for the translation and lay-out. It aims at what the compiler would have written if his language had been modern English; though no translation can be exact, for even a simple word like 'free' nowadays means freedom from different restrictions. Bishop Henry emphasized that his grandfather preferred 'ordinary words'; the nearest ordinary modern English is therefore chosen whenever possible. Words that are now obsolete, or have changed their meaning, are avoided, but measurements have to be transliterated, since their extent is often unknown or arguable, and varied regionally. The terse inventory form of the original has been retained, as have the ambiguities of the Latin.

Modern English commands two main devices unknown to 11th century Latin, standardised punctuation and paragraphs; in the Latin, *ibi* ('there are') often does duty for a modern full stop, *et* ('and') for a comma or semi-colon. The entries normally answer the Commissioners' questions, arranged in five main groups, (i) the place and its holder, its hides, ploughs and lordship; (ii) people; (iii) resources; (iv) value; and (v) additional notes. The groups are usually given as separate paragraphs.

King William numbered chapters 'for easy reference', and sections within chapters are commonly marked, usually by initial capitals, often edged in red. They are here numbered. Maps, indices and an explanation of technical terms are also given. Later, it is hoped to publish analytical and explanatory volumes, and associated texts.

The editor is deeply indebted to the advice of many scholars, too numerous to name, and especially to the Public Record Office, and to the publisher's patience. The draft translations are the work of a team; they have been co-ordinated and corrected by the editor, and each has been checked by several people. It is therefore hoped that mistakes may be fewer than in versions published by single fallible individuals. But it would be Utopian to hope that the translation is altogether free from error; the editor would like to be informed of mistakes observed.

The maps are the work of Jim Hardy and Frank Thorn.

The preparation of this volume has been greatly assisted by a generous grant from the Leverhulme Trust Fund.

This support, originally given to the late Dr. J. R. Morris, has been kindly extended to his successors. At the time of Dr. Morris's death in June 1977, he had completed volumes 2, 3, 11, 12, 19, 23, 24. He had more or less finished the preparation of volumes 13, 14, 20, 28. These and subsequent volumes in the series were brought out under the supervision of John Dodgson and Alison Hawkins, who have endeavoured to follow, as far as possible, the editorial principles established by John Morris.

Conventions

*	refers to a note to the Latin text		
[ ]	enclose words omitted in the MS.	( )	enclose editorial explanations.

NORTHANTSCIRE.

219 a

TEMPORE REGIS EDWARDI fuer̃ in *NORTHANTONE* in dn̄io regis LX. burgenſes. hn̄tes totid̄ manſiones. Ex his ſunt m̊. XIIII. uaſtæ. Reſiduæ ſunt. XL.VII. præter hos ſunt m̊ in nouo burgo. XL. burgenſes in dn̄io regis Witti.

In ipſo burgo hẽ Ep̄s conſtantienſis. XXIII. domos. de. XXIX. ſolid̄. 7 IIII. denar̃.

Ab̄b de S̄ Edmundo. I. domū de. XVI. denar̃. ⁊ uaſtæ.

Ab̄b de Burg. XV. dom9 de. XIIII. ſol 7 VIII. den̄. Duæ sẽ

Ab̄b de Rameſÿg. I. domū de. XVI. denar̃.

Ab̄b de Couentreu. IIII. dom9 de. XII. denar̃. Tres sẽ uaſtæ.

Ab̄b de Eueſham. I. domū uaſtā.

Ab̄b de Salebi. II. dom9. de XXXII. denar̃.

Comes Moriton. XXXVII. de. XLV. ſol 7 VIII. den̄. Duæ sẽ uaſtæ. De. IX. domibʒ harū hẽ rex ſochā.

Comes Hugo. I. domū de. IIII. denar̃.

Comitiſſa Judita. XVI. domos. de XII. ſol. Vna. ẽ uaſta.

Rob̄t9 de Todeni. IIII. dom9 de. IIII. ſol. Vna. ẽ uaſta.

Henric9 de fereires. VIII. dom9 de. IX. ſol 7 IIII. den̄ ⁊ ſocā.

Anſger9 capellan9 regis. I. domū de quá rex debet hab̄e

Witts peurel. XXXII. dom9. de. XXVIII. ſolid̄ 7 VIII. den̄.

Tres ex his ſunt uaſtæ. ⁊ redd̄. XVI. denar̃.

Witts fili9 boſelini. II. de feudo ep̄i baioc̄ 7 comitiſſe Judit

Witts inganie. I. dom̄ de Rob̄to de boci. 7 nil reddit.

B In NORTHAMPTON 219 a

1 there were 60 burgesses in the King's lordship before 1066, who had as many residences. Now 14 of them are derelict; 47 are left. Besides these, there are now 40 burgesses in the new Borough, in King William's lordship.

2 In this Borough the Bishop of Coutances has 23 houses at 29s 4d.

3 The Abbot of St. Edmund's, 1 house at 16d.

4 The Abbot of Peterborough, 15 houses at 14s 8d. Two are derelict.

5 The Abbot of Ramsey, 1 house at 16d.

6 The Abbot of Coventry, 4 houses at 12d. Three are derelict.

7 The Abbot of Evesham, 1 house, derelict.

8 The Abbot of Selby, 2 houses at 32d.

9 The Count of Mortain, 37 (houses) at 45s 8d. Two are derelict. The King has the jurisdiction of 9 of these houses.

10 Earl Hugh, 1 house at 4d.

11 Countess Judith, 16 houses at 12s. One is derelict.

12 Robert of Tosny, 4 houses at 4s. One is derelict.

13 Henry of Ferrers, 8 houses at 9s 4d.

14 Ansger the King's Chaplain, 1 house of which the King ought to have the jurisdiction.

15 William Peverel, 32 houses at 28s 8d. Three of them are derelict.

16 William son of Boselin, 2 (houses) from the Holding of the Bishop of Bayeux and of Countess Judith. They pay 16d.

17 William the Artificer, 1 house from Robert of Bucy. It pays nothing.

Wido de Rainbudcurt . IIII . dom̃ de . LXIIII . denar̃.
Walter̃ flandrensis . X . dom̃ de . VIII . sol̃ . Vna . ē uasta
Winemar̃ . XII . dom̃ de . III . sol̃ . Ex his . IIII . sunt uastæ.
Ricard̃ inganie . IIII . dom̃ de . IIII . solid̃.
Rob̃t de Aluers . I . domū de . XII . den̄.
Roger̃ de boscnorman . I . dom̄ de . XVI . den̄.
Goisfrid̃ de Wirce . IIII . dom̃ de . IIII . sol̃.
Goisfrid̃ alselin 7 Rad̃ nepos ej̃ . II . dom̃ de . II . sol̃.
Gilo fr̃ Ansculsi . III . dom̃ de . XXXII . denar̃.
Gunfrid̃ de Cioches . VIII . dom̃ de . VIII . sol̃ . Tres sī uastæ.
Sigar de Cioches . I . dom̄ de XVI . den̄.
Suain filĩ Azur XXI . dom̄ de . X . sol̃ . p̄tin̄ ad Stoches.
Ansfrid̃ de ualbadon . II . dom̃ de . II . sol̃ . de feudo ep̄i baioc̃.
Balduin̄ dimid̃ mansionē uastā . Lefstan̄ . I . dom̄ de . II . den̄.
Osb̄n gifard . I . dom̄ de . IIII . den̄ . Goduin̄ . I . domū de . XII . den̄.
Durand̃ p̄posit̃ . I . dom̄ de XVI . den̄ de feudo Rob̄ti Todeni.
Dodin . II . dom̃ de . XX . den̄ . Vna . ē de Judit . alta de Winemaro.
Hugo de Widuile . II . dom̃ de XXXII . denar̃.

NORTHANTONE SCIRE redd̃ firmā triū noctiū . XXX . lib̃ ad pondus . Ad canes . XL . II . lib̃ . albas de . XX . in Ora . De dono reginæ . 7 de feno : X . lib̃ 7 V . oras . De accipitre . X . lib̃ . De sūmario : XX . sol̃ . De elemosina : XX . sol̃ . De eq̃ uenator̃ . XX . sol̃ . De Maner̃ Eddid reginæ : XL . lib̃ . De Cliue : X . lib̃.

Burgenses de Hantone redd̃t uicecomiti p̄ ann̄ . XXX . lib̃ 7 X . solid̃ . Hoc p̄tin̄ ad firmā ipsius.

Judita comitissa h̄t . VII . lib̃ de exitib; ej̃d burgi.

18 Guy of Raimbeaucourt, 4 houses at 64d.

19 Walter the Fleming, 10 houses at 8s. One is derelict.

20 Winemar, 12 houses at 3s. Four of them are derelict.

21 Richard the Artificer, 4 houses at 4s.

22 Robert of Auvers, 1 house at 12d.

23 Roger of Bois-Normand, 1 house at 16d.

24 Geoffrey of La Guerche, 4 houses at 4s.

25 Geoffrey Alselin and Ralph his nephew, 2 houses at 2s.

26 Giles brother of Ansculf, 3 houses at 32d.

27 Gunfrid of Chocques, 8 houses at 8s. Three are derelict.

28 Sigar of Chocques, 1 house at 16d.

29 Swein son of Azor, 21 houses at 10s. They belong to Stoke (Bruerne).

30 Ansfrid of Vaubadon, 2 houses at 2s from the Bishop of Bayeux' Holding.

31 Baldwin, ½ residence, derelict. Leofstan, 1 house at 4d.

32 Osbern Giffard, 1 house at 4d. Godwin the priest, 1 house at 12d.

33 Durand the reeve, 1 house at 16d from Robert of Tosny's Holding.

34 Dodin, 2 houses at 20d. One is from Countess Judith, the other from Winemar.

35 Hugh of Gouville, 2 houses at 32d.

36 Northamptonshire pays three nights' revenue, £30 by weight; for dogs, 42 white pounds, at 20 (pence) to the *ora;* for a gift to the Queen and for hay, £10 and 5 *oras;* for a hawk, £10; for a packhorse, 20s; for alms, 20s; for a hunting horse, 20s; for Queen Edith's manor, £40; for (King's) Cliffe, £10.

37 The burgesses of Northampton pay the Sheriff £30 10s a year. This belongs to his revenue.

38 Countess Judith has £7 from the income of this Borough.

HIC ANNOTANT̃ TENENTES T̃RAS IN NORTHANT̃SCIRE.

.I. REX WILLELMVS.
.II. Ep̃s Baiocensis.
.III. Ep̃s Dunelmensis.
.IIII. Ep̃s Constantiensis.
.V. Ep̃s Lincoliensis.
.VI. Abbatia de Burg.
.VII. Abbatia de Westmonast̃.
.VIII. Abbatia de S̃ Edmundo.
.IX. Abbatia de Ramesÿ.
.X. Abbatia de Tornÿg.
.XI. Abbatia de Cruiland.
.XII Abbatia de Couentreu.
.XIII Abbatia de Euesham.
.XIIII Abbatia de Grestain.
.XV. Æccl̃a S̃ Remigii rem̃sis.
.XVI. Ansgerus capellanus.
.XVII Leuuin pb̃r 7 alii clerici.
.XVIII. Comes Moritoniensis.
.XIX Comes de Mellent.
.XX. Comes Alanus.
.XXI. Comes Albericus.
.XXII Comes Hugo.
.XXIII Hugo de Grentemaisnil.
.XXIIII. Hugo de Juri.
.XXV. Henricus de ferieres.
.XXVI Robertus de Todeni.
.XXVII Rob̃tus de Statford.
.XXVIII. Rob̃tus de Oilgi.
.XXIX Rob̃tus de Veci.
.XXX. Rob̃tus de Buci.
.XXXI. Radulfus Pagenel.
.XXXII Radulfus de Limesi.
.XXXIII. Rob̃tus albus.
.XXXIIII. Witts de Cahainges.
.XXXV. Witts Peurel.
.XXXVI. Witts filius Ansculfi.
.XXXVII Witts Loueth.
.XXXVIII Walterius de Aincurth.
.XXXIX Walterius flandrensis.
.XL. Winemarus.
.XLI. Wido de Renbodcurth.
.XLII. Eudo filius Huberti.
.XLIII. Ghilo fr̃ Ansculfi.
.XLIIII Goisfridus Alselin.
.XLV. Goisfridus de Manneuile.
.XLVI. Gislebertus de Gand.
.XLVII Goisfridus de Wirce.
.XLVIII Gunfridus de Cioches.
.XLIX. Sigar de Cioches.
.L. Suain.
.LI. Siboldus.
.LII. Ogerius brito
.LIII. Drogo de Beurere.
.LIIII Maino brito.
.LV. Eustachius de Huntedune.
.LVI. Judita comitissa.
.LVII Gislebertus coqus.
.LVIII David.
.LIX. Ricardus.
.LX. Witts 7 alii taini.

LIST OF LANDHOLDERS IN NORTHAMPTONSHIRE

1 King William
2 The Bishop of Bayeux
3 The Bishop of Durham
4 The Bishop of Coutances
5 The Bishop of Lincoln
6 Peterborough Abbey
7 Westminster Abbey
8 St. Edmund's Abbey
9 Ramsey Abbey
10 Thorney Abbey
11 Crowland Abbey
12 Coventry Abbey
13 Evesham Abbey
14 Grestain Abbey
15 St. Remy's Church, Rheims [16]
16 Ansger the Chaplain [15]
17 Leofwin the priest
and other clergy
18 The Count of Mortain
19 The Count of Meulan
20 Count Alan
21 Earl Aubrey
22 Earl Hugh
23 Hugh of Grandmesnil
24 Hugh of Ivry
25 Henry of Ferrers
26 Robert of Tosny
27 Robert of Stafford
28 Robert d'Oilly
29 Robert of Vessey
30 Robert of Bucy
31 Ralph Pagnell
32 Ralph of Limesy
33 Robert Blunt
34 William of Keynes
35 William Peverel
36 William son of Ansculf
37 William Lovett
38 Walter of Aincourt
39 Walter the Fleming
40 Winemar
41 Guy of Raimbeaucourt
42 Eudo son of Hubert
43 Giles brother of Ansculf
44 Geoffrey Alselin
45 Geoffrey de Mandeville
46 Gilbert of Ghent
47 Geoffrey of La Guerche
48 Gunfrid of Chocques
49 Sigar of Chocques
50 Swein
51 Sibold
52 Oger the Breton
53 Drogo of Beuvrière
54 Mainou the Breton
55 Eustace of Huntingdon
56 Countess Judith
57 Gilbert Cook
58 David
59 Richard
60 William and other thanes

REX ten CHETENE. Ibi sunt. VII. hidæ. Tra. ē XIII. car
In dnio sunt. II. 7 III. serui. 7 XII. sochemans 7 XXIIII. uill 7 V.
bord cū pbro hntes. XI. car. Ibi molin de. VI. sol 7 VIII. den.
7 XL. ac pti. Siluæ uilis. XVI. ac.
Huic m ptin TICHESOVRE. Ibi sunt. II. hidæ. Tra. ē. VIII. car.
Ibi. XVI. sochm cū. IIII. bord hnt. VI. car. Ibi molin de. V. sol.
7 VIII. ac pti. 7 III. ac spineti.
Tot T.R.E. ualb. C. sol. Modo. X. lib.
Rex ten BERCHEDONE. Ibi sunt. IIII. hidæ una v min. Tra. ē. X.
car. Ibi sunt. IX. uilli 7 X. sochi cū. III. bord hntes. VI. car 7 dim.
Ibi. XVI. ac pti. 7 VI. ac spineti. Huic m ptin h mēbra.
In SEIETON. I. hida 7 dimid 7 I. bouata træ. Tra. ē. VI. car 7 II. ac pti.
In TORP. una hida 7 una v træ. Tra. ē. IIII. car. 7 III. ac pti.
In MORCOTE. IIII. hidæ. Tra. ē VIII. car. 7 VI. ac pti.
In BITLESBROCH 7 GLADESTONE I. hida 7 dim. Tra. ē. IIII. car. 7 VIII. ac pti.
In LVFENHAM. IIII. hidæ. Tra. ē. X. car. 7 XVI. ac pti.
In his tris sunt. XV. sochi 7 XXXIII. uilli 7 XXIII. bord cū pbro
hntes. XIX. car. In Seietone. ē molin de XXXVI. den. Silua
★ una qz lg 7 una lat. Spinetū. 7 VI. qz lg. 7 II. qz lat.
Tot T.R.E. ualb. III. lib. Modo. VII. lib.
Rex ten LVFENHĀ 7 SCVLETORP. Ibi sunt. VII. hidæ 7 una v træ
Trā. ē. XIIII. car. Ibi sunt. XII. sochi 7 XVI. bord cū pbro
hntes. XII. car. Ibi. II. molini de XL. den. 7 X. ac pti.
T.R.E. ualb. XXX. sol. Modo. LX. solid. Hoēs opant opa regis
quæ ppositus jusserit. ⸋ de rege.
Has tras tenuit regina Eddid. Modo ten Hugo de porth ad firmā

[1] LAND OF THE KING

In WITCHLEY Wapentake

1 The King holds KETTON. 7 hides. Land for 13 ploughs.
In lordship 2; 3 slaves;
12 Freemen, 24 villagers and 5 smallholders with a priest who have 11 ploughs.
A mill at 6s 8d; meadow, 40 acres; poor woodland, 16 acres.

TIXOVER belongs to this manor. 2 hides. Land for 8 ploughs.
16 Freemen with 4 smallholders have 6 ploughs.
A mill at 5s; meadow, 8 acres; spinney, 3 acres.
Value of the whole before 1066, 100s; now £10.

2a The King holds BARROWDEN. 4 hides less 1 virgate.
Land for 10 ploughs.
9 villagers and 10 Freemen with 3 smallholders who have 6½ ploughs.
Meadow, 16 acres; spinney, 6 acres.
To this manor belong these members:-

b In SEATON 1½ hides and 1 bovate of land. Land for 6 ploughs.
Meadow, 4 acres.

c In THORPE (by Water) 1 hide and 1 virgate of land. Land for 4 ploughs.
Meadow, 3 acres.

d In MORCOTT 4 hides. Land for 8 ploughs. Meadow, 6 acres.

e In BISBROOKE and GLASTON 1½ hides. Land for 4 ploughs.
Meadow, 8 acres.

f In LUFFENHAM 4 hides. Land for 10 ploughs. Meadow, 16 acres.

g In these lands are 15 Freemen, 33 villagers and 23 smallholders with a priest who have 19 ploughs.
In SEATON a mill at 36d; woodland 1 furlong long and 1 wide; spinney 6 furlongs long and 2 furlongs wide.
Value of the whole before 1066 £3; now £7.

3 The King holds LUFFENHAM and 'SCULTHORP'. 7 hides and 1 virgate of land. Land for 14 ploughs.
12 Freemen and 16 smallholders with a priest who have 12 ploughs.
2 mills at 40d; meadow, 10 acres.
Value before 1066, 30s; now 60s.
The men perform the King's works as the reeve orders.
Queen Edith held these lands. Now Hugh of Port holds them from the King at a revenue.

Rex teñ *CASTRETONE*. Morcar com tenuit. Ibi sunt. III. hidæ 7 dim. Tra. ē. IX. car. In dñio. ē una. 7 XXIIII. uitti 7 II. sochi 7 II. bord cū pbro 7 II. seruis hnt. VII. car. Ibi molin de. XVI. solid. 7 XVI. ac pti. Spinetū. III. q̃z lḡ. 7 II. q̃z lat. ℣ de rege. Valuit. VI. lib. Modo. X. lib. Hugo. f. baldric teñ ad firmā

Rex ht in dñio de Portland. II. carucatas. 7 II. partes tciæ carucatæ. 7 XII. acs pti. Ad æcclam S Petri jacet. I. car træ. 7 ad æcclam ōmiū scoz dimid carucata. Portland cū pto T.R.E. reddeb XL. VIII. sol. 7 X. solid p feltris sōmarioz regis. Sup hæc debet rex habe. IX. lib 7 XII. sol. p aliis exitib burgi.

Rex teñ *NORTONE*. Rex. E. tenuit. Ibi sunt. VII. hidæ 7 una v træ. cū. II. mēbris Blachesleuue 7 Atenestone. Tra. ē In dñio sunt. III. car. 7 III. serui 7 II. ancillæ. 7 XIX. uitti 7 XV. sochi 7 V. bord hntes. XXI. car. Ibi molini. II. de. XV. sol. Silua. IIII. leuu lḡ. 7 III. leu lat. Cū onerat uat. LX. sol. 7 mel. IIII. sol. Sochi redd. XXX. sol. Valuit. XII. lib. Modo. XX. lib. Fabri reddeb. VII. lib. T.R.E.

Rex ten *TOVECESTRE*. Ibi sunt. VII. hidæ 7 dimid. Tra. ē. XXII. car. In dñio sunt. II. car. 7 XV. uitti cū. X. car. Ibi molin de. XIII. sol. 7 IIII. den. 7 XII. ac pti. Silua II. leuu lḡ. 7 una lat. Fabri reddeb. C. sol. m nichil. Ibi un sochs redd. V. sol. hns dimid hid 7 V. partē dim hidæ. T.R.E. ualb. XII. lib. Modo. XXV. lib.

Rex teñ *SVDTONE*. Ibi sunt. III. hidæ. Tra. ē. VI. car. In dñio sunt. II. cū. I. seruo. 7 VII. uitti 7 X. bord cū. II. car. Ibi molin de. X. sol 7 VIII. den. De ptis. XX. sol. De foro: XX. sol. In alia tra ejd ϖ. sunt. IIII. uitti cū. II. car. Huic ϖ ptin *WITEFELLE*: Ibi sunt. II. hidæ 7 inland. II. car. 7 hōibz tra. V. car. In dñio sunt. II. cū. I. seruo. 7 VIII. uitti 7 III. bord cū. III. car 7 dim. Silua. I. leuu lḡ.

4 The King holds CASTERTON. Earl Morcar held it. 3½ hides. 219 c
Land for 9 ploughs. In lordship 1.
24 villagers, 2 Freemen and 2 smallholders with a priest and 2 slaves have 7 ploughs.
A mill at 16s; meadow, 16 acres; spinney, 3 furlongs long and 2 furlongs wide.
The value was £6; now £10.
Hugh son of Baldric holds it from the King at a revenue.

5 In the lordship of *PORTLAND* the King has 2 carucates and 2 parts of a third carucate and
meadow, 12 acres.
1 carucate of land lies with (the lands of) St. Peter's Church, and ½ carucate with All Saints' Church.
PORTLAND with its meadow paid 48s before 1066, and 10s for horse-cloths for the King's packhorses. In addition the King ought to have £9 12s from the other income of the Borough.

The King holds
[in FOXLEY Hundred]

6 (Greens) NORTON. King Edward held it. 7 hides and 1 virgate of land with 2 members, BLAKESLEY and ADSTONE. Land for......
In lordship 3 ploughs, 3 male and 2 female slaves;
19 villagers, 15 Freemen and 5 smallholders who have 21 ploughs.
2 mills at 15s; woodland 4 leagues long and 3 leagues wide; when stocked, value 60s, and honey 4s. The Freemen pay 30s.
The value was £12; now £20; the smiths paid £7 before 1066.

[in TOWCESTER Hundred]

7 TOWCESTER. 7½ hides. Land for 22 ploughs. In lordship 2 ploughs;
15 villagers with 10 ploughs.
A mill at 13s 4d; meadow, 12 acres; woodland 2 leagues long and 1 wide.
The smiths paid 100s; now nothing. 1 Freeman who has ½ hide and the fifth part of ½ hide pays 5s.
Value before 1066 £12; now £25.

[in SUTTON Hundred]

8 (Kings) SUTTON. 3 hides. Land for 6 ploughs. In lordship 2, with 1 slave;
7 villagers and 10 smallholders with 2 ploughs.
A mill at 10s 8d; from meadows 20s; from the market place 20s.
In another of this manor's lands are 4 villagers with 2 ploughs.
WHITFIELD belongs to this manor. 2 hides. *Inland* 2 ploughs; for the men, land for 5 ploughs. In lordship 2, with 1 slave;
8 villagers and 3 smallholders with 3½ ploughs.

7 VII . q̃rent lat.
Tot T.R.E. ualb . XIX . lib . Modo . XXXII . lib de . XX . in ora.
Rex ten FALELAV . Ibi . ẽ . I . hida *IN GRAVESENDE HD.*
7 dimid . 7 qnta pars hidæ . Inland . ẽ ad . IIII . car . Ibi sunt
II . car . 7 VI . bord hnt . IIII . car . In alia tra ext dniu . sunt
VI . uitti cu pposito hntes . IIII . car . De pto . II . sol exeunt.
T.R.E. ualb . XV . lib . Nc redd totid lib de . XX . in ora.
Huic m ptin soca de . I . hida . min . I . bouata . redd . II . sol.
Rex ten HARDINGESTORP. *IN COLTREWESTAN HD.*
Ibi sunt . V . hidæ . Inland . T . IIII . car . Ibi sunt . II . car.
7 IIII . uitti 7 X . bord cu . IIII . car . Ibi . II . molini de . L . sol.
De ptis 7 pasturis . LXVI . den.
T.R.E. ualb . XXX . lib . Modo . XII . lib.
Witts peurel 7 Gunfrid de Cioches hnt ibi . II . hid 7 LX . acs
pti . dono regis ut dicunt. *IN CORBEI HVND.*
Rex ten GRETONE . Ibi sunt . III . hidæ 7 III . v træ . Tra . ẽ
XIIII . car . In dnio sunt . II . 7 una ancilla . 7 XV . uitti 7 V.
bord cu pbro hnt . VI . car . Ibi molin de . III . sol . 7 XX . ac
pti . Silua . I . leuu lg . 7 dim leu lat.
Valuit 7 ual . XX . lib . Plurima desunt huic m quæ T.R.E.
appendeb ibi . ta in silua 7 ferrariis quam 7 aliis reditib.
Rex ten CORBEI . Ibi . ẽ una hida 7 dim . Tra . ẽ . IX . car.
In dnio . ẽ una . 7 VII . uitti cu pbro 7 III . bord hnt . IIII . car.
Silua XVIII . q̃rent lg . 7 IIII . q̃z lat.
T.R.E. 7 modo . ual . X . lib . Multa desunt huic m quæ T.R.E.
ibi adiaceb . in silua 7 ferrariis 7 aliis causis.
Rex ten BRICSTOC . Ibi sunt . III . hidæ 7 dim . Tra . ẽ . IX . car.

219 d
In dnio sunt . III . car . 7 VI . seru . 7 XVI . uitti cu pbro 7 IIII.
bord hnt . V . car . Ibi molin de . V . sol . 7 VII . ac pti . Silua
XV . q̃rent lg . 7 una leu lat.

Woodland 1 league long and 7 furlongs wide.
Value of the whole before 1066 £19; now £32 at 20 (pence) to the *ora*.

in GRAVESEND Hundred

9 FAWSLEY. 1½ hides and the fifth part of a hide. *Inland* for 4 ploughs. 2 ploughs there.
6 smallholders have 4 ploughs.
In another land outside the lordship are 6 villagers with a reeve who have 4 ploughs.
From the meadow come 2s.
Value before 1066 £15; now it pays as many pounds at 20 (pence) to the *ora*.
To this manor belongs the jurisdiction of 1 hide, less 1 bovate; it pays 4s.

in COLLINGTREE Hundred

10 HARDINGSTONE. 5 hides. Land for 4 ploughs besides the *inland*. 2 ploughs there.
4 villagers and 10 smallholders with 4 ploughs.
2 mills at 50s; from the meadows and pastures 66d.
Value before 1066 £30; now £12.
William Peverel and Gunfrid of Chocques have 2 hides and 60 acres of meadow as a gift of the King, as they state.

in CORBY Hundred

11 GRETTON. 3 hides and 3 virgates of land. Land for 14 ploughs. In lordship 2; 1 female slave.
15 villagers and 5 smallholders with a priest have 6 ploughs.
A mill at 3s; meadow, 20 acres; woodland 1 league long and ½ league wide.
The value was and is £20.
Very much is lacking from this manor which belonged to it before 1066, both in woodland and iron-workings and in other payments.

12 CORBY. 1½ hides. Land for 9 ploughs. In lordship 1.
7 villagers with a priest and 3 smallholders have 4 ploughs.
Woodland 18 furlongs long and 4 furlongs wide.
Value before 1066 and now £10.
Much is lacking from this manor which was attached to it before 1066 in woodland, iron-workings and other things.

13a BRIGSTOCK. 3½ hides. Land for 9 ploughs. In lordship 3 ploughs; 219 d
6 slaves.
16 villagers with a priest and 4 smallholders have 5 ploughs.
A mill at 5s; meadow, 7 acres; woodland 15 furlongs long and 1 league wide.

Huic m̄ append̄ h̄ mēbra. *SLEPE*. Ibi . I. hida 7 III. v̄ træ.
In *GEITENTONE* . I. hida. In *STANERE*. I. virḡ træ 7 dim̄.
Tra. ē. VIII. car̄. Ibi sunt. IIII. sochi 7 IX. uitti 7 VII. borđ
Int̄ om̄s hn̄t. VII. car̄. In *SLEPE*. sunt. IIII. ac̄ p̄ti.
Tot̄ m̄ cū append̄. T.R.E. ualb̄ xv. lib̄. Modo. xx. lib̄.
Rex ten̄ *DODINTONE*. Ibi. ē una hida. *IN WILEBROC HD̄*.
Tra. ē. VIII. car̄. In dn̄io. ē. una. 7 x. uitti cū p̄bro 7 II. borđ
hn̄t. III. car̄. Ibi. x. ac̄ p̄ti. Silua. I. leū lḡ. 7 VI. q̄rent̄ lat̄.
Ibi molin̄ de. IIII. sol̄. H̄ tra ptin̄ ad Gretone m̄ sup̄dictū.
T.R.E. ualb̄. x. lib̄. 7 modo similit̄. Multa desunt ei
ptinent̄ ad firmā in siluis 7 aliis causis.
Rex ten̄ *RODEWELLE*. 7 *OVERTONE*. *IN RODEWELLE HD̄*.
Ibi sunt. VIII. hidæ 7 II. part̄. I. hidæ. Tra. ē. XL. car̄.
In dn̄io sunt. IIII. car̄. 7 XIX. uitti 7 XLV. borđ hn̄t. x. car̄
7 dimiđ. Ibi. II. molini de. IX. sol̄ 7 IIII. den̄. 7 VIII. ac̄ p̄ti.
Huic m̄ ptin̄ h̄ mēbra.
LODINTONE. de. I. hida 7 t̄cia parte. I. hidæ.
CLENDONE dē dim̄ hida 7 t̄cia parte. I. hidæ.
DRACTONE. de. I. hida 7 dimiđ v̄ træ.
ARNINGVORDE. de dimiđ v̄ træ. *DEREBVRG* dimiđ v̄ træ
KEILMERSE. de. II. hiđ 7 t̄cia parte uni v̄. 7 dimiđ.
OXENDONE de. I. hida 7 una v̄ træ. *CLIPESTONE*. de. I. v̄
CRANESLEG de. II. hiđ una v̄ træ. *BVRTONE* de dim̄ hida.
Tra. ē. XVIIII car̄ int̄ tot̄. Ibi sunt. XLVII. sochi. hn̄tes. XVIII. car̄.
Hoc m̄ Rodeuuelle cū append̄. T.R.E. ualb̄. xxx. lib̄. Modo. L. lib̄.
Rex ten̄ *BRICLESWORDE*. Ibi sunt. IX. hidæ *IN MALESLEA HD̄*.
7 dimiđ. Tra. ē. XXXV. car̄. In dn̄io sunt. II. 7 XIIII. uitti cū
p̄bro 7 XV. borđ hn̄tes. XV. car̄. Ibi. II. molini de. XXX. III. sol̄

To this manor belong these members:-
b ISLIP. 1 hide and 3 virgates of land.
c In GEDDINGTON 1 hide.
d In STANION 1½ virgates of land. Land for 8 ploughs.
4 Freemen, 9 villagers and 7 smallholders; between them they have 7 ploughs.
e In ISLIP, meadow, 4 acres.
Value of the whole manor with its dependencies before 1066 £15; now £20.

in WILLYBROOK Hundred

14 DUDDINGTON. 1 hide. Land for 8 ploughs. In lordship 1.
10 villagers with a priest and 2 smallholders have 3 ploughs.
Meadow, 10 acres; woodland 1 league long and 6 furlongs wide. A mill at 4s.
This land belongs to the manor of Gretton, above.
Value before 1066 £10; now the same.
Much is lacking from it which belongs to the revenue, in woodlands and other things.

in ROTHWELL Hundred

15a ROTHWELL and ORTON. 8 hides and 2 parts of 1 hide. Land for 40 ploughs. In lordship 4 ploughs.
19 villagers and 45 smallholders have 10½ ploughs.
2 mills at 9s 4d; meadow, 8 acres.
To this manor belong these members:-
b LODDINGTON, 1 hide and the third part of a hide.
c GLENDON, ½ hide and the third part of 1 hide.
d DRAUGHTON, 1 hide and ½ virgate of land.
e ARTHINGWORTH, ½ virgate of land.
f DESBOROUGH, ½ virgate of land.
g KELMARSH, 2 hides and the third part of 1 virgate.
h OXENDON, 1 hide and 1 virgate of land.
i CLIPSTON, 1½ virgates.
j CRANSLEY, 2 hides, 1 virgate of land.
k BROUGHTON, ½ hide.
l Between them all, land for 19 ploughs.
47 Freemen who have 18 ploughs.
Value of this manor of Rothwell with its dependencies before 1066 £30; now £50.

in MAWSLEY Hundred

16 BRIXWORTH. 9½ hides. Land for 35 ploughs. In lordship 2;
14 villagers with a priest and 15 smallholders who have 15 ploughs.
2 mills at 33s 4d; meadow, 8 acres.

7 IIII. den. 7 VIII. ac pti. / in foresta regis.

Ad hoc m ptin una silua que reddeb p ann. c. sol. H est m

Huic m ptin *HOLECOTE*. Ibi sunt. II. hide. 7 II. virg træ 7 dim.

Tra. e. x. car. Ibi sunt. XI. sochi cu. IIII. car.

Totu T.R.E. reddeb. xxx. lib. Modo. XXXVI. lib.

Rex ten *FEXTONE*. Ibi sunt. II. hidæ. Tra. e. XII. car. In dnio

sunt. III. car. 7 VI. serui. 7 VI. uitti 7 IX. bord cu. III. car.

Ibi. XVI. ac pti.

Huic m ptin *WALDGRAVE*. 7 *WALDA*. Ibi. II. hidæ 7 III. virg

træ 7 dimid. Tra. e. VII. car. Ibi sunt. XIIII. sochi cu. VI. car.

Ibi. XII. ac pti.

Totu. T.R.E. reddeb. XV lib. Modo. XVI. lib.

Rex ten *TORP*. Ibi sunt. IIII. hidæ 7 III. virg træ Tra. e. xx.

car. In dnio sunt. II. car. 7 XVI. uitti 7 VIII. bord cu. III. car.

Ibi. III. molini de. XLIII. sol. 7 IIII. denar. 7 V. ac pti.

Huic m ptin *MULTONE*. Ibi. e. I. hida. 7 dimid. 7 I. bouata træ.

7 *WESTONE* de. I. hida. similit ibi ptin. Tra. e. V. car int tot.

Ibi sunt. X. sochi cu. III. car. 7 III. ac pti.

Tot T.R.E. reddeb. x lib. Modo tantd.

Rex ten *OPTONE*. Ibi sunt. II. hidæ. Tra. e. X. car. In dnio. e una.

7 X. uitti 7 X. bord hnt. V. car. Ibi molin de. XII. sol 7 VIII. den.

7 VI. ac pti.

Huic m ptin *ERLESTONE*. Ibi. e dimid hida. Tra. e. II. car.

Ibi sunt. II. sochi cu. I. car. Tot T.R.E. ualb. XV. lib. Modo tntd.

Rex ten *NASSINTONE*. Ibi sunt. VI. hidæ. Tra. e. XVI. car.

In dnio sunt. II. 7 XXIIII. uitti cu pbro 7 II. bord hnt. XIIII. car.

Ibi. II. molini de. XXX. sol 7 VIII. den. 7 XL. ac pti. Silua. I. leuu

lg. 7 dimid leuu lat.

T.R.E. reddeb. XXVI. lib 7 XIII. sol ad numer. Modo. XXX. lib.

To this manor belongs 1 woodland which paid 100s a year; it is now in the King's Forest.
HOLCOT belongs to this manor. 2 hides and 2½ virgates of land. Land for 10 ploughs.
11 Freemen with 4 ploughs.
The whole paid £30 before 1066; now £36.

17 FAXTON. 2 hides. Land for 12 ploughs. In lordship 3 ploughs; 6 slaves;
6 villagers and 9 smallholders with 3 ploughs.
Meadow, 16 acres.

WALGRAVE and OLD belong to this manor. 2 hides and 3½ virgates of land. Land for 7 ploughs.
14 Freemen with 6 ploughs.
Meadow, 12 acres.
The whole paid £15 before 1066; now £16.

18 KINGSTHORPE. 4 hides and 3 virgates of land. Land for 20 ploughs. In lordship 2 ploughs;
16 villagers and 8 smallholders with 3 ploughs.
3 mills at 43s 4d; meadow, 5 acres.

MOULTON belongs to this manor. 1½ hides and 1 bovate of land.
WESTON (Favell), 1 hide, similarly belongs there.
Land for 5 ploughs between them.
10 Freemen with 3 ploughs.
Meadow, 3 acres.
The whole paid £15 before 1066; now as much.

[in NOBOTTLE Hundred]

19 UPTON. 2 hides. Land for 10 ploughs. In lordship 1.
10 villagers and 10 smallholders have 5 ploughs.
A mill at 12s 8d; meadow, 6 acres.

HARLESTONE belongs to this manor. ½ hide there. Land for 2 ploughs.
2 Freemen with 1 plough.
Value of the whole before 1066 £15; now as much.

[in WILLYBROOK Hundred]

20 NASSINGTON. 6 hides. Land for 16 ploughs. In lordship 2.
24 villagers with a priest and 2 smallholders have 14 ploughs.
2 mills at 30s 8d; meadow, 40 acres; woodland 1 league long and ½ league wide.
It paid £26 13s at face value before 1066; now £30.

In *BEREFORD*. ē. I. hida. Osl͞ac hanc tenuit cū. II. sochis: de q̄bȝ ipse socam habeƀ. Tra. ē. II. car̄. Ibi sunt. IIII. uitti 7 III. borđ cū. II. car̄. 7 molin̄ de. XXXII. den.
Hanc trā rex. W. ͞cceſſit Goduino.

In *RICSDONE*. ē dimiđ v trae soca ptin ad Bereforde.
Ibi. ē. I. sochs hn̄s. II. boues. Vat. x. soliđ.

In *PATORP*. sunt. II. hidæ ptinent ad Naſſintone.
Tra. ē. XII. car. In dn̄io sunt. II. 7. XVI. uitti 7 IIII. borđ cū. x. car. Ibi molin̄ de. VI. sol. 7 VI. ac p̄ti. Silua. I. leuu lḡ. 7 tntđ lat. T.R.E. ualƀ. XIII. liƀ 7 VII. soliđ.

Rex ten *TANESOVRE*. Ibi sunt. VI. hidæ. Tra. ē. XVIII. car. In dn̄io sunt. II. car. 7 XV. uitti 7 IIII. borđ cū. XIIII. car̄.
Ibi molin̄ de. x. sol. 7 XII. ac p̄ti. Silua. I. leuu lḡ. 7 dim leu lat. T.R.E. reddeƀ. XX. liƀ ad numerū.

Rex ten *BERNEWELLE*. Ibi sunt. VI. hidæ 7 una v træ.
Tra. ē. VI. car. In dn̄io sunt. II. 7 XII. uitti 7 II. borđ cū. IIII. car. Ibi. XXIIII. ac p̄ti. T.R.E. reddƀ. XIII. liƀ 7 VI. sol. 7 VI. denar ad numer̄. Modo. XXX. liƀ cū *TANESOVRE*.

Rex ten *CLIVE*. Ibi. ē. I. hida. 7 II. virg 7 dim. Algar com tenuit. Tra. ē. XIIII. car. In dn̄io sunt. II. car. cū. I. seruo.
7 VII. uitti cū p̄bro 7 VI. borđ hn̄tes. V. car. Ibi molinū de. XII. denar. 7 IIII. ac p̄ti. Silua. I. leuu lḡ. 7 dim leu lat.
T.R.E. reddƀ. VII. liƀ. Modo. x. liƀ.

Rex ten *ROCHINGEHA*͞. Ibi. ē. I. hida. Tra. ē. III. car.
Ibi sunt. V. uitti 7 VI. borđ cū. III. car.
Hanc trā tenuit Boui cū saca 7 soca. T.R.E. Waſta erat qdo rex. W. juſſit ibi caſtellū fieri. Modo uat. XXVI. sol.

[?In ROTHWELL Hundred]

21 In BARFORD 1 hide. Oslac White held it with 2 Freemen from whom he himself had the jurisdiction. Land for 2 ploughs. 220 a

4 villagers and 3 smallholders with 2 ploughs.

A mill at 32d.

King William granted this land to Godwin.

22 In RUSHTON ½ virgate of land. The jurisdiction belongs to Barford.

1 Freeman who has 2 oxen.

Value 10s.

[In WILLYBROOK Hundred]

23 In APETHORPE 2 hides which belong to Nassington. Land for 12 ploughs. In lordship 2;

16 villagers and 4 smallholders with 10 ploughs.

A mill at 6s; meadow, 6 acres; woodland 1 league long and as wide.

Value before 1066 £13 7s.

The King holds

24 TANSOR. 6 hides. Land for 18 ploughs. In lordship 2 ploughs;

15 villagers and 4 smallholders with 14 ploughs.

A mill at 10s; meadow, 12 acres; woodland 1 league long and ½ league wide.

It paid £20 at face value before 1066.

25 BARNWELL. 6 hides and 1 virgate of land. Land for 6 ploughs. In lordship 2;

12 villagers and 2 smallholders with 4 ploughs.

Meadow, 24 acres.

It paid £13 6s 6d at face value before 1066; now £30 with Tansor.

26 (King's) CLIFFE. 1 hide and 2½ virgates. Earl Algar held it. Land for 14 ploughs. In lordship 2 ploughs, with 1 slave;

7 villagers with a priest and 6 smallholders who have 5 ploughs.

A mill at 12d; meadow, 4 acres; woodland 1 league long and ½ league wide.

It paid £7 before 1066; now £10.

[in STOKE Hundred]

27 ROCKINGHAM. 1 hide. Land for 3 ploughs.

5 villagers and 6 smallholders with 3 ploughs.

Bovi held this land with full jurisdiction before 1066.

It was waste when King William ordered a castle to be built there.

Value now 26s.

In *STOCHE* . ē . I . hida de soca *CORBI* Maner̃ regis . Tra . ē
II . car̃ . Ibi sunt cū . v . sochis . q̃ reddt . LXIIII . den̄ ad *CORBI*.
In *WILBERTESTONE* sunt . III . virg̃ træ . Tra . ē . II . car̃.
Ibi sunt . v . sochi cū . III . bord̄ hñtes . I . car̃ 7 dimid̄.
Valuit 7 ual̄ . IIII . solid̄.
Rex ten̄ *BASSONHĀ* . Ibi . ē . I . hida . Tra . ē . XII . car̃.
In dñio . ē una . cū . I . seruo . 7 VIII . uilli 7 VI . bord̄ cū uno
libero hoc̄ hñtes . v . car̃ . Ibi molin̄ de . XIII . sol̄ 7 IIII . den̄.
7 XXX . ac̄ p̃ti . Silua . I . leuu̇ lḡ . 7 tntd̄ lat̃.
Huic ᗰ ptin̄ *POCHESLEI* . Ibi . ē dim' hida . Tra . ē . I . car̃.
Ibi . ē un⁹ sochs hñs dimid̄ car̃ . 7 redd̄ . v . sol̄
Tot̄ T.R.E . reddeb̄ . VIII . lib̄ ad numer̄ . Modo . x . lib̄.
Rex ten̄ *WICLEI* . Algar com⁹ tenuit. *IN CORBI HVND*
Ibi sunt . II . hidæ 7 dimid̄ . Tra . ē . VI . car̃ . In dñio sunt . II . car̃
7 IIII . serui . 7 XII . uilli 7 VI . bord̄ cū . IIII . car̃ . Ibi molin̄
de . LXIIII . denar̃ . Valuit . III . lib̄ . Modo . VI . lib̄.
Rex ten̄ *TINGDENE* . Eddid regina tenuit. *IN NEVESLVND HD̄*.
rq̃ Ibi sunt . XX.VII . hidæ . cū append̄ . Tra . ē . LIIII . car̃.
hid̄ num̃ In dñio sunt . III . hidæ . 7 ibi . IIII . car̃ . 7 VII . serui . 7 XXX.
uilli 7 XV . bord̄ cū . XI . car̃ . 7 L . sochi cū . XXIIII . car̃.
Ibi . II . molini de . XVIII . solid̄ . 7 t̃ciū de XVI . solid̄.
Ibi . L . ac̄ p̃ti . Silua . I . leuu̇ lḡ . 7 dim̄ leu̇ lat̃.
T.R.E . reddeb̄ . XX . lib̄ ad numerū . Modo . XL . lib̄ ad
pon⁹d de . XX . in ora . Ipsi L . sochi reddt p̄ ann̄ de soca
VIII . lib̄ 7 x . denar̃ . Hu⁹j ᗰ tra sic jacet.
In Hechā Hund̄ : x . hid̄ 7 dim̄ . In Hocheslau Hund̄ :
. I . hid̄ 7 dim̄ . In Geritone Hd̄ : una hida . In Rodeuuel hd̄ :
III . partes . I . hidæ . In Ordinbaro hd̄ : IIII . hid̄ 7 una v̇ træ.
In Neueslund hd̄ : IX . hidæ 7 dimidia.

28 In STOKE (Albany) 1 hide of the jurisdiction of Corby, a manor of the King's. Land for 2 ploughs; they are there, with
5 Freemen who pay 64d at Corby.

29 In WILBARSTON 3 virgates of land. Land for 2 ploughs.
5 Freemen with 3 smallholders who have 1½ ploughs.
The value was and is 4s.

[In CLEYLEY Hundred]

30 The King holds PASSENHAM. 1 hide. Land for 12 ploughs.
In lordship 1, with 1 slave;
8 villagers and 6 smallholders with 1 free man who have 5 ploughs.
A mill at 13s 4d; meadow, 30 acres; woodland 1 league long and as wide.

PUXLEY belongs to this manor. ½ hide. Land for 1 plough.
1 Freeman who has ½ plough and pays 5s.
The whole paid £8 at face value before 1066; now £10.

In CORBY Hundred

31 The King holds WEEKLEY. Earl Algar held it. 2½ hides.
Land for 6 ploughs. In lordship 2; 4 slaves;
12 villagers and 6 smallholders with 4 ploughs.
A mill at 64d.
The value was £3; now £6.

In NAVISLAND Hundred

32 The King holds FINEDON. Queen Edith held it. 27 hides with
num' its dependencies. Land for 54 ploughs. In lordship 3 hides;
4 ploughs there; 7 slaves;
30 villagers and 15 smallholders with 11 ploughs;
50 Freemen with 24 ploughs.
2 mills at 18s and a third at 16s. Meadow, 50 acres; woodland 1 league long and ½ league wide.
It paid £20 at face value before 1066; now £40 by weight at 20 (pence) to the *ora*. The 50 Freemen pay £8 and 10d a year for the jurisdiction.

The land of this manor lies as follows:-
In HIGHAM Hundred 10½ hides.
In HUXLOE Hundred 1½ hides.
In GRETTON Hundred 1 hide.
In ROTHWELL Hundred 3 parts of 1 hide.
In ORLINGBURY Hundred 4 hides and 1 virgate of land.
In NAVISLAND Hundred 9½ hides.

.II. TERRA EPI BAIOCENSIS

Eps Baiocensis ten de rege 7 Witts Peurel de eo . dimid hid in *HALECOTE* . Tra . e . I . car . Ipsa . e in dnio cu . IIII . bord . Ibi molin de . VIII . den . 7 VI . ac pti . Silua . I . qrent lg . 7 dim qrent lat . Valuit . VIII . sol . Modo . X . sol . Almar tenuit cu saca 7 soca .

De feudo epi ten Witts . I . hid 7 dim v tre in *HOHTONE* . Tra . e . IIII . car . In dnio . e una 7 II . serui . 7 IX . uitti 7 VI . bord cu . III . car . Ibi molin de . VIII . den . 7 XX . ac pti . Silua . I . qrent lg . 7 dimid qz lat . Valuit . XX . sol . Modo . XL . solid . Vlf . f . Azor tenuit cu saca 7 soc . Judit comit calūniat .

De feudo epi Baioc ten Witts . III . v træ in *BRACHESFELD* . Tra . e . II . car . Has hnt ibi . V . uitti cu . II . bord . Ibi . V . ac pti . Valuit 7 ual . XX . sol . Nigel calūniat ad op eo mitisse Judit . Vlf . f . Azor tenuit T . R . E .

De feudo epi Baioc ten Witts . II . hid in *GRENTEVORDE* . Tra . e . V . car . In dnio . e una . 7 II . serui . 7 X . uitti 7 V . bord cu . III . car . Valuit . IIII . lib . Modo . III . lib . Saulf libe tenuit . T . R . E .

De feudo epi Baioc ten Witts una v træ in *BRANDESTONE* . Huj soca jacet in Faleuuesle . Tra . e . I . car . Ipsa ibi . e cu . II . uittis 7 III . bord . Valuit 7 ual . XX . solid . Sauuin tenuit T . R . E .

De feudo epi Baioc ten Witts una v træ 7 qnta parte uni v in *WALTONE* . Huj soca jacet in Sutone . Tra . e

2 LAND OF THE BISHOP OF BAYEUX 220 b

[In CLEYLEY Hundred]

1 The Bishop of Bayeux holds ½ hide in HULCOTE from the King, and William Peverel from him. Land for 1 plough; it is there, in lordship, with

4 smallholders.

A mill at 8d; meadow, 6 acres; woodland 1 furlong long and ½ furlong wide.

The value was 8s; now 10s.

Aelmer held it, with full jurisdiction.

[In WYMERSLEY Hundred]

2 From the Holding of the Bishop, William holds 1 hide and ½ virgate of land in HOUGHTON. Land for 4 ploughs.

In lordship 1; 2 slaves;

9 villagers and 6 smallholders with 3 ploughs.

A mill at 8d; meadow, 20 acres; woodland 1 furlong long and ½ furlong wide.

The value was 20s; now 40s.

Ulf son of Azor held it, with full jurisdiction.

Countess Judith claims it.

From the Holding of the Bishop of Bayeux William holds

3 in BRAFIELD (on the Green) 3 virgates of land. Land for 2 ploughs.

5 villagers with 2 smallholders have them there.

Meadow, 5 acres.

The value was and is 20s.

Nigel claims it for Countess Judith's use. Ulf son of Azor held it before 1066.

[in WARDEN Hundred]

4 in GREATWORTH 2 hides. Land for 5 ploughs. In lordship 1; 2 slaves;

10 villagers and 5 smallholders with 3 ploughs.

The value was £4; now £3.

Saewulf held it freely before 1066.

[in GRAVESEND Hundred]

5 in BRAUNSTON 1 virgate of land. Its jurisdiction lies in Fawsley. Land for 1 plough; it is there, with

2 villagers and 3 smallholders.

The value was and is 20s.

Saewin held it before 1066.

[in SUTTON Hundred]

6 in WALTON (Grounds) 1 virgate of land and the fifth part of 1 virgate. Its jurisdiction lies in (Kings) Sutton.

.I.car̃. Ipſa ibi.ē cū.I.ſeruo 7 II.uiłłs. Ibi molin̄ de IIII.ſolid. Valuit.x.ſol. Modo.xv.ſolid. Vlfric tenuit de Alnod cantuarienſi.

De feudo epi Baioc ten idē Wiłłs.IIII.hid 7 dimid. 7 q̄ntā partē dimid hidæ in *HERTEWELLE*. Tra.ē x.car̃. In dn̄io ſunt.II.7 v.ſerui.7 xI.uiłłi 7 Ix.bord cū pbro hn̄tes.IIII.car̃ 7 dimid. Ibi.xII.ac p̄ti.7 molin̄ de xvII.ſol 7 IIII.denar. Silua.vIII.q̄z lḡ.7 III.lat. Valuit.IIII.lib. Modo.LXX.ſolid. Edmar libe tenuit.

De feudo epi Baioc ten Wiłłs dim hid *IN CLAILEI HD.* q̄ntā partē dim hidæ min in *POCHESLAI*. Tra.ē.I.car. Ibi.ē un uiłłs cū.I.bord hn̄s dim car. Valet.IIII.ſol. Almar tenuit T.R.E. In RODE ten de epo Stefan.I.hid Vaſta.ē In manu regis.ē.

IN GRAVESENDE HD.

De feudo epi Baioc ten Wiłłs dim hid in *EVERDONE*. Huj træ ſoca jac in Feleſleuue. Tra.ē.I.car. Ipſa.ē ibi cū.II.uiłłis 7 II.bord.7 vI.ac p̄ti. Valuit.v.ſol. Modo.x.ſolid. Bern tenuit T.R.E. *IN SVTONE HD.*

De feudo epi Baioc ten Adā in *CERLINTONE*.III.v træ 7 q̄ntā partē.I.virge. Soca jac in Sutone. Tra.ē.II. car. In dn̄io.ē una cū.II.bord. Valuit 7 uat.x.ſol.

De feudo epi Baioc ten Wiłłs *IN NIWEBOTE HVND* II.hid.7 unā v træ 7 dim in *HEIFORDE*. Tra.ē.IIII.car. In dn̄io ſunt.II.car 7 II.ſerui.7 vII.uiłłi 7 II.bord cū.I.car. Ibi.x.ac p̄ti. Valuit.x.ſol. Modo.xx.ſol. Biſcop 7 Ailet libe tenuer.T.R.E.

Land for 1 plough; it is there, with 1 slave and
2 villagers.
A mill at 4s.
The value was 10s; now 15s.
Wulfric held it from Alnoth of Canterbury.

7 also in HARTWELL 4½ hides and the fifth part of ½ hide.
Land for 10 ploughs. In lordship 2; 5 slaves;
11 villagers and 9 smallholders with a priest
who have 4½ ploughs.
Meadow, 12 acres; a mill at 17s 4d; woodland 8 furlongs long
and 3 wide.
The value was £4; now 70s.
Edmer held it freely.

in CLEYLEY Hundred

8 in PUXLEY ½ hide, less the fifth part of ½ hide. Land for 1 plough.
1 villager with 1 smallholder who has ½ plough.
Value 4s.
Aelmer held it before 1066.

9 In ROADE Stephen holds 1 hide from the Bishop. Waste. It is in the King's hands.

From the Holding of the Bishop of Bayeux

in GRAVESEND Hundred

10 William holds ½ hide in EVERDON. The jurisdiction of this land lies in Fawsley. Land for 1 plough; it is there, with
2 villagers and 2 smallholders.
Meadow, 6 acres.
The value was 5s; now 10s.
Bern held it before 1066.

in SUTTON Hundred

11 Adam holds 3 virgates of land and the fifth part of 1 virgate in CHARLTON. The jurisdiction lies in (Kings) Sutton. Land for 2 ploughs. In lordship 1, with
2 smallholders.
The value was and is 10s.

in NOBOTTLE Hundred

12 William holds 2 hides and 1½ virgates of land in HEYFORD.
Land for 4 ploughs. In lordship 2 ploughs; 2 slaves;
7 villagers and 2 smallholders with 1 plough.
Meadow, 10 acres.
The value was 10s; now 20s.
Bishop and Aelid held it freely before 1066.

.III. TERRA EPI DVNELMENSIS. *IN WICESLEA WAPENT.*

EPS DVNELMENSIS ten. II. hid de rege in *HORNE*. Tra. IIII. car. Nc in dnio. I. car. 7 XII. uitti cu pbro 7 I. socho 7 VII. bord 7 I. seruo. hnt IIII. car. Ibi. III. molini de. XX. solid. Silua. I. qz 7 XII. ptic lg. 7 XVII. ptic lat. Valuit 7 ual. IIII. lib. Langfer tenuit de rege. E. cu saca 7 soca.

220 c

.IIII. TERRA EPI CONSTANTIENSIS.

EPS Constant ten de rege *RANDE*. Ibi sunt. VI. hidæ 7 una v 7 dimid. Tra. e In dnio st. II. car. 7 IIII. serui. 7 IIII. uitti 7 VI. bord cu. II. car. Ibi molin de. XXX. IIII. sol. 7 VIII. den 7 C. anguill. Ibi. XX. ac pti.

De hac tra ten. III. sochi. II. hid. Robt. I. hid. Goisfrid. I. hid. Algar. una v 7 dimid. Ibi sunt in dnio. VI. car 7 dim 7 VII. uitti 7 IIII. bord cu. II. seruis hntes. II. car 7 molin de. XII. den. Valuit. LX. sol. Modo. C. sol.

De hac tra calun iat. W. sup epm. I. hid 7 dim v træ. Hoc m tenuit Burred cu saca 7 soca.

Ipse eps ten *DENEFORDE*. Ibi sunt. V. hidæ. Tra. e In dnio sunt. IIII. car 7 dim. 7 III. serui. 7 XII. uitti 7 XVIII. bord 7 IIII. sochi cu. XII. car. Ibi. II. molini de L. sol 7 VIII. den. 7 CC. L. anguillis. Burred libe tenuit hoc m Valuit. C. sol. modo. VIII. lib. *IN NARRESFORD HD.*

De ipso epo ten Albic. II. hid 7 dim 7 una bouata in *WADENHO*. Tra. e. V. car. In dnio sunt. III. 7 IIII. serui. 7 III. uitti 7 XIIII. bord cu pbro hnt. II. car. Ibi molin de. XII. den. 7 XI. ac pti. Valuit. III. lib. modo. IIII. lib.

Ad hanc tra ptin. III. virg træ in *SCALDEWELLE*. Tra e. I. car. Ipsa ibi. e cu. II. uittis 7 II. bord. Soca. e regis.

3 LAND OF THE BISHOP OF DURHAM

In WITCHLEY Wapentake

1 The Bishop of Durham holds 2 hides from the King in HORN.
Land for 4 ploughs. Now in lordship 1 plough.
12 villagers with a priest, 1 Freeman, 7 smallholders and 1 slave have 4 ploughs.
3 mills at 20s; woodland 1 furlong and 12 perches long and 17 perches wide.
The value was and is £4.
Langfer held it from King Edward, with full jurisdiction.

4 LAND OF THE BISHOP OF COUTANCES 220 c

[In HIGHAM Hundred]

1 The Bishop of Coutances holds RAUNDS from the King. 6 hides and 1½ virgates. Land for .... In lordship 2 ploughs; 4 slaves;
4 villagers and 6 smallholders with 2 ploughs.
A mill at 34s 8d and 100 eels. Meadow, 20 acres.
Of this land 3 Freemen hold 2 hides, Robert 1 hide, Geoffrey 1 hide, Algar 1½ virgates. In lordship 6½ ploughs;
7 villagers and 4 smallholders with 2 slaves who have 2 ploughs.
A mill at 12d.
The value was 60s; now 100s.
Of this land W(illiam) claims 1 hide and ½ virgate of land against the Bishop. Burgred held this manor, with full jurisdiction.

2 The Bishop holds DENFORD himself. 5 hides. Land for ....
In lordship 4½ ploughs; 3 slaves;
12 villagers, 18 smallholders and 4 Freemen with 12 ploughs.
2 mills at 50s 8d and 250 eels.
Burgred held this manor freely.
The value was 100s; now £8.

In NAVISFORD Hundred

3 Aubrey holds 2½ hides and 1 bovate from the Bishop himself in WADENHOE. Land for 5 ploughs. In lordship 3; 4 slaves.
3 villagers and 14 smallholders with a priest have 2 ploughs.
A mill at 12d; meadow, 11 acres.
The value was £3; now £4.
To this land belong 3 virgates of land in SCALDWELL.
Land for 1 plough; it is there, with
2 villagers and 2 smallholders.
The jurisdiction is the King's.

De eod epo ten id Alberic . II . hid 7 dim v træ in Wadenho.
Tra . ẽ . VI . car . In dñio sunt . II . car . 7 IIII . serui.
7 IX . uitti 7 III . bord cũ . I . socho hñtes . II . car 7 dimid.
Ibi molin de . XIII . sol 7 IIII . den . 7 LXV . anguitt.
Ibi . XVI . ac pti . Silua . III . qrent lg . 7 una leuu lat.
Valuit . XX . sol . Modo . LX . solid . Burred libe tenuit . T.R.E.

De ipso epo ten Walchelin . II . hid *IN ORDINBARO HD.*
7 III . v træ in *HARGINDONE* . Tra . ẽ . VI . car . In dñio
sunt . III . car . 7 XII . uitti 7 XIII . bord cũ . I . car 7 dimid.
Ibi molin de . VIII . sol. II . uittis 7 I . bord.

De hac tra ten un miles . III . virg træ . 7 ibi ht . I . car cũ
Valuit . LX . sol . Modo . C . solid . Eduin libe tenuit.

De ipso epo ten Walchel . I . hid 7 dim in alia *HARGDONE.*
Tra . ẽ . III . car . 7 ipse sunt ibi in dñio . H tra cũ supiori . ẽ appciat.

De ipso (feudo) epi ten Hardeuuin hõ Walchel . I . hid 7 unã v
træ in ead uilla . Tra . ẽ . II . car . 7 ipse sunt in dñio . cũ . I .
seruo . 7 IIII . uitti cũ . I . bord hñt dim car . Ibi . V . ac pti.
Valuit . XX . solid . Modo . XL . solid . Siuerd libe tenuit T.R.E.

De ipso epo ten Walchel . III . v træ in *HISHA* . Tra . ẽ . I . car.
7 ipsa . ẽ in dñio cũ . IIII . bord q hñt dim car . Valuit . V . sol.
Modo . XX . solid . Burred tenuit cũ saca 7 soca.

De ipso epo ten Walchel . II . hid 7 III . v træ . In *BURTONE.*
Tra . ẽ . V . car . In dñio sunt . II . cũ . I . seruo . 7 I . ancilla . Ibi . IX .
uitti 7 V . bord hñt . III . car 7 dim . Ibi . XV . ac pti.
Valuit . XX . sol . Modo . XL . sol . Burred tenuit cũ saca 7 soca.

4 Aubrey also holds 2 hides and ½ virgate of land from the Bishop in WADENHOE. Land for 6 ploughs. In lordship 2 ploughs; 4 slaves;
9 villagers and 3 smallholders with 1 Freeman who have 2½ ploughs.
A mill at 13s 4d and 65 eels. Meadow, 16 acres; woodland 3 furlongs long and 1 league wide.
The value was 20s; now 60s.
Burgred held it freely before 1066.

In ORLINGBURY Hundred

5 Walkelin holds 2 hides and 3 virgates of land from the Bishop himself in HARROWDEN. Land for 6 ploughs.
In lordship 3 ploughs;
12 villagers and 13 smallholders with 1½ ploughs.
A mill at 8s.
Of this land a man-at-arms holds 3 virgates of land.
He has 1 plough, with
2 villagers and 1 smallholder.
The value was 60s; now 100s.
Edwin held it freely.

6 Walkelin holds 1½ hides from the Bishop himself in another HARROWDEN. Land for 3 ploughs; they are there, in lordship.
This land is assessed with that above.

7 From this Holding of the Bishop's, Hardwin, Walkelin's man, holds 1 hide and 1 virgate of land in this village.
Land for 2 ploughs; they are in lordship, with 1 slave.
4 villagers with 1 smallholder have ½ plough.
Meadow, 5 acres.
The value was 20s; now 40s.
Siward held it freely before 1066.

From the Bishop himself

8 Walkelin holds 3 virgates of land in ISHAM. Land for 1 plough; it is (there), in lordship, with
4 smallholders who have ½ plough.
The value was 5s; now 20s.
Burgred held it, with full jurisdiction.

9 Walkelin holds 2 hides and 3 virgates of land in BURTON (Latimer).
Land for 5 ploughs. In lordship 2, with 1 male and 1 female slave.
9 villagers and 5 smallholders have 3½ ploughs.
Meadow, 15 acres.
The value was 20s; now 40s.
Burgred held it, with full jurisdiction.

De ipso epo ten Walchet dimid hid *IN STODFALDE HD*.
7 III. partes. I. virg in *CLIPESTONE*. Tra. e. III. car. In dnio. e
una. 7 IIII. uitti 7 II. bord hnt. I. car 7 dim. Huic træ adjacet
una v træ 7 II. partes uni v. Valuit. x. sol. Modo. xx. solid.

De ipso epo ten Walchet. II. hid in *HOCECOTE*. *IN WARDONE HD*.
Tra. e. v. car. In dnio sunt. II. cu. II. seruis. 7 XXI. uittis 7 II. bord
hnt. III. car. Ibi molin de. x. sol. 7 VI. ac pti. Valuit 7 uat. IIII. lib.
Burred tenuit cu saca 7 soca. Similit 7 supiores.

220 d

De ipso epo ten Ricard. I. hid 7 dim in *BURTONE*. *IN NEVESLUND HD*.
Tra. e. III. car. In dnio. e una. cu. I. seruo. 7 III. uitti cu. I. bord
hnt. I. car. Ibi. VI. ac pti. Valuit 7 uat. x. sol.

De ipso epo ten Ricard dimid hid in *TINGDENE*. Tra. e. II.
car. In dnio. e una. cu. III. bord. Ibi molin de. v. sol. 7 III. ac
pti. Valuit. v. sol. Modo. xx. solid. Burred utrunq tenuit

De ipso epo ten Goisfrid. I. hid 7 dim v træ in *HANTONE*.
Tra. e. IIII. car. In dnio sunt. II. 7 III. serui. 7 IIII. uitti 7 II.
bord cu. II. car. Ibi. IIII. ac pti. Valuit. xx. sol. Modo. xxx. sol.
Aluuin cubold tenuit *IN WIMERESLE HD*.

De eod epo ten Winemar dim hid in *HACHELINTONE*.
Tra. e. I. car. 7 ipsa ibi. e cu. I. seruo 7 III. bord.
Valuit. XVI. den. Modo. x. sol. Burred tenuit.

De ipso epo ten Winemar. I. hid in *PRESTONE*. 7 p. I. hida
se defdb. T.R.E. Tra. e. II. car. In dnio. e una. 7 II. serui.

in STOTFOLD Hundred

10 Walkelin holds ½ hide and three parts of 1 virgate in CLIPSTON. Land for 3 ploughs. In lordship 1.

4 villagers and 2 smallholders have 1½ ploughs.

Attached to this land are 1 virgate of land and two parts of 1 virgate.

The value was 10s; now 20s.

in WARDEN Hundred

11 Walkelin holds 2 hides in EDGCOTE. Land for 5 ploughs. In lordship 2, with 2 slaves,

21 villagers and 2 smallholders have 3 ploughs.

A mill at 10s; meadow, 6 acres.

The value was and is £4.

Burgred held it, with full jurisdiction; like the above (manors).

in NAVISFORD Hundred

12 Richard holds 1½ hides in BURTON (Latimer). 220 d

Land for 3 ploughs. In lordship 1, with 1 slave.

3 villagers with 1 smallholder have 1 plough.

Meadow, 6 acres.

The value was and is 10s.

13 Richard holds ½ hide in FINEDON. Land for 2 ploughs.

In lordship 1, with

3 smallholders.

A mill at 5s; meadow, 3 acres.

The value was 5s; now 20s.

Burgred held both.

14 Geoffrey holds 1 hide and ½ virgate of land in *HANTONE*.

Land for 4 ploughs. In lordship 2; 3 slaves;

4 villagers and 2 smallholders with 2 ploughs.

Meadow, 4 acres.

The value was 20s; now 30s.

Alwin Cobbold held it.

In WYMERSLEY Hundred

15 Also from the Bishop, Winemar holds ½ hide in HACKLETON.

Land for 1 plough; it is there, with 1 slave and

3 smallholders.

The value was 16d; now 10s.

Burgred held it.

From the Bishop himself

16 Winemar holds 1 hide in PRESTON (Deanery). Before 1066 it answered for 1 hide. Land for 2 ploughs. In lordship 1; 2 slaves;

7 IIII . uitti cū . I . car . Ibi . VI . ac pti . Valuit . II . sol . M XX . sol
Wluuara uidua tenuit . T.R.E.

De ipso epo ten Robt *BERTONE* . Ibi sunt . IIII . hidæ 7 dim . Tra . ē . x . car . In dnio sunt . IIII . car 7 VII . serui . 7 I . ancilla . 7 XXIII . uitti cū . III . bord hnt . VI . car . Ibi . II . molini de . x . sol . 7 XL . ac pti . 7 VIII . ac siluæ . Valuit . XL . sol . Modo . c . sol .

De ipso epo ten Robt *IN NEVESLVND HD.* Burred tenuit unā v træ in *CRANEFORD* . Tra . ē . I . car . Ibi sunt . v . uitti 7 . I . sochs cū . II . bord . hnt . II . car . Valet . x . sol . Vasta . fuit .

De ipso epo ten Norgot . I . v træ *IN HANVERDESHO HD.* in *WENDLESBERIE* . Tra . ē dim car . Ibi sunt . II . sochi cū ea . Valet . II . sol . Soca ptin ad Hargintone . cō epi .

De ipso epo ten Witts . II . hid dimid v min in *NIWETONE* . Tra . ē . II . car . In dnio sunt . II . car . 7 VIII . uitti 7 VI . bord . cū . II . car . Silua ibi . II . q̃z lg . 7 una q̃z lat . Valuit . XX . sol . Modo . XL . solid . Azor tenuit . T.R.E. *IN NEVESLVND HVND.*

De feudo epi ten Hugo . I . hid 7 dim in *EDINTONE* . Tra . ē II . car . In dnio . ē una . 7 VI . uitti cū . I . bord hnt . III . car . Ibi molin de . XVI . den . 7 IIII . ac pti . Valuit x . sol . M . XL . sol .

De feudo epi ten Osmund . I . hid 7 unā v træ in alia *EDINTONE* . Tra . ē . III . car . In dnio . ē una . 7 IIII . uitti hnt . II . car . Ibi . II . ac pti . Valuit . x . sol . Modo . XX . sol . Azor tenuit de rege . E .

4 villagers with 1 plough.
Meadow, 6 acres.
The value was 2s; now 20s.
Wulfwara, a widow, held it before 1066.

17 Robert holds BARTON (Seagrave). 4½ hides. Land for 10 ploughs.
In lordship 4 ploughs; 7 male slaves, 1 female.
23 villagers with 3 smallholders have 6 ploughs.
2 mills at 10s; meadow, 40 acres; woodland, 8 acres.
The value was 40s; now 100s.
Burgred held it.

in NAVISLAND Hundred

18 Robert holds 1 virgate of land in CRANFORD.
Land for 1 plough.
5 villagers and 1 Freeman with 2 smallholders have 2 ploughs.
Value 10s. It was waste.

in HAMFORDSHOE Hundred

19 Norigot holds 1 virgate of land in WELLINGBOROUGH.
Land for ½ plough;
2 Freemen there with it.
Value 2s.
The jurisdiction belongs to HARROWDEN, a manor of the Bishop's.

[in HIGHAM Hundred]

20 William holds 2 hides, less ½ virgate, in NEWTON (Bromswold).
Land for 2 ploughs. In lordship 2 ploughs;
8 villagers and 6 smallholders with 2 ploughs.
Woodland 2 furlongs long and 1 furlong wide.
The value was 20s; now 40s.
Azor held it before 1066.

In NAVISLAND Hundred

21 Hugh holds 1½ hides in ADDINGTON from the Bishop's
Holding. Land for 2 ploughs. In lordship 1.
6 villagers with 1 smallholder have 3 ploughs.
A mill at 16d; meadow, 4 acres.
The value was 10s; now 40s.

22 Osmund holds 1 hide and 1 virgate of land in another ADDINGTON
from the Bishop's Holding. Land for 3 ploughs. In lordship 1.
4 villagers have 2 ploughs.
Meadow, 2 acres.
The value was 10s; now 20s.
Azor held it from King Edward.

De eođ epo ten Radulf. i. hiđ 7 vnā v tre in *WODEFORD*.
Tra. ē. ii. car. In dn̄io sunt. ii. car. 7 un uitts cū pbro 7 v. borđ
hn̄t. i. car 7 dim. Ibi. vi. ac pti. 7 una ac siluæ. ad Burg.
Valuit. x. soliđ. Modo. xxx. sol. Burred tenuit. sed soca ptinuit
De eođ epo ten Odelin. iii. virg træ in *KAPESTONE*. Tra
ē. ii. car. In dn̄io. ē una. 7 ii. serui. 7 un uitts cū. iiii. borđ
ht. i. car. Valuit. xii. den. Modo. x. sol. Burred libe tenuit.
De eođ epo ten Eduin unā v træ 7 dim in *STANERE*. Tra. ē. ii.
car. In dn̄io. ē una. 7 iii. borđ hn̄t. i. car. Ibi molin de. xxxii. den.
Silua. iiii. qrent lg. 7 ii. qrent lat. Valuit. ii. sol. Modo. x. sol.
Idem libe tenuit T.R.E. *IN HOCHESLAV HVND*.
De eođ epo ten Eduin 7 Algar. ii. hiđ unā v min in *LVHWIC*.
Tra. ē. iii. car. In dn̄io. ē una car 7 una ancilla. 7 vii. uitti
7 ii. borđ cū. ii. car. Ibi molin de. lxiiii. den. Silua. v. qrent
lg. 7 iii. qrent lat. Valuit. x. sol. Modo. xxv. soliđ.
De eođ epo ten Algar. i. hiđ 7 una v træ in *ISLEP*. Tra. ē. ii.
car. In dn̄io. ē una. 7 ii. serui. 7 v. uitti cū. ii. borđ hn̄t. i. car.

221 a

De eođ epo ten Turbn. iii. v træ in *HORTONE*. Tra. ē. i. car.
Ibi. ē ipsa. cū. ii. uittis 7 ii. borđ. Valuit. vi. sol. Modo. x. sol.
Frano tenuit. T.R.E. *IN SVDTONE HD*.
in CREVELTONE.
De epo ten Aluric. iiii. partes dim hidæ. Tra. ē dim car.
Ibi sunt. iii. borđ cū. i. car. Valet. x. soliđ. Idē tenuit
de filio Burred. 7 n̄ poterat discedere.

Also from the Bishop

23 Ralph holds 1 hide and 1 virgate of land in WOODFORD.
Land for 2 ploughs. In lordship 2 ploughs.
1 villager with a priest and 5 smallholders have 1½ ploughs.
Meadow, 6 acres; woodland, 1 acre.
The value was 10s; now 30s.
Burgred held it, but the jurisdiction belonged to Peterborough.

[in NAVISFORD Hundred]

24 Odelin holds 3 virgates of land in THRAPSTON.
Land for 2 ploughs. In lordship 1; 2 slaves.
1 villager with 4 smallholders has 1 plough.
The value was 12d; now 10s.
Burgred held it freely.

[in CORBY Hundred]

25 Edwin holds 1½ virgates of land in STANION.
Land for 2 ploughs. In lordship 1.
3 smallholders have 1 plough.
A mill at 32d; woodland 4 furlongs long and 2 furlongs wide.
The value was 2s; now 10s.
He also held it freely before 1066.

in HUXLOE Hundred

26 Edwin and Algar hold 2 hides, less 1 virgate, in LOWICK.
Land for 3 ploughs. In lordship 1 plough; 1 female slave;
7 villagers and 2 smallholders with 2 ploughs.
A mill at 64d; woodland 5 furlongs long and 3 furlongs wide.
The value was 10s; now 25s.

27 Algar holds 1 hide and 1 virgate of land in ISLIP.
Land for 2 ploughs. In lordship 1; 2 slaves.
5 villagers with 2 smallholders have 1 plough.

(in WYMERSLEY Hundred)

28 Thorbern holds 3 virgates of land in HORTON. 221 a
Land for 1 plough; it is there, with
2 villagers and 2 smallholders.
The value was 6s; now 10s.
Fran held it before 1066.

From the Bishop

in SUTTON Hundred

29 Aelfric holds four parts of ½ hide in CROUGHTON. Land for ½ plough.
3 smallholders with 1 plough.
Value 10s.
He also held it from Burgred's son and could not leave.

De epo ten Robt *FINEMERE* . Ibi sunt . VIII . hidæ . Tra . ẽ IX . car . In dnio sunt . II . 7 IIII . serui . 7 X . uitti 7 V . bord cu . VI . car . Ibi molin de . XIIII . solid . 7 C . ac pasturæ . Silua . I . qrent lg . 7 una lat . Valuit 7 ualet . VIII . lib.
Vluuard libe tenuit . T.R.E.

De epo ten Rogeri *HEDHA* . Ibi sunt . VIII . hidæ.
Tra . ẽ . VIII . car . In dnio sunt . II . cu . I . seruo . 7 VIII . uitti 7 V . bord cu . I . car . Ibi . XX . ac pasturæ . Valuit 7 ual . VIII . lib . Vluuard libe tenuit.

De epo ten Herluin *SCILDESWELLE* . Ibi sunt . X . hidæ.
Tra . ẽ . VII . car . In dnio sunt . III . car . 7 II . serui . 7 VII . uitti 7 VII . bord cu . IIII . car . Valuit . C . sol . Modo . X . lib.
Eduin . f . Burred tenuit.

De epo ten Witts *GLINTONE* . Ibi sunt . X . hidæ.
Tra . ẽ . VI . car . In dnio sunt VI . car . 7 VI . serui . 7 XV . uitti 7 V . bord cu . V . car . Ibi molin de . V . sol . 7 XVIII . ac pti . Silua . VI . qz lg . 7 tntd lat . Valuit . VI . lib . M . VIII . lib.
Vluuard libe tenuit de rege . E.

De epo ten Witts 7 Ilger *OITONE* . Ibi sunt . V . hidæ.
Tra . ẽ . VI . car . In dnio sunt . II . 7 II . serui . 7 XIIII . uitti 7 II . bord cu . V . car . Ibi . XXX . ac pti . 7 XIII . ac pasturæ.
Valuit . IIII . lib . Modo . C . solid . Vluuard libe tenuit.

De epo ten Turstin dimid hid . in *HORTONE* . Tra . ẽ dimid car . Ibi sunt . VI . ac pti . Valuit . V . sol . m . X . sol.
Leuiget libe tenuit.

De epo ten Robt . V . hid in *EGFORDE* . Tra . ẽ . VI . car.
In dnio sunt . III . car . 7 V . serui . 7 V . uitti 7 VII . bord cu . II . car . Ibi molin de . XX . sol . 7 XXX . ac pti.
Valuit 7 ual . VI . lib . Eduin . f . Burred libe tenuit.

(In OXFORDSHIRE)

30 Robert holds FINMERE. 8 hides. Land for 9 ploughs.
In lordship 2; 4 slaves;
10 villagers and 5 smallholders with 6 ploughs.
A mill at 14s; pasture, 100 acres; woodland 1 furlong long and 1 wide.
The value was and is £8.
Wulfward held it freely before 1066.

31 Roger holds HETHE. 8 hides. Land for 8 ploughs.
In lordship 2, with 1 slave;
8 villagers and 5 smallholders with 1 plough.
Pasture, 20 acres.
The value was and is £8.
Wulfward held it freely.

32 Herlwin holds SHELSWELL. 10 hides. Land for 7 ploughs.
In lordship 3 ploughs; 2 slaves;
7 villagers and 7 smallholders with 4 ploughs.
The value was 100s; now £10.
Edwin son of Burgred held it.

33 William holds GLYMPTON. 10 hides. Land for 6 ploughs.
In lordship 6 ploughs; 6 slaves;
15 villagers and 5 smallholders with 5 ploughs.
A mill at 5s; meadow, 18 acres; woodland 6 furlongs long and as wide.
The value was £6; now £8.
Wulfward held it freely from King Edward.

34 William and Ilger hold WOOTTON. 5 hides. Land for 6 ploughs.
In lordship 2; 2 slaves;
14 villagers and 2 smallholders with 5 ploughs.
Meadow, 30 acres; pasture, 13 acres.
The value was £4; now 100s.
Wulfward held it freely.

35 Thurstan holds ½ hide in ?WORTON. Land for ½ plough.
Meadow, 6 acres.
The value was 5s; now 10s.
Leofgeat held it freely.

36 Robert holds 5 hides in HEYFORD. Land for 6 ploughs.
In lordship 3 ploughs; 5 slaves;
5 villagers and 7 smallholders with 2 ploughs.
A mill at 20s; meadow, 30 acres.
The value was and is £6.
Edwin son of Burgred held it freely.

.V. TERRA EPI LINCOLIENSIS. *IN GISLEBURG HD 7 DIM.*

EPS LINCOLIE ten de rege *HOLEWELLE* . Ibi . ē . I . hida. 7 II . partes de dim hida . Tra . ē . III . car . Ibi sunt IIII . uitti cū . I . bord hntes . I . car . Valuit 7 uat . x . sot. Bardi libe tenuit.

De ipso epo ten Walteri . II . hid in *LIDENTONE*. Ibi ptin *STOCHE* . Smelistone . Caldecote . Tra . ē . XVI . car int totū . In dnio sunt . VI . car . 7 IIII . serui . 7 XXVI . uitti 7 XXIIII . bord hntes . IX . car . Ibi . II . molini de . VIII . solid . 7 XXVIII . ac pti . Silua . III . qrent lg . 7 II . qz lat. Valet tot . VIII . lib . Bardi tenuit cū saca 7 soca.

De eod epo ten Walteri . I . hid in *ESINDONE* . Tra . ē VI . car . In dnio sunt . II . cū . I . seruo . 7 XVI . uitti 7 V . bord cū . IIII . car . Ibi molin de . XVI . solid . 7 III . ac pti. Silua . VI . qz lg . 7 IIII . qrent lat . Valuit . IIII . lib. Modo . C . solid . Bardi tenuit cū saca 7 soca.

221 b *IN ELBOLDESTON . HD.*

De eod epo ten Godefrid . IIII . hid in *CEWECUBE* . Tra . ē X . car . In dnio sunt . II . 7 IIII . serui . 7 XX . uitti 7 IX . bord cū . VIII . car . Ibi . III . molini de . XVI . sot . 7 IX . ac pti. Valuit . X . lib . Modo . VII . lib . Bardi libe tenuit.

.VI. TERRA SCI PETRI DE BURG. *IN STOCHE HUND.*

ABBATIA S PETRI DE BURG ten uillā quæ uocat *BURG* . Ibi sunt . VIII . hidæ . Tra . ē . XVI . car . In dnio sunt . V.
* 7 VII . serui . 7 XXXVII . uitti 7 VIII . bord cū . II . car.
Ibi molin de . V . solid . 7 XL . ac pti . Silua . I . leuu lg . 7 IIII . qrent lat . Valuit . XX . sot . Modo . X . lib.

5 LAND OF THE BISHOP OF LINCOLN

In GUILSBOROUGH Hundred and a half

1 The Bishop of Lincoln holds HOLLOWELL from the King. 1 hide and two parts of ½ hide. Land for 3 ploughs.
4 villagers with 1 smallholder who have 1 plough.
The value was and is 10s.
Bardi held it freely.

[In WITCHLEY Wapentake]

2 Walter holds 2 hides in LYDDINGTON from the Bishop himself. STOKE (Dry), 'SNELSTON' and CALDECOTT belong to it. Land for 16 ploughs in total. In lordship 6 ploughs; 4 slaves;
26 villagers and 24 smallholders who have 9 ploughs.
2 mills at 8s; meadow, 28 acres; woodland 3 furlongs long and 2 furlongs wide.
Value of the whole £8.
Bardi held it with full jurisdiction.

3 Walter holds 1 hide in ESSENDINE from the Bishop also. Land for 6 ploughs. In lordship 2, with 1 slave;
16 villagers and 5 smallholders with 4 ploughs.
A mill at 16s; meadow, 3 acres; woodland 6 furlongs long and 4 furlongs wide.
The value was £4; now 100s.
Bardi held it with full jurisdiction.

In ALBOLDSTOW Hundred 221 b

4 Godfrey holds 4 hides in CHACOMBE from the Bishop also. Land for 10 ploughs. In lordship 2; 4 slaves;
20 villagers and 9 smallholders with 8 ploughs.
3 mills at 16s; meadow, 9 acres.
The value was £10; now £7.
Bardi held it freely.

6 LAND OF PETERBOROUGH [ABBEY]

In STOKE Hundred

1 The Abbey of Peterborough holds the town called PETERBOROUGH. 8 hides. Land for 16 ploughs. In lordship 5; 7 slaves;
37 villagers and 8 smallholders with 11 ploughs.
A mill at 5s; meadow, 40 acres;
woodland 1 league long and 4 furlongs wide.
The value was 20s; now £10.

Ipſa æccła ten̄ *COTINGEHĀ*. Ibi ſunt . VII . hidæ . Tra . ē . XIIII . car̄ . In dn̄io ſunt . II . 7 IIII . ſerui . 7 XXIX . uitti 7 X . borđ cū . X . car̄ . Ibi molin̄ de . XL . den̄ . 7 XII . ac̄ p̄ti . Silua . I . leuū lḡ . 7 dim̄ leū lat̄ . Valuit . X . ſol . Modo . LX . ſol.

Ipſa æccła ten̄ *TORP* . Ibi . II . hiđ . Tra . ē . IIII . car̄ . In dn̄io ſunt . II . 7 IIII . ſerui . 7 XII . uitti 7 II . borđ cū . II . car̄ . Ibi p̄tū III . q̄z lḡ . 7 una q̄z lat̄ . Silua . VI . q̄z lḡ . 7 IIII . q̄z lat̄ . Ibi ſunt . III . ſochi cū . II . car̄ . Valuit . XL . ſol . Modo . L . ſol.

Ipſa æccła ten̄ *CASTRE* . Ibi ſunt . III . hidæ . Tra . ē . XII . car̄ . In dn̄io ſunt . II . cū . I . ſeruo . 7 XIII . uitti 7 II . borđ cū . III . car̄ 7 dim̄ . Ibi molin̄ de . VIII . ſol . 7 XV . ac̄ p̄ti . Silua . VI . q̄rent̄ lḡ . 7 IIII . q̄z lat̄ . Valuit . XX . ſol . Modo . L . ſoliđ.

Ipſa æccła ten̄ *EGLESWORDE* . Ibi ſunt . VI . hidæ . Tra . ē . XII . car̄ . In dn̄io ſunt . II . car̄ . 7 XVII . uitti 7 II . borđ 7 VIII . ſochi cū . XII . car̄ . Ibi . II . molini de . XII . ſol . 7 XV . ac̄ p̄ti . Silua . III . q̄rent̄ lḡ . 7 II . q̄z lat̄ . Valuit . XX . ſol . Modo . LXX . ſoliđ.

Ipſa æccła ten̄ . VI . hiđ in *PILLESGETE* . Tra . ē . VI . car̄ . In dn̄io . ē una . cū . I . ſeruo . 7 IX . uitti 7 II . borđ 7 XXVI . ſochi hn̄t XI . car̄ . Ibi molin̄ de . X . ſol . 7 XL . ac̄ p̄ti . 7 V . ac̄ ſiluæ . Valuit . XX . ſol . Modo . IIII . lib̄.

Ipſa æccła ten̄ . III . hiđ in *GLINTONE* . In hac cū appenđ . T.R.E. fuer̄ . XXX . car̄ . Tra . ē . XII . car̄ . In dn̄io ſt̄ . III . car̄ . 7 II . ancillæ . 7 X . uitti 7 VI . borđ 7 VIII . ſochi cū . V . car̄ . Ibi ſunt . C . ac̄ p̄ti . Silua . X . q̄z lḡ . 7 IX . q̄z lat̄ . Valuit 7 uał . LX . ſoliđ.

Ipſa æccła ten̄ . VIII . hiđ 7 unā v̄ træ in *WIDERINTONE*. Ibi cū appenđ fuer̄ . XXX . car̄ T.R.E. Tra . ē . XII . car̄ . In dn̄io ſt̄ . V . car̄ . 7 IIII . ſerui . 7 XXX . uitti 7 IIII . borđ 7 XIX . ſochi hn̄tes XIX . car̄ . Silua . II . leuū lḡ . 7 una leū lat̄ . Valuit . IIII . lib̄ . Modo . VII . lib̄.

The Church itself holds

in STOKE Hundred

2 COTTINGHAM. 7 hides. Land for 14 ploughs. In lordship 2; 4 slaves;
29 villagers and 10 smallholders with 10 ploughs.
A mill at 40d; meadow, 12 acres;
woodland 1 league long and ½ league wide.
The value was 10s; now 60s.

[in UPTON Hundred]

3 THORPE. 2 hides. Land for 4 ploughs. In lordship 2; 4 slaves;
12 villagers and 2 smallholders with 2 ploughs.
Meadow 3 furlongs long and 1 furlong wide;
woodland 6 furlongs long and 4 furlongs wide.
3 Freemen with 2 ploughs.
The value was 40s; now 50s.

4 CASTOR. 3 hides. Land for 12 ploughs. In lordship 2, with 1 slave;
13 villagers and 2 smallholders with 3½ ploughs.
A mill at 8s; meadow, 15 acres;
woodland 6 furlongs long and 4 furlongs wide.
The value was 20s; now 50s.

5 AILSWORTH. 6 hides. Land for 12 ploughs. In lordship 2 ploughs;
17 villagers, 2 smallholders and 8 Freemen with 12 ploughs.
2 mills at 12s; meadow, 15 acres;
woodland 3 furlongs long and 2 furlongs wide.
The value was 20s; now 70s.

6 in PILSGATE 6 hides. Land for 6 ploughs. In lordship 1, with 1 slave.
9 villagers, 2 smallholders and 26 Freemen have 11 ploughs.
A mill at 10s; meadow, 40 acres; woodland, 5 acres.
The value was 20s; now £4.

7 in GLINTON 3 hides. In this (land), with its dependencies, there
were 30 ploughs before 1066. Land for 12 ploughs.
In lordship 3 ploughs; 2 female slaves;
10 villagers, 6 smallholders and 8 Freemen with 5 ploughs.
Meadow, 100 acres; woodland 10 furlongs long and 9 furlongs wide.
The value was and is 60s.

8 in WERRINGTON 8 hides and 1 virgate of land. With its dependencies
there were 30 ploughs there before 1066. Land for 12 ploughs.
In lordship 5 ploughs; 4 slaves;
30 villagers, 4 smallholders and 19 Freemen who have 19 ploughs.
Woodland 2 leagues long and 1 league wide.
The value was £4; now £7.

Ipsa æccl̄a ten̄ in *ADELINTONE*.I.hid̄ 7 dimid̄.Tra.ē.III.car̄.
Ibi sunt.VI.sochi cū.III.car̄.7 VIII.ac̄ p̄ti.Valuit.II.sol̄.m̊.x.sol̄.
Ipsa æccl̄a ten̄.VI.hid̄ in *VNDELE*.Tra.ē.IX.car̄.In dn̄io sun̄
III.car̄.7 III.serui.7 XXIII.uitti.7 X.bord̄ cū.IX.car̄.Ibi molin̄
de.XX.sol̄.7 CC.L.anguitt.7 ibi.L.ac̄ p̄ti.Silua.III.leū lḡ.
7 II.leū lat̄.Cū onerat̄.ual̄.XX.sol̄.De mercato.XXV.sol̄.
Valuit.V.sol̄.Modo.XI.lib̄.
Huic ω ptin̄ dimid̄ hida in Terninge.Tra.ē dim̄ car̄.Ibi.ē
un̄ uitts.Valuit.II.sol̄.Modo.XL.denar̄. *IN WICESLE HVND̄*
Ipsi ω ptin̄.II.hidæ 7 una v̄ træ.in *STOCHE*.Tra.ē.VIII.car̄.

221 c

In dn̄io.ē una car̄.7 X.uitti 7 II.bord̄ cū.II.car̄ 7 dimid̄.
Ibi.X.ac̄ p̄ti.Silua.I.leuū lḡ.7 V.q̄rent̄ lat̄.
Valuit.X.sol̄.Modo.C.X.solid̄.
Ipsa æccl̄a ten̄.VII.hid̄ 7 dimid̄ in *WERMINTONE*.Tra.ē.XVI.
car̄.In dn̄io sunt.IIII.car̄.7 III.serui.7 XXXII.uitti cū.VIII.car̄.
Ibi molin̄ de.XL.sol̄.7 CCC.XXV.anguitt.7 XL.ac̄ p̄ti.7 una
ac̄ siluæ.Valuit.V.sol̄.Modo.XI.lib̄.
Ipsa æccl̄a ten̄.IIII.hid̄ 7 dim̄.in *ASCETONE*.Tra.ē.VIII.car̄.
In dn̄io sunt.II.car̄.cū.I.seruo.7 XI.uitti 7 II.bord̄ cū.VI.car̄.
Ibi.II.molini de.XL.sol̄.7 CCC.XXV.anguitt.7 XVI.ac̄ p̄ti.
7 IIII.or ac̄ siluæ.Valuit.VIII.sol̄.Modo.VII.lib̄. *IN WICESLE HD̄.*
Ipsa æccl̄a ten̄ *TEDINWELLE*.Ibi sunt.V.hidæ 7 una v̄ træ.
Tra.ē.VIII.car̄.In dn̄io sunt.II.æ 7 XXIIII.uitti 7 XI.bord̄ cū.VII.
car̄.Ibi.II.molini de.XXIIII.sol̄ 7 XX.ac̄ p̄ti.Valuit.X.sol̄.Modo
Ipsa æccl̄a ten̄.I.hid̄ 7 unā v̄ træ in *SLIPTONE*. ⌐VII.lib̄.

[?in WILLYBROOK Hundred]

9 in ELTON 1½ hides. Land for 3 ploughs.
6 Freemen with 3 ploughs.
Meadow, 8 acres.
The value was 2s; now 10s.

[in POLEBROOK Hundred]

10a in OUNDLE 6 hides. Land for 9 ploughs. In lordship 3 ploughs; 3 slaves;
23 villagers and 10 smallholders with 9 ploughs.
A mill at 20s and 250 eels; meadow, 50 acres;
woodland 3 leagues long and 2 leagues wide;
value when stocked, 20s. From the market 25s.
The value was 5s; now £11.

b To this manor belongs ½ hide in THURNING. Land for ½ plough.
1 villager.
The value was 2s; now 40d.

In WITCHLEY Hundred

c To this manor belong 2 hides and 1 virgate of land in STOKE (?Dry).
Land for 8 ploughs. In lordship 1 plough; 221 c
10 villagers and 2 smallholders with 2½ ploughs.
Meadow, 10 acres; woodland 1 league long and 5 furlongs wide.
The value was 10s; now 110s.

The Church itself holds

[in POLEBROOK Hundred]

11 in WARMINGTON 7½ hides. Land for 16 ploughs.
In lordship 4 ploughs; 3 slaves;
32 villagers with 8 ploughs.
A mill at 40s and 325 eels; meadow, 40 acres; woodland, 1 acre.
The value was 5s; now £11.

2 in ASHTON 4½ hides. Land for 8 ploughs.
In lordship 2 ploughs, with 1 slave;
11 villagers and 2 smallholders with 6 ploughs.
2 mills at 40s and 325 eels; meadow, 16 acres; woodland, 4 acres.
The value was 8s; now £7.

in WITCHLEY Hundred

3 TINWELL. 5 hides and 1 virgate of land. Land for 8 ploughs.
In lordship 2;
24 villagers and 11 smallholders with 7 ploughs.
2 mills at 24s; meadow, 20 acres.
The value was 10s; now £7.

[in HUXLOE Hundred]

4 in SLIPTON 1 hide and 1 virgate of land.

Tra.ē.II.car.7 ipse sunt ibi cū.VI.sochis.Ibi.IIII.ac siluæ.
Ipsa æccla ten.V.hid 7 unā v træ in *ERDIBVRNE*. Valet.V.sol.
Tra.ē.XV.car.In dnio sunt.II.7 II.serui.7 IX.uitti 7 VIII.
bord 7 IIII.sochi cū.V.car int oms.Ibi molin de.XVIII.sol.
Valuit.III.lib.Modo.VI.lib.

Ipsa æccla ten.I.hid 7 unā v træ in *STANWIGE*.Tra.ē.III.
car.In dnio sunt.II.car cū.I.seruo.7 VIII.uitti 7 IIII.bord
cū.I.car 7 II.bobz.Ibi molin de.XX.sol.7 VIII.ac pti.
Valuit.XL.solid.Modo.C.solid.

Ipsa æccla ten.X.hid in *CATERINGE*.Tra.ē.XVI.car.
In dnio est una.7 I.ancilla.7 XXXI.uitti cū.X.car.
Ibi.II.molini de.XX.sol.7 CVII.ac pti.7 III.ac siluæ.
Valuit.X.lib.Modo.XI.lib.

TERRA HOMINV EJVSD ÆCCLÆ.

In *CASTRE* ten.V.milit.III.hid de abbe.7 ibi hnt.V.car
in dnio.7 IX.uill 7 V.bord 7 III.seru cū.II.car 7 dimid.
Valb.X.sol.Modo.XL.sol.

Roger ten de abbe *MELETONE*.Ibi sunt.II.hidæ.Tra.ē.III.car.
In dnio sunt.II.cū.I.seruo.7 V.uill 7 VI.soch cū.II.car.Silua
III.qrent lg.7 una lat.Valuit.XX.sol.Modo.XL.sol.

In *EGLESWORDE* ten.III.milit abbis.III.hid.7 ibi hnt.III.car.

Anschitill ten de abbe *WITHERINGHĀ*. Vat.III.lib.
Ibi sunt.IX.hidæ.Tra.ē.XVI.car.T.R.E.fuer ibi.XXX.In dnio
sunt.III.car.7 V.serui.7 XII.uitti 7 VII.bord 7 XX.sochi cū.XII.
car int oms.Ibi.III.molini de.XIX.solid.Silua.II.leuu lg.7 una
lat.Valuit.III.lib.Modo.XI.lib.

Land for 2 ploughs. They are there, with
6 Freemen.
Woodland, 4 acres.
Value 5s.

[in NAVISLAND Hundred]

15 in IRTHLINGBOROUGH 5 hides and 1 virgate of land.
Land for 15 ploughs. In lordship 2; 2 slaves;
9 villagers, 8 smallholders and 4 Freemen with 5 ploughs between them.
A mill at 18s.
The value was £3; now £6.

[?in HIGHAM Hundred]

16 in STANWICK 1 hide and 1 virgate of land. Land for 3 ploughs.
In lordship 2 ploughs, with 1 slave;
8 villagers and 4 smallholders with 1 plough and 2 oxen.
A mill at 20s; meadow, 8 acres.
The value was 40s; now 100s.

[in NAVISLAND Hundred]

17 in KETTERING 10 hides. Land for 16 ploughs.
In lordship 1; 1 female slave;
31 villagers with 10 ploughs.
2 mills at 20s; meadow, 107 acres; woodland, 3 acres.
The value was £10; now £11.

[6a] LAND OF THIS CHURCH'S MEN

[In UPTON Hundred]

1 In CASTOR five men-at-arms hold 3 hides from the Abbot.
In lordship they have 5 ploughs;
9 villagers, 5 smallholders and 3 slaves with 2½ ploughs.
The value was 10s; now 40s.

2 Roger holds MILTON from the Abbot. 2 hides. Land for 3 ploughs.
In lordship 2, with 1 slave;
5 villagers and 6 Freemen with 2 ploughs.
Woodland 3 furlongs long and 1 wide.
The value was 20s; now 40s.

3 In AILSWORTH three of the Abbot's men-at-arms hold 3 hides;
they have 3 ploughs.
Value £3.

4 Ansketel holds WITTERING from the Abbot. 9 hides. Land for 16 ploughs.
Before 1066 there were 30 there. In lordship 3 ploughs; 5 slaves;
12 villagers, 7 smallholders and 20 Freemen with 12 ploughs between them.
3 mills at 19s; woodland 2 leagues long and 1 wide.
The value was £3; now £11.

In *BVRGLEA*. ten̄ Goisfrid. III. v̄ træ de abb̄e. Tra. ē. II. car̄. In dn̄io est una. 7 III. serui. 7 VII. uitt̄i. cū. I. bord̄ hn̄t. I. car̄. Ibi. VI. ac̄ p̄ti. 7 III. ac̄ siluæ. Valuit. X. sol̄. Modo. XL. solid̄.

In *SVDTORP* ten̄ Goisfr̄ 7 II. alij milit̄. II. hid̄ 7 dimid̄ de abb̄e. Tra. ē. VI. car̄. T.R.E. fuer̄. XII. In dn̄io sunt. III. car̄. 7 IIII. uitt̄i 7 II. bord̄ 7 XVIII. sochi cū. VII. car̄. Ibi. II. molini 7 dim̄ de. III. sol̄. 7 XX. ac̄ p̄ti. Silua. II. q̄rent̄ lḡ. 7 una lat̄. Valuit. XL. sol̄. M̊. VI. lib̄.

221 d

In *GLINTONE* ten̄. III. milites abb̄is X. hid̄ 7 unā v̄ træ. Ibi hn̄t. VI. car̄ in dn̄io. 7 XXXIII. soch̄ cū. IX. car̄ 7 dim̄. Ibi. II. molini de. XI. sol̄ 7 IIII. den̄. Valuit. XL. sol̄. M̊. X. lib̄.

In *WIDERINTONE* ten̄. IIII. milit̄ abb̄is. III. hid̄. 7 ibi hn̄t IIII. car̄. 7 XII. ac̄s p̄ti. Valuit. XX. sol̄. Modo. IIII. lib̄.

In *WRITORP* ten̄ Aluuin̄ de abbate. III. v̄ træ q̄ ꝑtin̄ ad *WITERINGHĀ*. Ibi hn̄t. III. soch̄ cū. I. car̄ 7 dimid̄. 7 IIII. ac̄s p̄ti. Valet. VIII. solid̄.

In *CODESTOCHE* ten̄. II. milit̄ de abb̄e. III. hid̄. Tra. ē VI. car̄. In dn̄io sunt. III. 7 X. uitt̄i 7 IIII. bord̄. cū. VI. car̄ 7 dimid̄. Ibi. XXIIII. ac̄ p̄ti. Silua. VI. q̄z lḡ. 7 IIII. q̄z lat̄. Valuit. V. solid̄. Modo. LX. solid̄.

In *LIDINTONE* ten̄ Witt̄s de abb̄e. II. hid̄ 7 dim̄. Tra. ē VI. car̄. In dn̄io. ē una cū. I. seruo. 7 VIII. uitt̄i 7 II. bord̄ cū. II. car̄. 7 VI. sochi cū. II. car̄. 7 XII. ac̄ p̄ti. Soca huj̄ træ ꝑtin̄ ad Vndel. Valuit. X. sol̄. Modo. XL. sol̄.

In *WARMINTONE* ten̄. II. milit̄ de abb̄e. I. hidā quæ jacet ad Walebroc. Tra. ē. II. car̄. Ipsæ sunt ibi cū. II. uitt̄is. 7 III. sochis. Valuit. II. sol̄. Modo. XXX. sol̄.

5 In BURGHLEY Geoffrey holds 3 virgates of land from the Abbot. Land for 2 ploughs. In lordship 1; 3 slaves.
7 villagers with 1 smallholder have 1 plough.
Meadow, 6 acres; woodland, 3 acres.
The value was 10s; now 40s.

6 In SOUTHORPE Geoffrey and two other men-at-arms hold 4½ hides from the Abbot. Land for 6 ploughs. Before 1066 there were 12. In lordship 3 ploughs;
4 villagers, 2 smallholders and 18 Freemen with 7 ploughs.
2½ mills at 3s; meadow, 20 acres; woodland 2 furlongs long and 1 wide.
The value was 40s; now £6.

7 In GLINTON three of the Abbot's men-at-arms hold 10 hides 221 d
and 1 virgate of land. In lordship they have 6 ploughs;
33 Freemen with 9½ ploughs.
2 mills at 11s 4d.
The value was 40s; now £10.

8 In WERRINGTON four of the Abbot's men-at-arms hold 3 hides; they have 4 ploughs and
meadow, 12 acres.
The value was 20s; now £4.

9 In WOTHORPE Alwin holds 3 virgates of land from the Abbot which belong to Wittering. He has
3 Freemen with 1½ ploughs and
meadow, 4 acres.
Value 8s.

[In WILLYBROOK Hundred]

10 In COTTERSTOCK two men-at-arms hold 3 hides from the Abbot. Land for 6 ploughs. In lordship 3;
10 villagers and 4 smallholders with 6½ ploughs.
Meadow, 24 acres; woodland 6 furlongs long and 4 furlongs wide.
The value was 5s; now 60s.

11 In LUTTON William holds 2½ hides from the Abbot. Land for 6 ploughs. In lordship 1, with 1 slave;
8 villagers and 2 smallholders with 2 ploughs;
6 Freemen with 2 ploughs.
Meadow, 12 acres.
The jurisdiction of this land belongs to Oundle.
The value was 10s; now 40s.

12 In WARMINGTON two men-at-arms hold from the Abbot 1 hide which lies in Willybrook (lands). Land for 2 ploughs; they are there, with
2 villagers and 3 Freemen.
The value was 2s; now 30s.

In *Pochebroc* ten̄ Eustachi̊ de abbe . IIII . hid̄ unā v̄
min̄ . Tra . ē . VIII . car̄ . In dnio . ē una . cū . I . seruo . 7 V . uitti
7 II . bord̄ 7 III . sochi cū VIII . uittis hn̄t IIII . car̄ 7 dim̄ int̄
om̄s . Ibi . V . ac̄ p̄ti . Valuit . V . sol̄ . Modo . XL . solid̄.
De hac t̄ra ten̄ Goisfrid̄ unā v̄ træ
In *Mermeston* 7 *Chingestorp* ten̄ . V . milit̄ de abbe
V . hid̄ de soca . T̄ra . ē . VIII . car̄ . In dnio sunt . V . 7 IX . uitti
7 III . bord̄ . 7 VI . sochi cū . III . car̄ int̄ om̄s . Ibi . III . ac̄ p̄ti.
Valuit . X . sol̄ . Modo . XL . solid̄.
In *Hinintone* ten̄ . III . milit̄ de abbe . II . hid̄ 7 dim̄.
7 ē Soca de Vndel . T̄ra . ē . IIII . car̄ . In dnio sunt . II . car̄.
7 V . uitti cū . II . car̄ . Ibi . X . ac̄ p̄ti . Valuit . X . sol̄ . m̄ . XL . sol̄.
In *Lullintone* ten̄ Walteri̊ de abbe . I . hid̄ 7 dimid̄.
quæ ptin̄ ad Vndel . T̄ra . ē . III . car̄ . In dnio . ē una . 7 VII.
uitti cū . I . car̄ 7 dim̄ . Valuit . X . sol̄ . Modo . XXX . sol̄.
In *Winewiche* ten̄ Eustachi̊ de abbe dimid̄ hidā.
Soca . ē de Vndel . Ibi . II . sochi cū . II . uittis . hn̄t . II . car̄.
Valuit . V . sol̄ . Modo . X . sol̄.
Isenbard 7 Rozelin̊ ten̄ . I . hid̄ 7 dim̄ de abbe 7 ptin̄
ad *Wermintone* . Ibi cū . III . uittis hn̄t . II . car̄.
Valuit . V . sol̄ . Modo . XL . solid̄.
Duo milit̄ 7 II . seruient̄ cū . I . socho ten̄ . II . hid̄ 7 III . v̄
t̄ræ quæ ptin̄ ad *Stoche* . Ibi hn̄t . II . car̄ 7 dim̄ . 7 VIII.
uittos 7 IIII . bord̄ cū . III . car̄ . Ibi . X . ac̄ p̄ti . Valuit . V . sol̄.
In *Pilchetone* ten̄ Rogeri̊ de abbe Modo . L . solid.
II . hid̄ 7 dimid̄ . T̄ra . ē . V . car̄ . In dnio . ē una . 7 VI . uitti
7 II . bord̄ 7 II . sochi cū . IIII . car̄ . Ibi . VIII . ac̄ p̄ti . Silua
XIIII . q̄rent̄ lḡ . 7 IIII . q̄z lat̄ . Valuit . V . sol̄ . Modo . LX . sol̄.

[In POLEBROOK Hundred]

13 In POLEBROOK Eustace holds 4 hides, less 1 virgate, from the Abbot. Land for 8 ploughs. In lordship 1, with 1 slave.
5 villagers, 2 smallholders and 3 Freemen with 8 villagers have 4½ ploughs between them.
Meadow, 5 acres.
The value was 5s; now 40s.
Of this land, Geoffrey holds 1 virgate of land.

14 In ARMSTON and KINGSTHORPE, five men-at-arms hold from the Abbot 5 hides of the jurisdiction. Land for 8 ploughs. In lordship 5;
9 villagers, 3 smallholders and 6 Freemen with 3 ploughs between them.
Meadow, 3 acres.
The value was 10s; now 40s.

15 In HEMINGTON three men-at-arms hold 2½ hides from the Abbot. It is a jurisdiction of Oundle. Land for 4 ploughs. In lordship 2 ploughs;
5 villagers with 2 ploughs.
Meadow, 10 acres.
The value was 10s; now 40s.

16 In LUDDINGTON (in the Brook) Walter holds 1½ hides from the Abbot which belong to Oundle. Land for 3 ploughs. In lordship 1;
7 villagers with 1½ ploughs.
The value was 10s; now 30s.

17 In WINWICK Eustace holds ½ hide from the Abbot. It is a jurisdiction of Oundle.
2 Freemen with 2 villagers have 2 ploughs.
The value was 5s; now 10s.

18 Isenbard and Rozelin hold 1½ hides from the Abbot; they belong to WARMINGTON; with
3 villagers they have 2 ploughs.
The value was 5s; now 40s.

19 Two men-at-arms and 2 servants with 1 Freeman hold 2 hides and 3 virgates of land which belong to STOKE (Doyle). They have 2½ ploughs;
8 villagers and 4 smallholders with 3 ploughs.
Meadow, 10 acres.
The value was 5s; now 50s.

[?In NAVISFORD Hundred]

20 In PILTON Roger holds 2½ hides from the Abbot. Land for 5 ploughs. In lordship 1;
6 villagers, 2 smallholders and 2 Freemen with 4 ploughs.
Meadow, 8 acres; woodland 14 furlongs long and 4 furlongs wide.
The value was 5s; now 60s.

In *WADENHO* ten Roger de abbe unā v træ 7 dimiđ.
7 ibi hT dimiđ car cū . I . borđ . Ibi . II . ac pti . Valet . v . sot.

In *ASECHIRCE* . ten Azelin 7 II . Angli de abbe . VI . hiđ
7 dim . Tra . ē . x . car . In dn̄io sunt . III . car . 7 III . serui.
7 x . uilti 7 XI . borđ cū . v . car . Ibi . xx . ac pti . 7 VI . ac siluæ.
Valuit . LX . sot . Modo . C . soliđ.

222 a

In *TIRCEMESSE* ten Azelin de abbe . III . hiđ 7 unā v træ.
Tra . ē . v . car . In dn̄io sunt . II . 7 III . serui . 7 VII . uilti 7 III . borđ
cū . II . car . 7 III . sochi cū . I . car . Ibi . x . ac pti . Valuit . xx . sot
Modo . LV . sot.

In *CLOTONE* ten Eustac de abbe . III . hiđ 7 III . v træ . 7 tciā
partē dim hidæ . Tra . ē . v . car . In dn̄io . ē una . 7 un miles
7 VIIII . uilti 7 XII . borđ 7 III . soch cū . IIII . car . Valuit . x . sot.

In eađ uilla ten Elmar de abbe dim hiđ. Modo . XL . sot.
7 ibi hT . I . car . 7 II . uilt 7 III . borđ cū dim car . In tota uilla
sunt . XXVI . ac pti . Valet h pars Ælmari . x . sot.

In *PIHTESLEA* ten Azo de abbe . v . hiđ 7 unā v træ.
Tra . ē . XIII . car . In dn̄io sunt . II . 7 II . serui . 7 v . uilti 7 totiđ
borđ cū . III . car . Ibi molin de . VIII . sot . 7 XI . ac pti.
Ibiđ hT azo . I . hiđ 7 dim . 7 ibi sunt . IIII . sochi cū . I . car.
Valuit tot cū recep . VIII . lib . Modo . C . soliđ.
Hoc M fuit de firma monachoꝝ . 7 ibi fuit dn̄icū ædificiū.

In *CATEWORDE* ten Eustach . I . hiđ 7 dim . Tra . ē . III . car.
Ibi sunt . IIII . sochi cū . I . car . Valuit . x . sot . Modo . v . sot.

In *ELDEWINCLE* sunt . III . hidæ . Tra . ē . x . car . In dn̄io . ē una.
7 IX . uilti 7 II . borđ 7 II . sochi cū . IIII . car 7 dimiđ . Ibi . xx . ac
pti . Silua . II . leuu lḡ . 7 una lat . Vat . xv . sot cū onerat.

21 In WADENHOE Roger holds 1½ virgates of land from the Abbot.
He has ½ plough, with
1 smallholder.
Meadow, 2 acres.
Value 5s.

22 In ACHURCH Azelin and 2 Englishmen hold 6½ hides from the Abbot.
Land for 10 ploughs. In lordship 3 ploughs; 3 slaves;
10 villagers and 11 smallholders with 5 ploughs.
Meadow, 20 acres; woodland, 6 acres.
The value was 60s; now 100s.

23 In TITCHMARSH Azelin holds 3 hides and 1 virgate of land 222 a
from the Abbot. Land for 5 ploughs. In lordship 2; 3 slaves;
7 villagers and 3 smallholders with 2 ploughs;
3 Freemen with 1 plough.
Meadow, 10 acres.
The value was 20s; now 55s.

24 In CLOPTON Eustace holds from the Abbot 3 hides and 3 virgates of
land and the third part of ½ hide. Land for 5 ploughs. In lordship 1;
1 man-at-arms, 9 villagers, 12 smallholders and 3 Freemen
with 4 ploughs.
The value was 10s; now 40s.
In the same village Aelmer holds ½ hide from the Abbot.
He has 1 plough, and
2 villagers and 3 smallholders with ½ plough.
In the whole village, meadow, 26 acres.
Value of Aelmer's part 10s.

[In ORLINGBURY Hundred]

25 In PYTCHLEY Azo holds 5 hides and 1 virgate of land from the Abbot.
Land for 13 ploughs. In lordship 2; 2 slaves;
5 villagers and as many smallholders with 3 ploughs.
A mill at 8s; meadow, 11 acres.
There Azo also has 1½ hides.
4 Freemen with 1 plough.
Value of the whole when acquired £8; now 100s.
This manor was (part) of the monks' revenue and a household
building was there.

[In NAVISFORD Hundred]

26 In CATWORTH Eustace holds 1½ hides. Land for 3 ploughs.
4 Freemen with 1 plough.
The value was 10s; now 5s.

[?In HUXLOE Hundred]

27 In ALDWINCLE 3 hides. Land for 10 ploughs. In lordship 1;
9 villagers, 2 smallholders and 2 Freemen with 4½ ploughs.
Meadow, 20 acres; woodland 2 leagues long and 1 wide; value
when stocked 15s.

Valuit . xx . sol . Modo . xxx . sol . Si bene exerceret . c . sol ualet. H tra fuit de uictu monachoꝝ T.R.E. Ferron ten p jussu regis: ctra uoluntate abbis.

In *WODEFORD* ten Roger . VII . hid de abbe . Tra . e . XII. car . In dnio sunt . II . car 7 dim . 7 IIII . serui . 7 XII . uilli 7 III. bord 7 XII . sochi cu . IX . car 7 dim . Ibi molin de . II . solid 7 xx . ac pti . Valuit . xx . sol . Modo . LX . sol.

In ead uilla ten Roger 7 Hugo 7 Siuuard . III . v trae de abbe 7 ibi hnt . I . car . 7 valet . x . sol . Tot m uuast fuit cu accepun.

In *EDINTONE* ten Hugo de abbe . III . hid . Tra . e . VIII . car. In dnio sunt . II . cu . I . seruo . 7 VIII . uilli 7 IIII . bord 7 I . sochs cu . IIII . car . Ibi molin de . XII . den 7 cc . anguill . 7 VIII . ac pti . Valuit . x . sol . Modo . XL . solid.

In *ERDINBVRNE* ten . IIII . milit de abbe . v . hid una v min . Ibi hnt . VI . car in dnio . 7 VIII . uill 7 II . bord cu . II . car. Ibi molin de . v . sol . Valuit . xx . sol . Modo . c . sol . Soca jacet in Burg.

In *CRANEFORD* ten Robt de abbe . III . hid . 7 I . mil de eo. Tra . e . VI . car . Ibi sunt . xv . sochi hntes . VI . car . Valuit . v . sol.

In *CRANEFORD* . e . I . hida 7 dim . Godric ten de rege. Modo . XL . sol. Tra . e . III . car . In dnio . e una 7 IIII. bord hnt alia car . Ibi molin de . II . sol . 7 IIII . ac pti . 7 totid siluæ . Valuit . x . sol . Modo . xx . solid.

In *DAILINTONE* ten Ricard de abbe . IIII . hid . Tra . e . VIII. car . In dnio sunt . II . 7 III . serui . 7 XVIII . uilli cu pbro 7 IIII. bord hnt . VI . car . Ibi molin de . xx . sol . 7 v . ac pti. Valuit . XL . sol . Modo . c . solid.

In *ASCETONE* . ten Iuo dim hid de abbe . Valet . IIII . solid.

The value was 20s; now 30s; if well managed, value 100s.
Before 1066 this land was for the supplies of the monks.
Ferron holds by the King's order, against the Abbot's will.

[In NAVISLAND Hundred]

28 In WOODFORD Roger holds 7 hides from the Abbot.
Land for 12 ploughs. In lordship 2½ ploughs; 4 slaves;
12 villagers, 3 smallholders and 12 Freemen with 9½ ploughs.
A mill at 2s; meadow, 20 acres.
The value was 20s; now 60s.
In the same village Roger, Hugh and Siward hold 3 virgates of land from the Abbot. They have 1 plough.
Value 10s.
The whole manor was waste when they received it.

29 In ADDINGTON Hugh holds 3 hides from the Abbot.
Land for 8 ploughs. In lordship 2, with 1 slave;
8 villagers, 4 smallholders and 1 Freeman with 4 ploughs.
A mill at 12d, and 200 eels; meadow, 8 acres.
The value was 10s; now 40s.

30 In IRTHLINGBOROUGH four men-at-arms hold 5 hides, less 1 virgate, from the Abbot. They have 6 ploughs in lordship and
8 villagers and 2 smallholders with 2 ploughs.
A mill at 5s.
The value was 20s; now 100s.
The jurisdiction lies in Peterborough.

31 In CRANFORD Robert holds 3 hides from the Abbot, and 1 man-at-arms from him. Land for 6 ploughs.
15 Freemen who have 6 ploughs.
The value was 5s; now 40s.

32 In CRANFORD 1½ hides. Godric holds from the King .....
Land for 3 ploughs. In lordship 1.
4 smallholders have another plough.
A mill at 2s; meadow, 4 acres; woodland, as many.
The value was 10s; now 20s.

[In NOBOTTLE Hundred]

33 In DALLINGTON Richard holds 4 hides from the Abbot. Land for 8 ploughs. In lordship 2; 3 slaves.
18 villagers with a priest and 4 smallholders have 6 ploughs.
A mill at 20s; meadow, 5 acres.
The value was 40s; now 100s.

[In POLEBROOK Hundred]

34 In ASHTON Ivo holds ½ hide from the Abbot.
Value 4s.

.VII. TERRA S PETRI DE WESTMON. *IN CORBIE HVND.*

ABBATIA S PETRI de WESTMON. ten *DENE*. Ibi sunt
II. hidæ 7 dimid. Tra. ē. VIII. car. In dñio sunt. II. 7 XVII. uitti
cũ pbro 7 VI. bord hñt. VI. car. 7 Duo fabri reddt. XXXII. sol.
Ibi molin de. III. sol. Silua. I. leuũ lg. 7 VIII. qrent lat.
Valuit 7 uat. VI. lib. Sep tenuit æccta. *IN HOCHESLAV HD*
Ipsa æccta ten in *SVTBVRG*. III. hid. Tra. ē. VIII. car.
In dñio. ē una. 7 XII. uitti 7 V. sochi cũ. II. bord hñt. VI. car.
Ibi molin de. VI. sol. Silua. VII. qrent lg. 7 VI. lat.
Valuit 7 uat. C. solid.

.VIII. TERRA SCI EDMVNDI. *IN RODEWELLE HD.*

ABBATIA S EDMVNDI ten de rege. I. hid de soca in
BOCTONE. Tra. ē. II. car. Ibi sunt. VI. uitti 7 II. bord
cũ. II. car. Ibi molin de XII. den. Silua. I. qrent lg. 7 I. lat.
Valuit. LXIIII. den. Modo. XII. solid. Algar [com] tenuit.
In *GADINTONE* ten abb. I. hid 7 unã v træ de soca. Tra. ē. II.
car. Ipsæ ibi sunt cũ. V. soch 7 IIII. bord. Valuit 7 uat. VI. sol.
In *ERNIWADE* ten abb dim v træ de soca. Ibi. ē. I. uitts
cũ. II. bord hns dimid car. Valuit 7 uat. III. solid.
In *SCADEWELLE* ten abb. I. hid 7 III. v træ. Tra. ē. III. car.
Ibi sunt ipsæ cũ. IX. sochis 7 IX. bord. Valuit 7 uat. XVI. sol.
Algar [com 9] tenuit. W. rex ded S Edmundo p anima [regine] Mathild.
In *HOHTONE* ten abb. I. hid 7 dim v træ. Tra. ē. II. car.
Has hñt ibi. III. sochi 7 XII. bord. Valuit 7 uat. XII. sol.

7 LAND OF ST. PETER'S OF WESTMINSTER 222 b

In CORBY Hundred

1 St. Peter's Abbey, Westminster, holds DEENE. 2½ hides.
Land for 8 ploughs. In lordship 2.
17 villagers with a priest and 6 smallholders have 6 ploughs.
2 smiths pay 32s.
A mill at 3s; woodland 1 league long and 8 furlongs wide.
The value was and is £6.
The Church has always held it.

In HUXLOE Hundred

2 The Church holds 3 hides itself in SUDBOROUGH. Land for 8 ploughs.
In lordship 1.
12 villagers and 5 Freemen with 2 smallholders have 6 ploughs.
A mill at 6s; woodland 7 furlongs long and 6 wide.
The value was and is 100s.

8 LAND OF ST. EDMUND'S

In ROTHWELL Hundred

1 St. Edmunds's Abbey holds from the King 1 hide of the jurisdiction
in BOUGHTON. Land for 2 ploughs.
6 villagers and 2 smallholders with 2 ploughs.
A mill at 12d; woodland 1 furlong long and 1 wide.
The value was 64d; now 12s.
Earl Algar held it.

The Abbey holds

2 in GEDDINGTON 1 hide and 1 virgate of land of the jurisdiction.
Land for 2 ploughs; they are there, with
5 Freemen and 4 smallholders.
The value was and is 6s.

3 in ARTHINGWORTH ½ virgate of land of the jurisdiction.
1 villager with 2 smallholders who has ½ plough.
The value was and is 3s.

[? in MAWSLEY Hundred]

4 in SCALDWELL 1 hide and 3 virgates of land. Land for 3 ploughs;
they are there, with
9 Freemen and 9 smallholders.
The value was and is 16s.
Earl Algar held it. King William gave it to St. Edmund's
for the soul of Queen Matilda.

5 in (Hanging) HOUGHTON 1 hide and ½ virgate of land.
Land for 2 ploughs.
3 Freemen and 12 smallholders have them there.
The value was and is 12s.

In *Langeport* ten abb unā v træ 7 unā bouatā. Tra. ē. I. car. Hanc hnt ibi. III. sochi. Valuit 7 uat. XL. denar.

In *Badebroc* ten abb dim v træ de soca. Tra. ē dim car. Hanc ht ibi. I. sochs. Valuit 7 uat. III. sot. *In Stodfald Hund.*

In *Ferendone* ten abb de soca dim hid 7 tciā partē uni v. Tra. ē. I. car. Ibi. ē. I. car 7 dim cū. III. soch. Valuit 7 uat. x. sot.

In *Vdetorp* ten abb. III. v tre 7 dimid Algar tenuit. de Soca. Tra. ē. I. car. Ibi. ē. I. sochs cū dim car. Valuit 7 uat. II. sot.

In *Clipestone* ten abb. II. v træ 7 dimid. Tra. ē. I. car. Ibi sunt. v. sochi cū. I. car 7 dimid. Valuit 7 uat. x. solid.

In *Calme* ten abb dimid hid de Soca. Tra. ē. dim car. I Ibi. v. sochi hnt. I. car. Valuit 7 uat. VI. solid. Valuit 7 uat. VI. den.

In *Medewelle* ten abb tciā partē uni v. Ibi. ē un sochs.

Ipse abb ten de rege *Werchintone*. *In Neveslund Hund.* Ibi sunt. III. hidæ 7 dim. Tra. ē. IX. car. In dnio sunt. II. car. 7 XVI. uitti 7 VIII. bord cū. VII. car. 7 III. serui. Ibi molin de. XII. solid. 7 XX. ac pti. Silua. III. qrent lg. 7 II. qz lat. Valuit. VII. lib. Modo. VIII. lib. Ælueua mat Morcari tenuit.

.IX. Terra S Benedicti De Ramesyg. *In Wilibroc Hd.*

Abbatia De Ramesyg ten unā v træ 7 dim in *Hala*. Tra. ē. I. car. Ipsa. ē ibi in dnio. 7 I. uitts 7 II. bord hnt dim car. Valuit 7 uat v. solid.

In *Lvditone* ten abb dim hid. Tra. ē dimid car. Hanc ht ibi un uitts. Valuit 7 uat. II. solid.

6 in LAMPORT 1 virgate of land and 1 bovate. Land for 1 plough.
3 Freemen have it there.
The value was and is 40d.

[in ROTHWELL Hundred]

7 in BRAYBROOKE ½ virgate of land of the jurisdiction. Land for ½ plough.
1 Freeman has it there.
The value was and is 3s.

in STOTFOLD Hundred

8 in (East) FARNDON ½ hide and the third part of 1 virgate of the jurisdiction. Land for 1 plough. 1½ ploughs there, with
3 Freemen.
The value was and is 10s.
Earl Algar held it.

9 in HOTHORPE 3½ virgates of land of the jurisdiction. Land for 1 plough.
1 Freeman with ½ plough.
The value was and is 2s.

10 in CLIPSTON 2½ virgates of land. Land for 1 plough.
5 Freemen with 1½ ploughs.
The value was and is 10s.

11 in *CALME* ½ hide of the jurisdiction. Land for ½ plough.
5 Freemen have 1 plough.
The value was and is 6s.

12 in MAIDWELL the third part of 1 virgate.
1 Freeman.
The value was and is 6d.

In NAVISLAND Hundred

13 The Abbey itself holds WARKTON from the King. 3½ hides.
Land for 9 ploughs. In lordship 2 ploughs;
16 villagers and 8 smallholders with 7 ploughs; 3 slaves.
A mill at 12s; meadow, 20 acres; woodland 3 furlongs long and 2 furlongs wide.
The value was £7; now £8.
Aelfeva, Morcar's mother, held it.

9 LAND OF ST. BENEDICT'S OF RAMSEY

In WILLYBROOK Hundred

1 Ramsey Abbbey holds 1½ virgates of land in HALEFIELD.
Land for 1 plough; it is there, in lordship.
1 villager and 2 smallholders have ½ plough.
The value was and is 5s.

The Abbey holds

2 in LUTTON ½ hide. Land for ½ plough.
1 villager has it there.
The value was and is 2s.

In *ADELINTONE* ten abb dimid hid. Tra. e dim car: Tam. II. uilli hnt ibi. I. car. 7 VI. acs pti. Valuit. III. sol. Val. V. sol. *IN POCHEBROC*

In *HEMINTONE* ten abb. II. hid. 7 dimid. Tra. e. IIII. car. *HVND.*

In dnio. e una. 7 VIII. uilli cu. I. bord hnt. III. car. Ibi. X. ac pti.

Valuit. X. sol. Modo. XX. solid. *IN HOCHESLAV HD.*

In *BERNEWELLE* ten abb. VI. hid. Tra. e. VIII. car. In dnio st. II. car.

7 III. serui. 7 XV. uilli cu pbro 7 VI. bord hnt. VI. car. Ibi. II. molini

de. XXIIII. solid. 7 XL. ac pti. Silua. VI. qz lg. 7 III. qz 7 dim lat.

Valuit. XXX. sol. modo. IIII. lib. *IN WIMERLEV HD.*

In *WICETONE* 7 *DODINTONE* ten abb. III. hid. Tra. e. VI. car.

In dnio sunt. II. 7 III. serui. 7 XX. uilli 7 VIII. bord 7 III. sochi cu. V. car.

222 c
Ibi molin de. XX. sol. 7 XX. ac pti. Silua n pastil una qz

lg. 7 una lat. Valuit. XXX. solid. Modo. IIII. lib.

In Brachefeld. e una dom ptin ad *WICETONE*. cu. V. acris

træ. De dimid acra ht soca Judit comitissa.

.X. TERRA ÆCCLE DE TORNIG. *IN HOCHESLAV HD.*

ABBATIA DE THORNYG ten in *TVIWELLA*. III. hid.

vna v 7 dim min. Tra. e. VII. car. In dnio sunt. II. 7 IX. uilli

7 V. bord cu. V. car. Ibi. II. molini de. VII. sol 7 IIII. den.

7 II. ac siluæ. Valuit. X. sol. Modo. XL. sol. *IN GRAVESEND*

Ipsa abbatia ten dimid hid in *CERWELTONE*. *HVND.*

7 Balduin de ea. Tra. e. I. car. In dnio. e dim. 7 I. uills cu. I.

bord ht dim car. Valuit. XII. denar. Modo. V. solid.

In *SALWEBRIGE*. ten Turchil de abbe. V. hid. Tra. e. V.

car. Ibi sunt. XII. uilli 7 V. bord cu. IIII. car. 7 VIII. ac pti.

Valuit. L. sol. Modo. LX. solid.

3 in ELTON ½ hide. Land for ½ plough.
2 villagers have 1 plough there, however, and meadow, 6 acres.
The value was 3s; value 5s.

in POLEBROOK Hundred

4 in HEMINGTON 2½ hides. Land for 4 ploughs. In lordship 1.
8 villagers with 1 smallholder have 3 ploughs.
Meadow, 10 acres.
The value was 10s; now 20s.

in HUXLOE Hundred

5 in BARNWELL 6 hides. Land for 8 ploughs. In lordship 2 ploughs; 3 slaves.
15 villagers with a priest and 6 smallholders have 6 ploughs.
2 mills at 24s; meadow, 40 acres; woodland 6 furlongs long and 3½ furlongs wide.
The value was 30s; now £4.

in WYMERSLEY Hundred

6 in WHISTON and DENTON 3 hides. Land for 6 ploughs.
In lordship 2; 3 slaves;
20 villagers, 8 smallholders and 3 Freemen with 5 ploughs.
A mill at 20s; meadow, 20 acres; woodland without 222 c
pasture 1 furlong long and 1 wide.
The value was 30s; now £4.
In Brafield (on the Green) is a house which belongs to Whiston with 5 acres of land. Countess Judith has the jurisdiction of ½ acre.

10 LAND OF THORNEY CHURCH

In HUXLOE Hundred

1 The Abbey of Thorney holds 3 hides, less 1½ virgates, in TWYWELL.
Land for 7 ploughs. In lordship 2;
9 villagers and 5 smallholders with 5 ploughs.
2 mills at 7s 4d; woodland, 2 acres.
The value was 10s; now 40s.

In GRAVESEND Hundred

2 The Abbey holds ½ hide itself in CHARWELTON, and Baldwin from it. Land for 1 plough. In lordship ½.
1 villager with 1 smallholder has ½ plough.
The value was 12d; now 5s.

3 In SAWBRIDGE Thorkell holds 5 hides from the Abbot.
Land for 5 ploughs.
12 villagers and 5 smallholders with 4 ploughs.
Meadow, 8 acres.
The value was 50s; now 60s.

.XI. TERRA ÆCCL̄Æ DE CRVILAND. *IN OPTONGREN HD̄.*

ABBATIA DE CRVILAND teñ in *WRIDTORP* .I.hiđ
7 dimiđ . Tra . ē . II . car . In dn̄io . ē una 7 XI . uitti 7 II . borđ
cū . II . car . Ibi . VI . ac̄ p̄ti . 7 molin̄ de . v . sol . Valet . XL . sol.
In *ELMINTONE* teñ abb̄ . I . hiđ . Tra . ē . I . car . Hæc . ē ibi
in dn̄io . 7 II . uitti 7 II . borđ cū . I . car . 7 VI . ac̄ p̄ti ibi.
Valuit . VIII . sol . Modo . XVI . soliđ.
In *ELMINTONE* teñ abb̄ . II . hiđ . Tra . ē . III . car . Ibi st̄
.V . uitti 7 IIII . borđ . cū . III . car . Ibi XII . ac̄ p̄ti.
Valuit . XII . sol . Modo . XX . soliđ. *IN NEVESLVND HD̄.*
In *EDINTONE* teñ abb̄ . II . hiđ . Tra . ē . IIII . car . In dn̄io
est una . 7 II . serui . 7 VI . uitti 7 III . borđ cū . I . socho hn̄t
III . car . Ibi . VI . ac̄ p̄ti . 7 molin̄ de . XIII . sol . 7 IIII . deñ.
Valuit . XV . sol . Modo . XL . soliđ.
In *WENDLEBERIE* teñ abb̄ . V . hiđ 7 dimiđ . Tra . ē
XII . car . In dn̄io . ē una car cū . I . seruo . 7 XXI . uitti
cū p̄bro 7 VII . borđ 7 XI . sochis hn̄t . XI . car . Ibi . II.
molini de . XVI . soliđ . 7 XXX . ac̄ p̄ti.
Valuit . L . sol . 7 post . XL . sol . Modo . VI . lib̄.
In *BADEBI* . teñ abb̄ . IIII . hiđ. *IN GRAVESEND HD̄*
Tra . ē . X . car . In dn̄io sunt . IIII . car 7 VIII . serui . 7 V.
ancillæ . 7 XII . uitti 7 VIII . borđ cū . VI . car.
Ibi molin̄ de . II . soliđ . 7 XXVIII . ac̄ p̄ti . Silua . IIII.
q̄rent lḡ . 7 II . q̄z lat . Valuit 7 ual . VIII . lib̄.

.XII. TERRA ÆCCL̄E DE COVENTREV *IN GISLEBVRG HD̄ 7 DIM̄.*

ABBATIA DE COVENTREV teñ . III . hiđ 7 unā v̄ træ
in *WINEWICHE* . Tra . ē . VI . car 7 dimiđ . Ibi sunt in

1 LAND OF CROWLAND CHURCH

In UPTON Hundred

1 Crowland Abbey holds 1½ hides in WOTHORPE.
Land for 2 ploughs. In lordship 1;
11 villagers and 2 smallholders with 2 ploughs.
Meadow, 6 acres; a mill at 5s.
Value 40s.

The Abbey holds

[in WILLYBROOK Hundred]

2 in ELMINGTON 1 hide. Land for 1 plough. It is there, in lordship.
2 villagers and 2 smallholders with 1 plough.
Meadow, 6 acres.
The value was 8s; now 16s.

3 in ELMINGTON 2 hides. Land for 3 ploughs.
5 villagers and 4 smallholders with 3 ploughs.
Meadow, 12 acres.
The value was 12s; now 20s.

in NAVISLAND Hundred

4 in ADDINGTON 2 hides. Land for 4 ploughs.
In lordship 1; 2 slaves.
6 villagers and 3 smallholders with 1 Freeman have 3 ploughs.
Meadow, 6 acres; a mill at 13s 4d.
The value was 15s; now 40s.

[?in HAMFORDSHOE Hundred]

5 in WELLINGBOROUGH 5½ hides. Land for 12 ploughs.
In lordship 1 plough, with 1 slave.
21 villagers with a priest, 7 smallholders and 11 Freemen have 11 ploughs.
2 mills at 16s; meadow, 30 acres.
The value was 50s; later 40s; now £6.

in GRAVESEND Hundred

6 in BADBY 4 hides. Land for 10 ploughs. In lordship 4 ploughs;
8 male and 5 female slaves;
12 villagers and 8 smallholders with 6 ploughs.
A mill at 2s; meadow, 28 acres; woodland 4 furlongs long and 2 furlongs wide.
The value was and is £8.

2 LAND OF COVENTRY CHURCH

In GUILSBOROUGH Hundred and a half

1 Coventry Abbey holds 3 hides and 1 virgate of land in WINWICK.
Land for 6½ ploughs. In lordship 3 ploughs.

dñio . III . car . 7 XVI . uitti 7 V . bord hnt . III . car.

In *Essebi* ten abb . II . hid 7 dim . 7 ptin ad ⁊ Valet . L . sol.
Wineuuiche . Tra . e . V . car . Ibi sunt . IIII . uitti 7 V . bord
cu . II . car . Valet . X . sol. *In Alvratlev hd.*

In *Chidesbi* ten abb . II . hid . Tra . e . V . car . In dnio st . II
7 III . serui . 7 X . uitti 7 VIII . bord cu . III . car . Ibi . VIII . ac pti.

In *Eddone* ten abb . II . hid . Tra . e . IIII . car. ⁊ Valet . L . sol.
Ibi st . IIII . uitti cu . II . bord 7 IIII . sochis hnt . IIII . car . Val . XX . sol.
Vna ex his hid redd soca in Wineuuiche.

222 d

.XIII. TERRA ÆCCLÆ DE EVESHAM. *IN GRAVESEND HD*

Abbatia De Evesha ten . IIII . hid in *Liceberge*.
Tra . e . X . car . In dnio sunt . II . 7 VIII . uitti 7 VI . bord
cu . V . car . Valuit 7 ual . XL . sol . Leuenot libe tenuit T.R.E.

.XIIII. TERRA ÆCCLÆ DE GRESTAIN.

Abbatia S marie De Grestain ten de rege
in elemos *Nevbote* . Ibi sunt . II . part uni hidæ
Tra . e . I . car 7 dim . In dnio . e una . 7 III . uitti cu . I . bord
hnt dimid car . Ibi molin de . II . solid . Valuit 7 ual . VI . sol.

In *Baiebroc* ten ipsa æccta . II . hid . Tra . e . IIII . car.
In dnio . e una . cu . I . seruo . 7 IIII . uitti 7 IIII . bord cu . III .
car . Valuit . VI . sol . Modo . X . sol . Vlchet tenuit has tras.

In *Clenedone* ten ipsa æccta dim hid 7 tcia parte
uni hidæ . Tra . e . II . car . Ibi sunt . IIII . uitti 7 IIII . bord

16 villagers and 5 smallholders with a priest have 3 ploughs.
Value 50s.

2 In (Cold) ASHBY the Abbey holds 2½ hides; they belong to Winwick.
Land for 5 ploughs.
4 villagers and 5 smallholders with 2 ploughs.
Value 10s.

In ALWARDSLEY Hundred

3 In KILSBY the Abbey holds 2 hides. Land for 5 ploughs.
In lordship 2; 3 slaves;
10 villagers and 8 smallholders with 3 ploughs.
Meadow, 8 acres.
Value 50s.

[In GUILSBOROUGH Hundred and a half]

4 In (West) HADDON the Abbey holds 2 hides. Land for 4 ploughs.
4 villagers with 2 smallholders and 4 Freemen have 4 ploughs.
Value 20s.
One of these hides pays jurisdiction in Winwick.

13 LAND OF EVESHAM CHURCH 222 d

In GRAVESEND Hundred

1 Evesham Abbey holds 4 hides in LITCHBOROUGH.
Land for 10 ploughs. In lordship 2;
8 villagers and 6 smallholders with 5 ploughs.
The value was and is 40s.
Leofnoth held it freely before 1066.

14 LAND OF GRESTAIN CHURCH

[In ROTHWELL Hundred]

1 The Abbey of St. Mary of Grestain holds NEWBOTTLE from the King
in alms. 2 parts of 1 hide. Land for 1½ ploughs. In lordship 1.
3 villagers with 1 smallholder have ½ plough.
A mill at 2s.
The value was and is 6s.

The Church itself holds

2 in BRAYBROOKE 2 hides. Land for 4 ploughs. In lordship 1,
with 1 slave;
4 villagers and 4 smallholders with 3 ploughs.
The value was 6s; now 10s.
Ulfketel held these lands.

3 in GLENDON ½ hide and the third part of 1 hide. Land for 2 ploughs.
4 villagers and 4 smallholders with 1 slave who have 1 plough.

cū . i . seruo hn̄tes . i . car̄ . Valuit . v . sol̄ . Modo . x . sol̄.

In *Ristone* ten̄ ipsa æccl̄a dim̄ v̄ ⌈Vlf lib̄e tenuit.

træ . Tra . ē dimid̄ car̄ . Ibi sunt . ii . bord̄ . Valet . xvi . den̄.

Ipsa æccl̄a ten̄ *Arintone*. *In Rodewelle Hund̄*.

Ibi sunt . v . hidæ . 7 tcia pars uni̇ hidæ . Tra . ē . x . car̄.

In dn̄io sunt . iii . car̄ . 7 xii . uilli 7 xiii . bord̄ cū . v . car̄.

7 iiii . sochi cū . ii . car̄ . Ibi . iiii . molini de . ii . solid̄.

Valuit . xxx . sol̄ . Modo . vi . lib̄ . Vlf tenuit.

In *Westone* ten̄ ipsa æccl̄a . i . hid̄ 7 dim̄ . Tra . ē . iii . car̄.

In dn̄io . ē una 7 dim̄ . 7 ii . serui . 7 iiii . uilli 7 ii . bord̄

cū dim̄ car̄ . Ibi . v . ac̄ p̄ti . Valuit . xx . sol̄ . Modo . xxx . sol̄.

Vlf tenuit T.R.E.

.XV. Terra Ansgeri Capellani *In Stotfald hd̄*.

Ansgervs clericus ten̄ de rege . i . hid̄ 7 iii . v̄ træ in *Mede welle* . 7 ibi h̄t . ii . car̄ 7 ii . seruos . 7 v . uill̄ 7 ii . bord̄ cū . ii . car̄ . Valet . xx . solid̄ . Godric tenuit T.R.E.

.XVI. Terra S̄ Remigii Remis. *In Coduuestan hd̄*.

Æccl̄a S̄ Remigii ten̄ de rege *Lepelie* . Similit̄ tenuit T.R.E . Ibi cū append̄ sunt . iii . hidæ . Tra . ē . vi . car̄. In dn̄io sunt . iii . car̄ . 7 v . serui . 7 xviii . uilli 7 ix . bord̄ cū . viii . car̄ . Ibi . xvi . ac̄ p̄ti . Nem̄ . iii . q̄rq̄ lḡ . 7 totid̄ lat̄ . Valet . l . solid̄.

In *Mersetone* ten̄ . ii . hoēs S̄ Remigii . i . hid̄ . Tra . ē . i . car̄ . Valet . v . sol̄ . Goduin̄ tenuit cū soca 7 saca.

The value was 5s; now 10s.
Ulf held it freely.

4 in RUSHTON ½ virgate of land. Land for ½ plough.
2 smallholders.
Value 16d.

in ROTHWELL Hundred

5 HARRINGTON. 5 hides and the third part of 1 hide. Land for 10 ploughs.
In lordship 3 ploughs;
12 villagers and 13 smallholders with 5 ploughs;
4 Freemen with 2 ploughs.
4 mills at 2s.
The value was 30s; now £6.
Ulf held it.

[in SPELHOE Hundred]

6 in WESTON (Favell) 1½ hides. Land for 3 ploughs.
In lordship 1½; 2 slaves;
4 villagers and 2 smallholders with ½ plough.
Meadow, 5 acres.
The value was 20s; now 30s.
Ulf held it before 1066.

15 LAND OF ANSGER THE CHAPLAIN

In STOTFOLD Hundred

1 Ansger the Clerk holds 1 hide and 3 virgates of land in MAIDWELL from the King. He has 2 ploughs, 2 slaves,
5 villagers and 2 smallholders with 2 ploughs.
Value 20s.
Godric held it before 1066.

16 LAND OF ST. REMY'S OF RHEIMS

In CUTTLESTONE Hundred *(STAFFORDSHIRE)*

1 The Church of St. Remy holds LAPLEY from the King. It held it similarly before 1066. With dependencies 3 hides.
Land for 6 ploughs. In lordship 3 ploughs; 5 slaves;
18 villagers and 9 smallholders with 8 ploughs.
Meadow, 16 acres; wood 3 furlongs long and as many wide.
Value 50s.

2 In MARSTON two of St. Remy's men hold 1 hide. Land for 1 plough.
Value 5s.
Godwin held it, with full jurisdiction.

.XVII. TERRA ELEMOSINAR REGIS. *IN FOXLE HVND.*

LEWIN pbr ten de rege unã v træ in *ETENESTONE*. Ibi dimid car poteſt. ee. Valet. VI. ſol. *IN GRAVESEND HD.*

GODVIN pbr ten de rege. IIII. partes dimid hidæ in *FELVES LEA*. Tra. ē. I. car. 7 ibi. ē cũ. IIII. bord. Valet. x. ſolid.

GODVIN pbr 7 Vluuin ten de rege. III. v træ. 7 qntã partẽ uni v in *SVTONE*. Tra. ē. II. car. 7 ibi ſunt cũ. IX. bord. Ibi moliñ de. XXXII. den. Valet. XV. ſol. *IN CLAILEA HD.*

RAINALD ten de rege dimid hid in *PASSEHÃ*. 7 ibi hĩ. I. car cũ. IIII. bord. Valet. x. ſolid. *IN SPELEHOV HD.*

GODVIN pbr ten de rege. unã v træ 7 dim in *BVCHETONE*. 7 ibi hĩ dimid car. Valet. v. ſolid

223 a

.XVIII. TERRA COMITIS MORITON. *IN ANVESDESOV HD.*

COMES MORITON ten. IIII. hid in *SNEWELLE*. Tra ē. x. car. In dñio ſunt. III. car. 7 VI. ſerui. 7 XVIII. uilli 7. II. bord cũ. III. car. Ibi. XX. ac pti. Valuit. XX. ſol Modo. VI. lib. Oſmund. f. Leuric tenuit cũ ſoca 7 ſaca. Huj træ. II. hidæ sĩ in dñio. Judit comit' calũniat Soc. uni v 7 dim.

In *BELINGE* ten com dim hid 7 dim v træ. Tra. ē. I. car.

* Ibi ſunt. III. uilli cũ. II. bob. 7 XX. ac pti. Valuit. II. ſolid Modo. x. ſol. Oſmund libe tenuit. *IN NIVEBOT HD*

In *BVCHEBROC* ten com. IIII. hid. Tra. ē. x. car. In dñio

17 LAND OF THE KING'S ALMSMEN

In FOXLEY Hundred

1 Leofwin the priest holds from the King 1 virgate of land in ADSTONE. ½ plough possible.
Value 6s.

In GRAVESEND Hundred

2 Godwin the priest holds from the King 4 parts of ½ hide in FAWSLEY. Land for 1 plough; it is there, with
4 smallholders.
Value 10s.

[In SUTTON Hundred]

3 Godwin the priest and Wulfwin hold from the King 3 virgates of land and the fifth part of 1 virgate in (Kings) SUTTON. Land for 2 ploughs; they are there, with
9 smallholders.
A mill at 32d.
Value 15s.

In CLEYLEY Hundred

4 Reginald holds from the King ½ hide in PASSENHAM.
He has 1 plough, with
4 smallholders.
Value 10s.

In SPELHOE Hundred

5 Godwin the priest holds from the King 1½ virgates of land in BOUGHTON. He has ½ plough.
Value 5s.

18 LAND OF THE COUNT OF MORTAIN 223 a

In HAMFORDSHOE Hundred

1 The Count of Mortain holds 4 hides in SYWELL. Land for 10 ploughs.
In lordship 3 ploughs; 6 slaves;
18 villagers and 2 smallholders with 3 ploughs.
Meadow, 20 acres.
The value was 20s; now £6.
Osmund son of Leofric held it, with full jurisdiction.
Of this land 2 hides are in lordship. Countess Judith claims the jurisdiction of 1½ virgates.

The Count holds

2 in BILLING ½ hide and ½ virgate of land. Land for 1 plough.
3 villagers with 2 oxen.
Meadow, 10 acres.
The value was 2s; now 10s.
Osmund held it freely.

in NOBOTTLE Hundred

3 in BUGBROOKE 4 hides. Land for 10 ploughs. In lordship

ſunt.III.car.7 IIII.ſerui.7 XXX.uitti 7 XIIII.bord cū.X.
car.Ibi.II.molini de.XL.ſol.7 XXX.ac pti.7 IIII.ac ſiluæ.
In *Westone* ten com.II.hid 7 dim. *In Spelho Hund.*
Tra.ē.V.car.In dn̄io ſunt.II.7 IIII.ſerui.7 XII.uitti 7 II.bord
cū.III.car 7 dim.Ibi.X.ac pti.Valuit.XL.ſol.Modo.LX.ſol.
In *Bellica*.ē Soca huj ↄn.II.v træ 7 dim. Leuric libe tenuit.
Tra.ē.I.car.Ibi ſunt.II.uitti cū.I.bord.7 VII.ac pti.
Valuit 7 ual.X.ſol. *In Niwebotle Hd.*
In *Eddone* ten com.II.hid 7 dim.Ex his.I.in dn̄io.ē.Tra.ē.V.
car.In dn̄io ſunt.III.car.7 IX.ſerui.7 VII.uitti cū pbro 7 VII.
bord hn̄t.II.car.Ibi molin de.X.ſolid.7 VIII.ac pti.7 X.ac
minutæ ſiluæ.Valuit XL.ſol.Modo.IIII.lib.
In *Ravenestorp* ten.C.dim.hid.Tra.ē.II.car.Ibi.ē un uitts
cū.II.bord.Valuit 7 ual.V.ſol.Edmar libe tenuit utraſq; tras.
In *Brantone* ten.C.IIII.hid.V.acs min.Tra.ē.VIII.car.
In dn̄io.ē una hida 7 ibi.II.car.7 II.ſerui.7 III.uitti 7 V.bord
7 XII.ſochi cū.III.car 7 dim int oms.Ibi molin de.XXVIII.ſol.
7 X.ac pti.7 V.ac minutæ ſiluæ.Valuit.LX.ſol.modo.C.ſol.
Huj tre dimid hid tenuit Vlmar T.R.E.Reliq tota jac 7 jacuit
in Cretone 7 Eddone. appciata.ē.
In altera *Haiford* ten.C.tciā partē uni v.quæ cū capitali ↄn
In *Aldritone*.ten.C.II.hid 7 dim v træ. *In Cailæ Hund*
Tra.ē.VIII.car.In dn̄io ſunt.II.hide 7 dim v.7 ibi.III.car.
cū.I.ſeruo.7 III.uitti 7 III.bord cū.II.car.Ibi.XII.ac pti.Silua
III.qrent lg.7 tntd lat.Valuit.XL.ſol.Modo.L.ſolid.
Edmar 7 Eduin libe tenuer *In Elboldestov Hd.*
In *Elmedene* ten Com.IIII.hid.Tra.ē.X.car.In dn̄io ſunt.II.hidæ

3 ploughs; 4 slaves;
30 villagers and 14 smallholders with 10 ploughs.
2 mills at 40s; meadow, 30 acres; woodland, 4 acres.
[Value......]

in SPELHOE Hundred

4 in WESTON (Favell) 2½ hides. Land for 5 ploughs.
In lordship 2; 4 slaves;
12 villagers and 2 smallholders with 3½ ploughs.
Meadow, 10 acres.
The value was 40s; now 60s.
Leofric held it freely.

In BILLING is a jurisdiction of this manor. 2½ virgates of land.
Land for 1 plough.
2 villagers with 1 smallholder.
Meadow, 7 acres.
The value was and is 10s.

in NOBOTTLE Hundred

5 in (East) HADDON 2½ hides. One of these is in lordship.
Land for 5 ploughs. In lordship 3 ploughs; 9 slaves.
7 villagers with a priest and 7 smallholders have 2 ploughs.
A mill at 10s; meadow, 8 acres; underwood, 10 acres.
The value was 40s; now £4.

6 in RAVENSTHORPE ½ hide. Land for 2 ploughs.
1 villager with 2 smallholders.
The value was and is 5s.
Edmer held both lands freely.

7 in BRAMPTON 4 hides, less 5 acres. Land for 8 ploughs.
In lordship 1 hide; 2 ploughs there; 2 slaves;
3 villagers, 5 smallholders and 12 Freemen with 3½ ploughs between them.
A mill at 28s; meadow, 10 acres; underwood, 5 acres.
The value was 60s; now 100s.
Wulfmer held ½ hide of this land before 1066; all the rest lies and lay in Creaton and (East) Haddon (lands).

8 in the other HEYFORD the third part of 1 virgate which is assessed with the head manor.

in CLEYLEY Hundred

9 in ALDERTON 2 hides and ½ virgate of land. Land for 8 ploughs.
In lordship 2 hides and ½ virgate; 3 ploughs there, with 1 slave;
3 villagers and 3 smallholders with 2 ploughs.
Meadow, 12 acres; woodland 3 furlongs long and as wide.
The value was 40s; now 50s.
Edmer and Edwin held it freely.

in ALBOLDSTOW Hundred

10 in HELMDON 4 hides. Land for 10 ploughs. In lordship 2 hides;
5 ploughs there; 2 slaves;

7 ibi.v.car.7 II.serui.7 VII.uitti 7 II.bord cu.II.car.Ibi molin de.XII.den.Valuit 7 ual.VI.lib.Aluuin 7 Goduin libe tenuer.

In *CELVERDESCOTE* ten Com.IIII.hid.Tra.e.x.car. *IN GRAVESEND HD.*

In dnio sunt.II.hidæ huj træ.7 ibi un seru.7 IX.uitti 7 III.bord cu pbro hnt.IIII.car 7 dim.Ibi.VI.ac pti.Silua.II.qz lg. 7 una qz 7 dim lat.Valuit.XL.sol.Modo.LX.solid. Turbern 7 Alli libe tenuer. *IN CLAILEA HUND.*

In *COVESGRAVE* ten.IIII.partes dim hidæ.Tra.e.I.car.quæ ibi.e cu.III.uittis.Valuit.v.sol.m.IIII.sol.Goduin libe tenuit.

IN STOCHE HUND.

HUNFRID ten de comite Morit.III.v træ in *CARLINTONE*. Tra.e.III.car.In dnio sunt.II.7 VII.sochi cu.VI.bord hnt.IIII. car.Ibi molin de.XVI.den.7 VIII.ac pti.Silua.II.qz lg.7 dim qrent lat.Valuit.x.sol.Modo.xx.sol.Leuric libe tenuit.

Idem ten.I.hid 7 tcia parte hidæ.7 una bouat 7 dim in *DINGLEI*. Tra.e.III.car.In dnio.e una.7 v.uitti hnt alia.Ibi.IIII.ac pti. 7 v.ac siluæ.Valuit.x.solid.Modo.xx.solid.Eduin libe tenuit.

Idem ten.II.hid 7 una v træ 7 II.partes uni v in *ARNIWORDE*.

223 b

Tra.e.v.car.In dnio sunt.II.car.cu.I.seruo.7 IX.uitti cu.I.bord 7 VIII.sochis cu.III.car.Valuit 7 ual.xx.solid.Vlf 7 Fardein tenuer.

In *PIPEWELLE* ten ide.H.tcia parte uni hidæ.Tra.e.I.car. qua hnt ibi.IIII.bord Valuit.III.sol.Modo.v.sol.Vlchetel libe tenuit

Idem ten in *SIBERTOD*.III.hid una v min. *IN STOTFALD HD.*

7 villagers and 2 smallholders with 2 ploughs.
A mill at 12d.
The value was and is £6.
Alwin and Godwin held it freely.

in GRAVESEND Hundred

11 in *CELVERDESCOTE* 4 hides. Land for 10 ploughs. In lordship 2 hides of this land; 1 slave there.
9 villagers and 3 smallholders with a priest have 4½ ploughs.
Meadow, 6 acres; woodland 2 furlongs long and 1½ furlongs wide.
The value was 40s; now 60s.
Thorbern and Alli held it freely.

In CLEYLEY Hundred

12 In COSGROVE he holds 4 parts of ½ hide. Land for 1 plough, which is there, with
3 villagers.
The value was 5s; now 4s.
Godwin held it freely.

In STOKE Hundred

13 Humphrey holds 3 virgates of land in (East) CARLTON from the Count of Mortain. Land for 3 ploughs. In lordship 2.
7 Freemen with 6 smallholders have 4 ploughs.
A mill at 16d; meadow, 8 acres;
woodland 2 furlongs long and ½ furlong wide.
The value was 10s; now 20s.
Leofric held it freely.

14 He also holds 1 hide and the third part of a hide and 1½ bovates in DINGLEY. Land for 3 ploughs. In lordship 1.
5 villagers have another.
Meadow, 4 acres; woodland, 5 acres.
The value was 10s; now 20s.
Edwin held it freely.

[In ROTHWELL Hundred]

15 He also holds 2 hides and 1 virgate of land and 2 parts of 1 virgate
in ARTHINGWORTH. Land for 5 ploughs. In lordship 2 ploughs, 223 b
with 1 slave;
9 villagers with 1 smallholder and 8 Freemen with 3 ploughs.
The value was and is 20s.
Ulf and Farthin held it.

16 In PIPEWELL Humphrey also holds the third part of 1 hide. Land for 1 plough, which
4 smallholders have there.
The value was 3s; now 5s.
Ulfketel held it freely.

He also holds

in STOTFOLD Hundred

17 in SIBBERTOFT 3 hides, less 1 virgate. Land for 9 ploughs.

T͛ra.ē.ix.car͛. In d͞nio st͞.ii.7 iiii.ſerui.7 v.ancillæ.7 viii.uitti
cū p̄bro hn͞t.ii.car͛. Ibi.xx.ac͛ p̄ti. Valuit.v.ſol.m̄.xxx.ſol.
Idem ten͛.iii.v͛ træ 7 t͛cia͞ parte͞ uni⁹ v͛ in *FAREDONE*.
T͛ra.ē.ii.car͛. In d͞nio.ē una.7 iii.uitti hn͞t alia͞. Valuit.ii.ſol.
Modo.v.ſolid. Fregis 7 Brumage tenuer͞.
Idem ten͛.ii.hid 7 una͞ v͛ træ 7 t͛cia͞ parte͞ uni⁹ v͛ in *BVGEDONE*.
T͛ra.ē.vi.car͞.In d͞nio.ē una.cū.i.ſeruo.7 xi.uitti cū.i.
bord hn͞t.ii.car͞. Ibi molin͞ de.xvi.den͛.7 viii.ac͛ p̄ti.
7 iii.ſochi cū.ii.car͞. Valuit.lxiiii.den͛.Modo.xxx.ſol.
Idē ten͛.i.hid 7 t͛cia͞ parte͞ uni⁹ v͛ Goduin⁹ 7 Wlſin⁹ tenuer͞.
in *OXEDONE*.T͛ra.ē.ii.car͞.In d͞nio.ē una.nil a͞plius.
Valuit.xii.den͛.Modo.x.ſolid. Fregis tenuit.
Idem ten͛.iii.hid in *ESBECE*.T͛ra.ē.ix.car͞.In d͞nio st͞.ii.
7 ix.uitti 7 x.bord hn͞t.vii.car͛. Valuit.xx.ſol.M̊.xl.ſol.
Ælmar⁹ 7 Norman tenuer͞.T.R.E. Edric⁹ lib͞e tenuit. Vaſta.ē.
Idē ten͛ dimid bouat͛ træ in *HEROLVESTONE*.T͛ra.ē.ii.bob⁹.
Idē ten͛.ii.partes.i.hidæ in *OLLETORP*.T͛ra.ē.ii.car͛.
In d͞nio h͞t una͞ cū.iii.ſeruis.7 un⁹ miles h͞t alia͞ cū.iii.bord.
Ibi.viii.ac͛ p̄ti.7 ii.ac͛ ſpineti. Valuit.v.ſol. Modo.xx.ti ſol.
Toſti 7 Snoterman lib͞e tenuer͞. *IN CLAVESLEA HD̄*.
Idē ten͛.v.partes uni⁹ hidæ in *COVESGRAVE*.Soca jac͛ in Paſeha͞.
T͛ra.ē.i.car͛ 7 dim͛.7 tot ibi ſunt cū.iiii.bord.Ibi.x.ac͛
p̄ti.7 ii.q̄rent͛ ſiluæ minutæ.Valuit 7 ual.xx.ſol. Ailric
Idē ten͛ una͞ v͛ træ in *PIDEṢFORD*. *IN SPELHO HD̄*. lib͞e tenuit.
T͛ra.ē dim͛ car͛.7 ibi.ē cū.i.bord.Molin͞ de.ii.ſol.ibi.
Valuit.iii.ſolid.Modo.x.ſolid.Oſmund⁹ lib͞e tenuit.

In lordship 2; 4 male and 5 female slaves.
8 villagers with a priest have 2 ploughs.
Meadow, 20 acres.
The value was 5s; now 30s.

18 in (East) FARNDON 3 virgates of land and the third part of 1 virgate.
Land for 2 ploughs. In lordship 1.
3 villagers have another.
The value was 2s; now 5s.
Fregis and Brumage held it.

19 in (Little) BOWDEN 2 hides and 1 virgate of land and the third part of 1 virgate. Land for 6 ploughs. In lordship 1, with 1 slave.
11 villagers with 1 smallholder have 2 ploughs.
A mill at 16d; meadow, 8 acres; 3 Freemen with 2 ploughs.
The value was 64d; now 30s.
Godwin and Wulfwin held it.

20 in OXENDON 1 hide and the third part of 1 virgate.
Land for 2 ploughs. In lordship 1; nothing more.
The value was 12d; now 10s.
Fregis held it.

21 in HASELBECH 3 hides. Land for 9 ploughs. In lordship 2.
9 villagers and 10 smallholders have 7 ploughs.
The value was 20s; now 40s.
Aelmer and Norman held it before 1066.

[in NOBOTTLE Hundred]

22 in HARLESTONE ½ bovate of land. Land for 2 oxen.
Edric held it freely. It is waste.

23 in ALTHORP 2 parts of 1 hide. Land for 2 ploughs. In lordship he has 1, with 3 slaves. A man-at-arms has another, with 3 smallholders.
Meadow, 8 acres; spinney, 2 acres.
The value was 5s; now 20s.
Tosti and Snoterman held it freely.

in CLEYLEY Hundred

24 in COSGROVE 5 parts of 1 hide. The jurisdiction lies in Passenham.
Land for 1½ ploughs; they are all there, with 4 smallholders.
Meadow, 10 acres; underwood, 2 furlongs.
The value was and is 20s.
Alric held it freely.

in SPELHOE Hundred

25 in PITSFORD 1 virgate of land. Land for ½ plough; it is there, with 1 smallholder.
A mill at 2s.
The value was 3s; now 10s.
Osmund held it freely.

ALANVS ten de Comite unã v træ in *DESBVRG*.Tra.ẽ.I.
car.Ibi.ẽ dimiđ car.cũ.II.borđ.Valuit.III.sol m.v.sol.
Idẽ ten.I.hiđ in *WOLTONE*.Tra.ẽ.II.car.Fregis tenuit.
In dñio.ẽ una.7 II.serui.7 II.uilli cũ pbro 7 VI.borđ hñt
aliã car.Ibi.v.ac pti.7 molin de.XL.den.Valuit.x.sol.
Modo.LX.sol.Boui libe tenuit.
Idẽ ten.II.hiđ 7 IIII.partes dimiđ hidæ in *HECHÃ*.Tra.ẽ
VI.car.In dñio.ẽ una.7 IIII.uilli cũ pbro 7 III.borđ hñt.I.car.
Ibi.x.ac pti.Valuit.v.sol.Modo.xx.sol.Leuric libe tenuit.
Idẽ ten dimiđ hiđ in *WEDONE*.Tra.ẽ.I.car 7 dim.Ibi.ẽ.I.
car cũ.I.uillo 7 IIII.borđ.7 VI.ac pti.7 II.ac siluæ minutæ.
7 molin de.XL.denar.Valuit.XL.den.Modo.x.soliđ.
Idẽ ten.III.hiđ in *STAVERTONE*.Soca jac Estan libe tenuit.
in Faleuueslei.de.I.hida 7 dim.Tra.ẽ.VIII.car 7 dimiđ.
In dñio sunt.II.7 VI.uilli 7 XII.borđ cũ.IIII.car.Valuit.XL.
soliđ.Modo.LX.sol.Saulf Edric 7 Aluuin libe tenuer.

RADVLF ten de com.II.hiđ una v min in *HOHTONE*.Tra.ẽ
IIII.car.In dñio.ẽ una 7 dim.7 III.uilli cũ.II.borđ hñt tntđ.
Valuit.III.sol.modo.xx.soliđ.Fredgis libe tenuit.T.R.E.
De.II.v træ 7 dim.calũniat socã abb S Edmundi.
Idem ten.I.hidã 7 dim.7 unã bouatã træ *IN WARDVNE HD*.
in *FERENDONE*.Tra.ẽ.II.car.Ibi.ẽ una cũ.II.borđ.
Valuit.v.soliđ.Modo.xx.soliđ.Ordric tenuit de Stigand archiepo.

[In ROTHWELL Hundred]

26 Alan holds 1 virgate of land in DESBOROUGH from the Count.
Land for 1 plough. ½ plough there, with
2 smallholders.
The value was 3s; now 5s.
Fregis held it.

He also holds

[in NOBOTTLE Hundred]

27 in WHILTON 1 hide. Land for 2 ploughs. In lordship 1; 2 slaves.
2 villagers with a priest and 6 smallholders have another plough.
Meadow, 5 acres; a mill at 40d.
The value was 10s; now 60s.
Bovi held it freely.

[in TOWCESTER Hundred]

28 in (Cold) HIGHAM 2 hides and 4 parts of ½ hide. Land for 6 ploughs.
In lordship 1.
4 villagers with a priest and 3 smallholders have 1 plough.
Meadow, 10 acres.
The value was 5s; now 20s.
Leofric held it freely.

[In GRAVESEND Hundred]

29 in WEEDON (Bec) ½ hide. Land for 1½ ploughs. 1 plough there, with
1 villager and 4 smallholders.
Meadow, 6 acres; underwood, 2 acres; a mill at 40d.
The value was 40d; now 10s.
Estan held it freely.

30 in STAVERTON 3 hides. The jurisdiction of 1½ hides lies in Fawsley.
Land for 8½ ploughs. In lordship 2;
6 villagers and 12 smallholders with 4 ploughs.
The value was 40s; now 60s.
Saewulf, Edric and Alwin held it freely.

[In MAWSLEY Hundred]

31 Ralph holds 2 hides, less 1 virgate, in (Hanging) HOUGHTON from
the Count. Land for 4 ploughs. In lordship 1½.
3 villagers with 2 smallholders have as many.
The value was 3s; now 20s.
Fredegis held it freely before 1066. The Abbot of St. Edmund's
claims the jurisdiction of 2½ virgates of land.

In WARDEN Hundred

32 He also holds in (West) FARNDON 1½ hides and 1 bovate of land.
Land for 2 ploughs. 1 is there, with
2 smallholders.
The value was 5s; now 20s.
Orderic held it from Archbishop Stigand.

223 b

Idē ten̄ . I . hid̄ 7 dimid̄ . 7 v . partē uni͛ hidæ in *TIFELDE*.
Tra . ē . IIII . car̄ . Ibi . ē una car̄ cū . I . uillo . Valuit . v . sol.
Modo . x . solid̄ . Biscop 7 Leuing libe tenuer̄. *IN CLAILEA HD̄*
Idem ten̄ . II . hid̄ in *FORHO*. Tra . ē . VI . car̄ . In dn̄io . ē una,

223 c

7 IIII . serui . 7 II . uilli 7 III . bord̄ cū . I . car̄ . Ibi . VIII . ac̄ pti.
Valuit . x . sol . Modo . xxx . sol . Godeman 7 Godeua libe tenuer̄.
Idē . R . ten̄ de comite dim̄ hid̄ 7 unā bouatā in *WALETONE*.
Tra . ē . I . car̄ quæ ibi . ē cū . III . bord̄ . 7 una ac̄ pti . Valuit
III . sol . Modo . x . solid̄ . Aluuin͛ libe tenuit.
Idē ten̄ . II . hid̄ 7 IIII . partes dimd̄ hidæ in *CERVELTONE*. Tra . ē
VI . car̄ . In dn̄io sunt . II . cū . I . seruo . 7 VII . uilli cū . III . car̄.
Ibi molin̄ de . II . sol . Valuit . VI . solid̄ . Modo . LX . sol.
Idē ten̄ . II . hid̄ in *MIDELTONE*. Tra . ē . v . car̄. *IN SVDTONE HD̄*.
In dn̄io sunt . II . cū . I . seruo . 7 VII . uilli 7 VI . bord̄ cū . I . car̄.
Ibi . IIII . ac̄ pti . Valuit . L . sol . Modo . LX . solid̄ . Almar͛
7 Saulf͛ tenuer̄ . De huj͛ træ q̄nta parte jac̄ soca in Sutone.
Idē ten̄ . I . hid̄ 7 dimid̄ in *CERLINTONE*. Tra . ē . III . car̄ 7 dim̄.
Vasta . ē Tam̄ ualet 7 ualuit . v . sol . Quatuor teini libe tenuer̄.
Idē ten̄ . IIII . partes dim̄ hidē in *FOXESLEA*. *IN TOVECESTRE HD̄*.
Tra . ē . I . car̄ . Vasta . ē . Tam̄ ual . v . sol . Meresin libe tenuit.

[In TOWCESTER Hundred]

33 He also holds 1½ hides and the fifth part of 1 hide in TIFFIELD.
Land for 4 ploughs. 1 plough there, with
1 villager.
The value was 5s; now 10s.
Bishop and Leofing held it freely.

In CLEYLEY Hundred

34 He also holds 2 hides in FURTHO. Land for 6 ploughs.
In lordship 1; 4 slaves;
2 villagers and 3 smallholders with 1 plough. 223 c
Meadow, 8 acres.
The value was 10s; now 30s.
Godman and Godiva held it freely.

[In SUTTON Hundred]

35 Ralph also holds ½ hide and 1 bovate in WALTON (Grounds) from the Count. Land for 1 plough, which is there, with
3 smallholders.
Meadow, 1 acre.
The value was 3s; now 10s.
Alwin held it freely.

He also holds

[in GRAVESEND Hundred]

36 in CHARWELTON 2 hides and 4 parts of ½ hide. Land for 6 ploughs.
In lordship 2, with 1 slave;
7 villagers with 3 ploughs.
A mill at 2s.
The value was 6s; now 60s.

in SUTTON Hundred

37 in MIDDLETON (Cheney) 2 hides. Land for 5 ploughs.
In lordship 2, with 1 slave;
7 villagers and 6 smallholders with 1 plough.
Meadow, 4 acres.
The value was 50s; now 60s.
Aelmer and Saewulf held it. The jurisdiction of a fifth part of this land lies in (Kings) Sutton.

38 in CHARLTON 1½ hides. Land for 3½ ploughs. It is waste.
However, the value is and was 5s.
Four thanes held it freely.

in TOWCESTER Hundred

39 in FOXLEY 4 parts of ½ hide. Land for 1 plough. It is waste.
Value, however, 5s.
Merefin held it freely.

Idē ten̄ dim̄ hid̄ in *SIGRESHĀ*.Tra.ē.x.bob.Ibi.ē.i.uitts.
Silua.i.q̄rent lḡ.7 dimid̄ lat̄.Valuit.xx.sol.m̄.v.sol.
Idē ten̄ unā v̄ træ 7 ii.partes.i.virḡ in *HEIFORD*.ꝑ Leuenot ꝑ tenuit.
Soca jac̄ ad Bvchebroc.Tra.ē.i.car̄.7 ipsa ibi.ē.7 una
ac̄ p̄ti.Valuit.v.sol.Modo.x.solid̄.Vlstan tenuit.

IN ORDINBARO HD̄.

WILLELM̄ ten̄ de comite dimid̄ hid̄ in *HANITONE*.
Tra.ē.i.car̄.7 ibi.ē ipsa cū.i.uitto 7 ii.bord̄.7 una ac̄ p̄ti.
Valuit.xii.den̄.Modo.v.sol.Eduin̄ libe tenuit.ꝑ HD̄.
Idē ten̄.i.hid̄ 7 dim̄ in *HEROLVESTVNE*. *IN NIWEBOLD*
Tra.ē.iii.car̄.Has hn̄t ibi.ii.uitti 7 iii.bord̄.Ibi molin̄
de.ii.sol.7 iii.ac̄ p̄ti.Valuit.v.sol.Modo.xxx.sol.
Leuric 7 Orgar libe tenuer̄.
Idē ten̄ dim̄ hid̄ in *BRINTONE*.Tra.ē.iii.car̄.In dn̄io
est una.7 ii.serui.7 iii.uitti 7 iii.bord̄ cū.ii.car̄.Valuit
.v.sol.Modo.xx.solid̄.Aluric̄ libe tenuit.i.v̄ huj̄ træ.
Soca alteri̅ v̄ jac̄ ad *EDONE* ꝟ comitis.
Idē ten̄.iii.virḡ træ in *BROCOLE* 7 *MISECOTE*.Tra.ē.ii.
car̄.In dn̄io.ē una.7 vi.bord̄ hn̄t aliā.Ibi.vi.ac̄ p̄ti.
Valuit 7 ual.xl.solid̄.Leuric 7 Leuuin̄ libe tenuer̄.
Idē ten̄ dim̄ hid̄ in *CIFELINGEBERIE*.Tra.ē.i.car̄ 7 dim̄.
Vna.ē ibi cū.i.uitto 7 ii.bord̄ 7 ii.seruis.7 ii.ac̄ p̄ti.
Valuit.x.sol.Modo.xx.sol.Leuric libe tenuit.
Idē ten̄.iii.v̄ træ in *FLORA*.Tra.ē.ii.car̄.In dn̄io
est una.7 iiii.serui.7 ii.uitti 7 v.bord̄ hn̄t aliā.Ibi.iiii.

[in ALBOLDSTOW Hundred]

40 in SYRESHAM ½ hide. Land for 10 oxen.
1 villager.
Woodland 1 furlong long and ½ wide.
The value was 20s; now 5s.
Leofnoth held it.

[in NOBOTTLE Hundred]

41 in HEYFORD 1 virgate of land and 2 parts of 1 virgate.
The jurisdiction lies in Bugbrooke. Land for 1 plough; it is there.
Meadow, 1 acre.
The value was 5s; now 10s.
Wulfstan held it.

In ORLINGBURY Hundred

42 William holds ½ hide in HANNINGTON from the Count.
Land for 1 plough; it is there, with
1 villager and 2 smallholders.
Meadow, 1 acre.
The value was 12d; now 5s.
Edwin held it freely.

He also holds

in NOBOTTLE Hundred

43 in HARLESTONE 1½ hides. Land for 3 ploughs.
2 villagers and 3 smallholders have them.
A mill at 2s; meadow, 3 acres.
The value was 5s; now 30s.
Leofric and Ordgar held it freely.

44 in BRINGTON ½ hide. Land for 3 ploughs. In lordship 1; 2 slaves;
3 villagers and 3 smallholders with 2 ploughs.
The value was 5s; now 20s.
Aelfric held 1 virgate of this land freely. The jurisdiction of the other virgate lies in (East) Haddon, the Count's manor.

45 in BROCKHALL and MUSCOTT 3 virgates of land. Land for 2 ploughs.
In lordship 1.
6 smallholders have another.
Meadow, 6 acres.
The value was and is 40s.
Leofric and Leofwin held it freely.

46 in KISLINGBURY ½ hide. Land for 1½ ploughs; 1 there, with
1 villager, 2 smallholders and 2 slaves.
Meadow, 2 acres.
The value was 10s; now 20s.
Leofric held it freely.

47 in FLORE 3 virgates of land. Land for 2 ploughs.
In lordship 1; 4 slaves.
2 villagers and 5 smallholders have another.

ac̄ p̄ti. 7 molin̄ de. x. solid̄. Valuit. xx. sol. M̊. xl. sol.
Leuric lib̄e tenuit. 7 hanc quæ seq̇tur.

Idē ten̄. iii. v̄ træ in *Clachestorp*. 7 dim̄ hid̄ in ead̄ uilla. Tra. ē. iii. car̄. In dn̄io sunt. ii. 7 iii. serui. 7 i. uill̄ 7 un̄ bord̄. Valuit. xx. sol. Modo. xl. sol. Leuric 7 Turbern lib̄e tenuer̄.

Idē ten̄. iii. v̄ tre in *Celvrecot*. Tra. ē. i. car̄ 7 dim̄. 7 tant̄. ē ibi cū. i. uill̄o 7 iiii. bord̄. Ibi. ii. ac̄ p̄ti. Valuit 7 ual. x. sol. Tored lib̄e tenuit.

Idē ten̄ dimid̄ hid̄ in *Essebi*. Tra. ē. i. car̄. Ibi. ē dimid̄ car̄ cū. iii. uill̄is 7 uno bord̄. Valuit 7 ual. v. sol.

Idē ten̄. i. hid̄ 7 dim̄ in ead̄ uilla. Tra. ē. iii. car̄. Ibi s̄t iiii. uill̄i cū. ii. car̄. 7 iiii. ac̄ p̄ti. Valuit. ii. sol. M̊. x. sol. Has. ii. tras tenuit Aileua uidua.

IN FOXELE HVNĐ.

Idē ten̄. i. hid̄ in *Silvestone*. Tra. ē. iii. car̄. In dn̄io. ē una cū. i. seruo. Valuit. x. sol. Modo. xx. solid̄. Leuric lib̄e tenuit.

IN GISLEBVRG HVNĐ.

Idē. W. ten̄ dim̄ hid̄ in *Creptone*. 7 Hunfrid̄ de eo. Tra. ē. i. car̄. quæ ibi. ē cū. ii. seruis. 7 ii. bord̄. 7 x. ac̄ siluæ. Valuit. xvi. den̄. Modo. x. solid̄.

223 d

Idē Will̄s ten̄ dim̄ hid̄ in *Tifelde*. 7 v. partē uni⁹ hidæ. Tra ē. i. car̄ 7 dim̄. Vna car̄. ē ibi cū. i. uill̄o. 7 vii. ac̄ siluæ. Valuit. v. sol. Modo. x. solid̄. Leuuin⁹ lib̄e tenuit. Huj⁹ træ Soca p̄tin̄ ad Toucestre.

Idē ten̄ dim̄ hid̄ 7 iiii. partes dim̄ hidæ in *Forho*. Tra. ē. iii. car̄ 7 dim̄. In dn̄io. ē una.

Meadow, 4 acres; a mill at 10s.
The value was 20s; now 40s.
Leofric held it freely and that which follows.

48 in GLASSTHORPE(HILL) 3 virgates of land and ½ hide in the same village.
Land for 3 ploughs. In lordship 2; 3 slaves;
1 villager and 1 smallholder.
The value was 20s; now 40s.
Leofric and Thorbern held it freely.

[in GUILSBOROUGH Hundred and a half]

49 in YELVERTOFT 3 virgates of land. Land for 1½ ploughs;
as many there, with
1 villager and 4 smallholders.
Meadow, 2 acres.
The value was and is 10s.
Thored held it freely.

50 in (Cold) ASHBY ½ hide. Land for 1 plough; ½ plough there, with
3 villagers and 1 smallholder.
The value was and is 5s.

51 in the same village 1½ hides. Land for 3 ploughs.
4 villagers with 2 ploughs.
Meadow, 4 acres.
The value was 2s; now 10s.
Aeleva the widow held these two lands.

in FOXLEY Hundred

52 in SILVERSTONE 1 hide. Land for 3 ploughs. In lordship 1, with 1 slave.
The value was 10s; now 20s.
Leofric held it freely.

In GUILSBOROUGH Hundred

53 William also holds ½ hide in CREATON, and Humphrey from him.
Land for 1 plough, which is there, with 2 slaves;
2 smallholders.
Woodland, 10 acres.
The value was 16d; now 10s.

[In TOWCESTER Hundred]

54 William also holds ½ hide in TIFFIELD and the fifth part of 1 hide. 223 d
Land for 1½ ploughs; 1 plough there, with
1 villager.
Woodland, 7 acres.
The value was 5s; now 10s.
Leofwin held it freely. The jurisdiction of this land belongs
to Towcester.

He also holds

[in CLEYLEY Hundred]

55 in FURTHO ½ hide and 4 parts of ½ hide. Land for 3½ ploughs.
In lordship 1.

7 II . borđ hn̄t dim̄ car̄ . Ibi . VI . ac̄ p̄ti . Valuit . X . solid.
Modo . XXX . sol . Aluuin 7 Osulf libe tenuer̄.

Idē ten̄ . IX . partes . I . hidæ in eađ uilla . Tra . ē . II . car̄ . Ibi est una cū . I . uillo 7 III . borđ . Ibi . VIII . ac̄ p̄ti . Valuit . X . sol. Modo . LX . solid . Goduin libe tenuit.

Idē ten̄ . III . hid 7 unā v̄ træ in *FORDINESTONE* . Tra . ē . VIII . car̄ . In dn̄io . ē una cū . II . seruis . Ibi un miles ten̄ . I . hid 7 dim̄ 7 hr̄ . II . car̄ cū . II . seruis . 7 VI . uill 7 III . borđ cū . II . car̄. Ibi . XVI . ac̄ p̄ti . Silua . IIII . q̄rent lg . 7 III . lat̄ . Valuit . XX . solid . Modo . IIII . lib . Vluric libe tenuit . I . hid 7 dim̄ huj træ. Reliq tenuer̄ Orgar Tedgar 7 Godric . Soca ptin ad Fale

Idē ten̄ . III . hid in *DODEFORDE* . Tra . ē . VII . car̄ . / wesleie. In dn̄io st̄ . II . 7 IIII . serui . 7 XI . uilli cū pb̄ro 7 VI . borđ hn̄t . V . car̄ . Ibi . II . molini de . X . sol . 7 XII . ac̄ p̄ti . Valuit . XL . sol. Modo . IIII . lib . De hac tra . I . hid 7 dim̄ tenuit Turbern libe. Aliā trā tenuer̄ Orgar Aluric 7 Leuric . Soca jac̄ ad Faleuueslei.

Idē ten̄ . I . hid 7 II . v̄ træ 7 dim̄ in *ESTANESTONE* . Tra . ē . VI car̄ . In dn̄io . ē una 7 dim̄ . 7 II . serui . 7 VI . uilli cū . I . car̄ 7 dimid . Ibi molin̄ de . X . sol . 7 III . ac̄ p̄ti . Silua . III . q̄z 7 dim̄ lg . 7 II . q̄z 7 dim̄ lat̄ . Valuit 7 ual . XXX . solid.

Idē ten̄ unā v̄ træ 7 dim̄ in *SNOCHESCVBE*. *IN GRAVESEND HD̄.* Tra . ē . I . car̄ . quæ ibi . ē cū . I . seruo 7 I . uillo . 7 II . ac̄ siluæ minut. Valuit 7 ual . X . sol . Turb̄n libe tenuit has . II . tras.

2 smallholders have ½ plough.
Meadow, 6 acres.
The value was 10s; now 30s.
Alwin and Oswulf held it freely.

56 in the same village 9 parts of 1 hide. Land for 2 ploughs. 1 there, with
1 villager and 3 smallholders.
Meadow, 8 acres.
The value was 10s; now 60s.
Godwin held it freely.

[in GRAVESEND Hundred]

57 in FARTHINGSTONE 3 hides and 1 virgate of land. Land for 8 ploughs. In lordship 1, with 2 slaves. A man-at-arms holds 1½ hides and has 2 ploughs, with 2 slaves;
6 villagers and 3 smallholders with 2 ploughs.
Meadow, 16 acres; woodland 4 furlongs long and 3 wide.
The value was 20s; now £4.
Wulfric held 1½ hides of this land freely. Ordgar, Theodger and Godric held the rest. The jurisdiction belongs to Fawsley.

58 in DODFORD 3 hides. Land for 7 ploughs. In lordship 2; 4 slaves.
11 villagers with a priest and 6 smallholders have 5 ploughs.
2 mills at 10s; meadow, 12 acres.
The value was 40s; now £4.
Thorbern held 1½ hides of this land freely. Ordgar, Aelfric and Leofric held the other land. The jurisdiction lies in Fawsley.

[in CLEYLEY Hundred]

59 in EASTON NESTON 1 hide and 2½ virgates of land. Land for 6 ploughs. In lordship 1½; 2 slaves;
6 villagers with 1½ ploughs.
A mill at 10s; meadow, 3 acres;
woodland 3½ furlongs long and 2½ furlongs wide.
The value was and is 30s.

in GRAVESEND Hundred

60 in SNORSCOMB 1½ virgates of land. Land for 1 plough, which is there, with 1 slave and
1 villager.
Underwood, 2 acres.
The value was and is 10s.
Thorbern held these two lands freely.

223 d

Idē ten dim hid in *PRESTETONE*. Tra. ē. I. car. *IN SVTON HD*.
quæ ibi. ē cū. I. bord. 7 II. ac pti. Valuit 7 ual x. solid.
Soca jac in Sutone. Alric libe tenuit.
Idē ten dim hid in *WALTONE*. Tra. ē. I. car. quæ ibi. ē cū. II.
seruis. 7 II. bord. Valuit. x. sol. Modo. xx. sol. Soca in Sutone
jacet. Quinq; taini tenuer. 7 qlibet ire potuer.
Idē ten qntā partē. I. hidæ in *SVTONE*. Tra. ē dim car.
Ibi. ē un uitts. Valuit 7 ual. III. solid. Alric libe tenuit.
Idē ten. IIII. partes dim hide in *CRIWELTONE*. Tra. ē. I. car.
Ibi. ē un bord tant. Valuit. xx. sol. Modo. II. sol. Leuenot
libe tenuit Bereuuicha fuit in Euelaia. *IN HOLEBOLDEST HD*.
Idē ten. I. hid in *AVELAI*. Tra. ē. II. car 7 dim. In dnio. ē una.
7 un uitts 7 VII. bord cū dim car. Ibi molin de. XII. den.
Valuit. LX. sol. Modo. XXX. sol. Lefstan libe tenuit.
Idē ten dim hid in *CELVERTONE*. *IN GRAVESENDE HVND*.
Tra. ē. I. car. quā hnt ibi. IIII. uitti 7 II. bord. Valuit x. sol
Modo. xx. sol. Vluric libe tenuit.
ALVRED ten de com. II. partes uni hidæ in *TORP*. Tra. ē. II.
car quæ ibi st cū. v. uittis 7 III. bord. Valuit. v. sol. m. xx. sol.
Azor. F. Lefsi libe tenuit.
Idē ten unā v træ in *CILDECOTE*. Tra. ē dim car. quæ ibi. ē
cū. II. bord. Valet. II. sol. Turbern tenuit.

in SUTTON Hundred

61 in PURSTON ½ hide. Land for 1 plough, which is there, with
1 smallholder.
Meadow, 2 acres.
The value was and is 10s.
The jurisdiction lies in (Kings) Sutton. Alric held it freely.

62 in WALTON (Grounds) ½ hide. Land for 1 plough, which is there, with 2 slaves;
2 smallholders.
The value was 10s; now 20s.
The jurisdiction lies in (Kings) Sutton. Five thanes held it and could go where they would.

63 in (Kings) SUTTON the fifth part of 1 hide. Land for ½ plough.
1 villager.
The value was and is 3s.
Alric held it freely.

64 in CROUGHTON 4 parts of ½ hide. Land for 1 plough.
1 smallholder, only.
The value was 20s; now 2s.
Leofnoth held it freely. It was an outlier of Evenley.

in ALBOLDSTOW Hundred

65 in EVENLEY 1 hide. Land for 2½ ploughs. In lordship 1;
1 villager and 7 smallholders with ½ plough.
A mill at 12d.
The value was 60s; now 30s.
Leofstan held it freely.

in GRAVESEND Hundred

66 in CHARWELTON ½ hide. Land for 1 plough, which
4 villagers and 2 smallholders have there.
The value was 10s; now 20s.
Wulfric held it freely.

67 Alfred holds 2 parts of 1 hide in ?THRUPP (Grounds) from the Count.
Land for 2 ploughs, which are there, with
5 villagers and 3 smallholders.
The value was 5s; now 20s.
Azor son of Leofsi held it freely.

He also holds

[in GUILSBOROUGH Hundred and a half]

68 in 'CHILCOTES' 1 virgate of land. Land for ½ plough, which is there, with
2 smallholders.
Value 2s.
Thorbern held it.

Idē ten̄ . i . hid̄ 7 iii . v̄ træ in *ELTETONE*. Tra . ē . iii . car̄ 7 dim̄.
In dn̄io sunt . ii . 7 iii . serui . 7 x . uitti cū . i . car̄ 7 dimid̄.
Valuit 7 ual̄ . xl . sol̄ . Turbern libe tenuit.
Idē ten̄ unā v̄ træ in *LINEBVRNE* . Tra . ē . ii . car̄ 7 dimid̄.
7 totid̄ sť ibi cū . vii . uittis 7 i . bord̄ . 7 iii . ac̄ p̄ti.
Valuit . xii . denar̄ . Modo . x . solid̄ . Turbern tenuit
Idē ten̄ . iii . v̄ træ in *GELVRECOTE* . Tra . ē . i . car̄ . Ibi . ē una
7 dimid̄ . cū . i . seruo . 7 iiii . uittis . 7 ii . ac̄ p̄ti . Valuit . v . sol̄.
Modo . x . solid̄.

224 a

Idem Alvred̄ ten̄ . iii . v̄ træ in *BVCHEBI* . Tra . ē . i . car̄ 7 dim̄.
7 tn̄td̄ ibi . ē cū . vi . uittis 7 ii . bord̄ . Ibi . iiii . ac̄ p̄ti.
Valuit 7 ual̄ . xxx . solid̄ . Turbern 7 Alric libe tenuer̄.
Idē ten̄ unā v̄ træ 7 v . partē unius v̄ in *ETENESTONE*.
Tra . ē . i . car̄ 7 iii . ac̄ p̄ti quæ ibi . ē . Valuit . iiii . sol̄ . Modo . vi . solid̄.
Idē ten̄ unā v̄ træ 7 dim̄ in *PRESTETONE* . Tra . ē . i . car̄.
Idē ten̄ . iii . v̄ træ in *FORDINESTONE*. Vasta . ē.
Tra . ē . i . car̄ . quæ ibi . ē in dn̄io . 7 ii . serui . Valuit . x . solid̄.
Modo . xv . solid̄ . Ingelrann̄ ten̄ de eo . Leuric tenuit T . R . E.
Soca huj̄ træ jac̄ ad Feleuuesleie.
FVLCHER ten̄ de com̄ . i . hid̄ 7 tciā partē . i . hidæ in *ALIDETORP* . Tra . ē . iii . car̄ . In dn̄io . ē una . 7 ii . serui . 7 x . uitti
7 viii . bord̄ hn̄t . ii . car̄ . Valuit 7 ual̄ xxx . sol̄ . Eduin libe tenuit.
Idē ten̄ . iii . v̄ træ in *PICTESLEI* . Tra . ē . i . car̄ 7 dim̄

69 in ELKINGTON 1 hide and 3 virgates of land.
Land for 3½ ploughs. In lordship 2; 3 slaves;
10 villagers with 1½ ploughs.
The value was and is 40s.
Thorbern held it freely.

70 in LILBOURNE 1 virgate of land. Land for 2½ ploughs;
as many there, with
7 villagers and 1 smallholder.
Meadow, 3 acres.
The value was 12d; now 10s.
Thorbern held it.

71 in YELVERTOFT 3 virgates of land. Land for 1 plough. 1½ there,
with 1 slave and
4 villagers.
Meadow, 2 acres.
The value was 5s; now 10s.

72 Alfred also holds 3 virgates of land in (Long) BUCKBY. 224 a
Land for 1½ ploughs; as many there, with
6 villagers and 2 smallholders.
Meadow, 4 acres.
The value was and is 30s.
Thorbern and Alric held it freely.

[In FOXLEY Hundred]

73 He also holds 1 virgate of land and the fifth part of 1 virgate in
ADSTONE. Land for 1 plough, which is there.
Meadow, 3 acres.
The value was 4s; now 6s.

[In GRAVESEND Hundred]

74 He also holds 1½ virgates of land in PRESTON.
Land for 1 plough. Waste.

75 He also holds 3 virgates of land in FARTHINGSTONE.
Land for 1 plough; it is there, in lordship; 2 slaves.
The value was 10s; now 15s.
Ingelrann holds from him. Leofric held it before 1066.
The jurisdiction of this land lies in Fawsley.

[?In ROTHWELL Hundred]

76 Fulchere holds 1 hide and the third part of 1 hide
from the Count in THORPE (Malsor). Land for 3 ploughs.
In lordship 1; 2 slaves.
10 villagers and 8 smallholders have 2 ploughs.
The value was and is 30s.
Edwin held it freely.

[In ORLINGBURY Hundred]

77 He also holds 3 virgates of land in PYTCHLEY. Land for 1½ ploughs.

Duæ car̃ sť ibi cũ . I . socħo 7 II . borđ . 7 una ac̃ p̃ti.
Valuit . v . soliđ . Modo . x . soliđ . Eduin̄ liƀe tenuit . 7 hanc.
Idẽ ten̄ . III . v̄ træ in *ORDINBARO* . Tra . ẽ . I . car̃ 7 dimiđ.
7 tn̄tđ ibi . ẽ cũ . I . uilło 7 II . borđ . Ibi . II . ac̃ p̃ti . Silua . I.
q̃rent lg̃ . 7 dim̃ q̃z lať . Valuit . v . soł . Modo . x . soliđ.
ROBERT̃ ten̄ de com̃ dimiđ hiđ in *WOLDEGRAVE* . Tra . ẽ . II.
car̃ . Ibi . ẽ una cũ . I . seruo 7 uno borđ . 7 III . ac̃ p̃ti . Valuit
v . soliđ . Modo . x . soł . Martin̄ liƀe tenuit.
Idẽ ten̄ . II . hiđ in *NORTOT* . Tra . ẽ . IIII . car̃ . In dñio . ẽ una.
cũ . I . seruo . 7 IIII . uilłi 7 III . borđ cũ . I . car̃ . Ibi . VIII . ac̃ p̃ti.
7 molin̄ de . VIII . denar̃ . Valuit . III . soł . Modo . XXX . soliđ.
Huic træ p̃tin̄ æccła cũ una v̄ træ in *GISLEBVRG* . 7 sedes
molini cũ t̃cia parte uni̇̄ v̄ in *HOLEWELLE* . H̃ sunt vasta.
Leuuin̄ liƀe tenuit.
Idẽ ten̄ . II . virg̃ træ 7 dimiđ in *HIRECESTRE* . Tra . ẽ dim̃ car̃.
Ibi . ẽ un̄ uilłs . 7 III . ac̃ p̃ti 7 dim̃ . Valuit . XII . den̄ . M̊ . VIII . soł.
Siuuard̄ liƀe tenuit.
WALTERIVS ten̄ de com̃ . III . hiđ in *WESTONE* . Tra . ẽ . VI.
car̃ . In dñio . ẽ una . 7 XIIII . uilłi 7 IIII . borđ hñt . v . car̃.
Ibi . XV . ac̃ p̃ti . Valuit . XL . soł . Modo . LXX . soliđ . Lochi Scotel
7 Stanchil 7 II . socħi tenuer̃ . T.R.E. *IN NIVEBOTLEGRAVE HD̃.*
Idẽ ten̄ unã v̄ træ 7 III . partes uni̇̄ v̄ in *HAIFORD* . Tra . ẽ . I . car̃.
quæ ibi . ẽ cũ . II . seruis . 7 molin̄ de . XVI . soł . 7 IIII . ac̃ p̃ti.

2 ploughs there, with
1 Freeman and 2 smallholders.
Meadow, 1 acre.
The value was 5s; now 10s.
Edwin held this freely also.

78 He also holds 3 virgates of land in ORLINGBURY.
Land for 1½ ploughs; as many there, with
1 villager and 2 smallholders.
Meadow, 2 acres; woodland 1 furlong long and ½ furlong wide.
The value was 5s; now 10s.

[? In MAWSLEY Hundred]

79 Robert holds ½ hide from the Count in WALGRAVE.
Land for 2 ploughs. 1 there, with 1 slave and
1 smallholder.
Meadow, 3 acres.
The value was 5s; now 10s.
Martin held it freely.

[In GUILSBOROUGH Hundred]

80 He also holds 2 hides in NORTOFT. Land for 4 ploughs.
In lordship 1, with 1 slave;
4 villagers and 3 smallholders with 1 plough.
Meadow, 8 acres; a mill at 8d.
The value was 3s; now 30s.
To this land belong a church with 1 virgate of land in GUILSBOROUGH and the site of a mill with the third part of 1 virgate in HOLLOWELL. They are waste.
Leofwin held freely.

[In HIGHAM Hundred]

81 He also holds 2½ virgates of land in IRCHESTER. Land for ½ plough.
1 villager.
Meadow, 3½ acres.
The value was 12d; now 8s.
Siward held it freely.

[In SPELHOE Hundred]

82 Walter holds 3 hides from the Count in WESTON (Favell).
Land for 6 ploughs. In lordship 1.
14 villagers and 4 smallholders have 5 ploughs.
Meadow, 15 acres.
The value was 40s; now 70s.
Lokki, Scotel, Steinkell and two Freemen held it before 1066.

In NOBOTTLE Hundred

83 He also holds 1 virgate of land and 3 parts of 1 virgate in HEYFORD. Land for 1 plough, which is there, with 2 slaves.
A mill at 16s; meadow, 4 acres.

224 a

Valuit . x . sol . Modo . xxx . solid . Biscop tenuit . Soca jacet in Buchebroch.

RADVLF ten de com unā v træ 7 II . partes uni v in HAI FORD . Soca ē in Buchebroc . Tra . ē . I . car . Ibi . ē una 7 dim cū . I . uillo . Ibi . III . ac pti . Valuit . v . sol . Modo . x . solid.

Idē ten . IIII . partes uni hidæ . in PRESTETONE . Tra . ē . III . car. 7 ipse ibi sunt cū . III . seruis 7 IIII . uillis . 7 II . bord . In dnio . ē medietas caruc . Valuit . x . sol . Modo . XL . sol . Sauuata te nuit.

RADVLF ten . II . hid 7 unā v træ in ALDENESBI . Soca jac in EDONE . Tra . ē . VIII . car . In dnio st . II . 7 IIII . serui . 7 un uills 7 IX . sochi cū . II . car . Ibi . III . ac pti . 7 III . ac siluæ . Valuit xx . solid . Modo . XL . solid . Siuuard cū . IX . sochis libe tenuer.

RADVLF ten dimid hid in HADONE . Tra . ē . I . car . Hanc hnt ibi . II . uilli 7 IIII . bord . Valuit . XII . denar . Modo . v . solid.

Wills 7 Durand . ten . III . hid una v min in SPRETONE. Tra . ē . VI . car . In dnio . ē una 7 dim . cū . I . seruo . 7 VI . uilli 7 VI . bord cū . III . car 7 dimid . Ibi molin de . VI . solid . 7 VI . ac pti. Valuit . xx . solid . Modo . LX . solid . Osmund libe tenuit.

Wills ten . IIII . partes uni hidæ in GRASTONE . IN CLAILEA HD Tra . ē . II . car . In dnio . ē una cū . I . bord . Ibi . XI . ac pti . 7 xx . ac siluæ . Valuit . III . sol . Modo . XXVI . sol . Goduin libe tenuit.

224 b

NIGELL ten de com . I . hid 7 dim v træ in PRESTETONE . Tra est . III . car . In dnio sunt . II . 7 II . serui . 7 pbr cū . III . uillis ht . I . car. Ibi . I . ac siluæ . Valuit . VI . sol . Modo . XL . solid . Fregis tenuit.

The value was 10s; now 30s.
Bishop held it. The jurisdiction lies in Bugbrooke.

4 Ralph holds 1 virgate of land and 2 parts of 1 virgate from the Count in HEYFORD. The jurisdiction is in Bugbrooke.
Land for 1 plough. 1½ there, with
1 villager.
Meadow, 3 acres.
The value was 5s; now 10s.

[In GRAVESEND Hundred]

5 He also holds 4 parts of 1 hide in PRESTON. Land for 3 ploughs; they are there, with 3 slaves and
4 villagers and 2 smallholders. In lordship ½ plough.
The value was 10s; now 40s.
Saewata held it.

[In NOBOTTLE Hundred]

6 Ralph holds 2 hides and 1 virgate of land in HOLDENBY.
The jurisdiction lies in (East) Haddon. Land for 8 ploughs.
In lordship 2; 4 slaves;
1 villager and 9 Freemen with 2 ploughs.
Meadow, 3 acres; woodland, 3 acres.
The value was 20s; now 40s.
Siward with nine Freemen held it freely.

Ralph holds ½ hide in (East) HADDON. Land for 1 plough.
2 villagers and 4 smallholders have it there.
The value was 12d; now 5s.

[? In SPELHOE Hundred]

William and Durand hold 3 hides, less 1 virgate, in SPRATTON.
Land for 6 ploughs. In lordship 1½, with 1 slave;
6 villagers and 6 smallholders with 3½ ploughs.
A mill at 6s; meadow, 6 acres.
The value was 20s; now 60s.
Osmund held it freely.

In CLEYLEY Hundred

William holds 4 parts of 1 hide in GRAFTON (Regis).
Land for 2 ploughs. In lordship 1, with
1 smallholder.
Meadow, 11 acres; woodland, 20 acres.
The value was 3s; now 26s.
Godwin held it freely.

[In GRAVESEND Hundred]

Nigel holds 1 hide and ½ virgate of land from the Count in PRESTON. Land for 3 ploughs. In lordship 2; 2 slaves. 224 b
A priest with 3 villagers has 1 plough.
Woodland, 1 acre.
The value was 6s; now 40s.
Fregis held it.

In *ALDRITONE* ten un tain de com . I . hid . Tra . ē . II . car . Ibi . ē una . Valet . x . solid . Idem ipse tenuit.

In *ALDENESTONE* ten Ormar . I . hid 7 III . v træ . Tra . ē . IIII . car. In dnio sunt . II . 7 III . serui . 7 VI . uitti 7 v . bord cu . II . car. Ibi molin de . VIII . solid . 7 III . ac pti . 7 III . ac siluæ minutæ. Valuit . xx . solid . Modo . XL . solid . Siuuard libe tenuit.

In *EDONE* ten Alric . I . hid 7 dim de com . Tra . ē . III . car. In dnio . ē una . 7 v . serui . 7 IIII . uitti 7 VII . bord cu . II . car. Ibi . VI . ac pti . 7 IIII . ac siluæ minutæ . Valuit . xx . sol . m . XL . sol. Idē ten tcia partē uni v in *HOLEWELLE* . Vasta . ē.

In *BLACVLVESLEI* ten Sagrim de com . I . hid 7 dimid. Soca . ē regis in *NORTONE* . Tra . ē . III . car 7 dim . Vna car tant . ē ibi cu . II . uittis . 7 II . seruis . 7 II . ac pti . Valuit . x . solid . modo . xx . solid . Idem ipse tenuit . T . R . E.

In *BOTENDONE* ten Leuuin . II . hid de com . Tra . ē . v . car. In dnio sunt . II . 7 IIII . serui . 7 XI . uitti 7 v . bord cu . III . car 7 dimid . Ibi . x . ac pti . Valuit . c . solid . Modo . IIII . lib . Turi

In *SNOCHESCVBE* ten Alric dim v træ de com . ⁊ libe tenuit. Tra . ē . I . car . quæ ibi . ē cu . I . seruo 7 I . uitto . 7 una ac siluæ minutæ . Valet . v . sol . Idē ipse tenuit.

In *WALETONE* ten Vlmar de com dim v træ . v . acs min. Tra . ē dimid car . 7 tant ibi . ē cu . I . bord . 7 una ac pti. Valet . v . solid . Idē ipse libe tenuit.

[In CLEYLEY Hundred]

1 In ALDERTON a thane holds 1 hide from the Count.
Land for 2 ploughs. 1 there.
Value 10s.
He also held it himself.

[In NOBOTTLE Hundred]

2 In ?HOLDENBY Ordmer holds 1 hide and 3 virgates of land.
Land for 4 ploughs. In lordship 2; 3 slaves;
6 villagers and 5 smallholders with 2 ploughs.
A mill at 8s; meadow, 3 acres; underwood, 3 acres.
The value was 20s; now 40s.
Siward held it freely.

3 In (East) HADDON Alric holds 1½ hides from the Count.
Land for 3 ploughs. In lordship 1; 5 slaves.
4 villagers and 7 smallholders with 2 ploughs.
Meadow, 6 acres; underwood, 4 acres.
The value was 20s; now 40s.

[In GUILSBOROUGH Hundred and a half]

4 He also holds the third part of 1 virgate in HOLLOWELL. Waste.

[In FOXLEY Hundred]

5 In BLAKESLEY Saegrim holds 1½ hides from the Count.
The jurisdiction is the King's in (Greens) NORTON.
Land for 3½ ploughs. 1 plough only there, with
2 villagers and 2 slaves.
Meadow, 2 acres.
The value was 10s; now 20s.
He also held it himself before 1066.

[In WARDEN Hundred]

6 In BODDINGTON Leofwin holds 2 hides from the Count.
Land for 5 ploughs. In lordship 2; 4 slaves;
11 villagers and 5 smallholders with 3½ ploughs.
Meadow, 10 acres.
The value was 100s; now £4.
Thori held it freely.

[In GRAVESEND Hundred]

7 In SNORSCOMB Alric holds ½ virgate of land from the Count.
Land for 1 plough, which is there, with 1 slave and
1 villager.
Underwood, 1 acre.
Value 5s.
He also held it himself.

8 In WELTON Wulfmer holds ½ virgate of land, less 5 acres,
from the Count. Land for ½ plough; as much there, with
1 smallholder.
Meadow, 1 acre.
Value 5s.
He also held it freely himself.

224 b

In *BRANTONE* ten Vlmar de com dim hid. Tra. ē. I. car. Hæc ibi. ē. Valet. xx. sol. Idē ipse tenuit.

.XIX TERRA COMITIS DE MELLEND. *IN GRAVESENDE HVND*

COMES de MELLEND ten de rege in *NORTONE*. II. hid 7 dim 7 v. partē dimid hidæ. Tra. VII. car. Nc in dnio st. II. 7 una hida træ. Ibi XXIII. uitti cū pbro 7 IX. bord 7 I. seruo hnt. VI. car. Ibi molin de. x. solid. 7 XXV. ac pti. Valuit. VI. lib. Modo. VIII. lib. Agemund libe tenuit.

.XX TERRA ALANI COMITIS. *IN CLAILEA HD.*

COMES ALANVS ten de rege. IIII. partes dim hidæ in *WACAFELD*. 7 Radulf dapifer de eo. Tra. ē. II. car. In dnio. ē una. 7 III. uitti cū. I. bord hnt aliā car. Ibi. I. ac pti. Silua. v. qrent lg. 7 dim. 7 in lat III. qrent. Valuit. v. solid. Modo. x. sol.

.XXI. TERRA ALBERICI COMITIS. *IN ODBOLDESTOV HVND.*

COMES ALBERICVS tenuit de rege. II. hid in *HASOV*. 7 II. hid in *SIGRESHĀ*. 7 I. hid in *BRACHELAI*. cū æccla 7 molino de. x. sol. In his. v. hid. ē Tra. XII. car 7 dimid. In dnio sunt. II. 7 VI. serui. 7 XX. uitti cū pbro 7 X. bord hnt. VI. car. Ibi. XX. ac pti. Silua. II. qrent 7 dim lg. 7 una qz 7 dim lat. Ibi Osmund ten tciā partē. II. hidar. In *SIGREHĀ*. Tot ualuit. XII. lib qdo recep. Modo. IX. lib. Azor libe tenuit.

In *BRACHELAI* sunt. II. hidæ. Tra. v. car. In dnio sunt. II. 7 VI. serui. 7 X. uitti 7 VIII. bord cū. III. car. Ibi. x. ac pti. Valuit. c. sol qdo recep. Modo. IIII. lib.

In *LILLEBVRNE* sunt. II. hidæ 7 dim v træ. Tra. ē. IIII. car. 7 II. bou. In dnio. ē una. 7 VIII. uitti 7 VI. bord 7 III. sochi hnt. III. car. Ibi. XII. ac pti. Valuit. II. sol. Modo. xxx. sol.

[In NOBOTTLE Hundred]

99 In BRAMPTON Wulfmer holds ½ hide from the Count.
Land for 1 plough; it is there.
Value 20s.
He also held it himself.

19 LAND OF THE COUNT OF MEULAN

In GRAVESEND Hundred

1 The Count of Meulan holds 2½ hides and the fifth part of ½ hide from the King in NORTON. Land for 7 ploughs. Now in lordship 2 and 1 hide of land.
23 villagers with a priest, 9 smallholders and 1 slave have 6 ploughs.
A mill at 10s; meadow, 25 acres.
The value was £6; now £8.
Agemund held it freely.

⊕ *(19, 2-3, are entered after ch. 21, at the foot of cols. 224a,b)*

20 LAND OF COUNT ALAN

In CLEYLEY Hundred

1 Count Alan holds 4 parts of ½ hide from the King in WAKEFIELD, and Ralph the Steward from him. Land for 2 ploughs. In lordship 1.
3 villagers with 1 smallholder have another plough.
Meadow, 1 acre; woodland 5½ furlongs long and 3 furlongs in width.
The value was 5s; now 10s.

21 LAND OF EARL AUBREY

In ALBOLDSTOW Hundred

1 Earl Aubrey held from the King 2 hides in HALSE, 2 hides in SYRESHAM and 1 hide in BRACKLEY, with a church and a mill at 10s.
In these 5 hides, land for 12½ ploughs. In lordship 2; 6 slaves.
20 villagers with a priest and 10 smallholders have 6 ploughs.
Meadow, 20 acres; woodland 2½ furlongs long and 1½ furlongs wide.
Osmund holds the third part of 2 hides in SYRESHAM.
Value of the whole when acquired £12; now £9.
Azor held it freely.

2 In BRACKLEY 2 hides. Land for 5 ploughs. In lordship 2; 6 slaves;
10 villagers and 8 smallholders with 3 ploughs.
Meadow, 10 acres.
Value when acquired, 100s; now £4.

[In GUILSBOROUGH Hundred and a half]

3 In LILBOURNE 2 hides and ½ virgate of land. Land for 4 ploughs and 2 oxen. In lordship 1.
8 villagers, 6 smallholders and 3 Freemen have 3 ploughs.
Meadow, 12 acres.
The value was 2s; now 30s.

In eađ uilla.ē una v træ 7 dim. Radulf ten de rege. Tra.ē
vi. bou. Ibi.ē un uitts 7 ii.borđ.7 iiii.ac pti. Valet.iiii.sol.
In *Evelai* st.iii.v træ. Gislebt ten. *In Svtone hd.*
Tra.ē.ii.car.Ibi.ē.i.borđ cū.i.seruo. Valuit.x.sol. Modo.iiii.st.
In *Ferningeho* st.iiii.hidæ.Tra.x.car.In dnio st.iii.car
7 x.serui.7 xv.uitti cū pbro 7 viii.borđ hnt.v.car.
Ibi.xx.ac pti.Valuit.x.lib.qdo recep.Modo.vii.lib.
H Terræ fvervnt Alberici comit.Modo svnt in Manv Regis.

224 a, b

⊕ Idē comes de Mellend ten *Berchewelle* in dnio.
Ibi st.iiii.hidæ.Harū.iii.hiđ ht in dnio.Tra.viii.car.
In dnio.ē una.7 iiii.serui.7 vii.uitti cū.iii.borđ hnt.i.car.
Ibi.v.ac pti.Silua i.leu lg.7 una leu lat.Valet.xl.sol.
Idē comes ten in *Witacre* dimiđ hiđ uastā.7 uat.xii.den.
Has tras Leuenot libe tenuit.T.R.E.

224 c

.XXXIII. Terra Hvgonis De Grentmaisn.

※Hvgo de Grentemaisnil ten unā v træ 7 dim in *Ferendon*.
Tra.ē.i.car.Hanc hnt ibi.ii.uitti.Valuit 7 uat.v.soliđ.
In *Mersitone* 7 in *Torp* ten Hugo de Hug *In Stotfald hd.*
ii.hiđ 7 unā v træ.7 tciā partē uni v.Tra.ē.iiii.car 7 dim.
In dnio sunt.ii.7 ii.serui.7 xxiii.uitti 7 xvii.borđ hnt
vii.car.Ibi.x.ac pti. Valuit.xx.sol. Modo.lx.soliđ.
Oslac libe tenuit. *In Gravesende hd.*
Idē ten.iii.hiđ 7 dim in *Wedone*.qp excābit de Wadford.

4 In the same village 1½ virgates of land. Ralph holds from the King. Land for 6 oxen.
1 villager and 2 smallholders.
Meadow, 4 acres.
Value 4s.

In SUTTON Hundred

5 In EVENLEY 3 virgates of land. Gilbert holds them. Land for 2 ploughs.
1 smallholder with 1 slave.
The value was 10s; now 4s.

6 In FARTHINGHOE 4 hides. Land for 10 ploughs.
In lordship 3 ploughs; 10 slaves.
15 villagers with a priest and 8 smallholders have 5 ploughs.
Meadow, 20 acres.
Value when acquired £10; now £7.

These lands were Earl Aubrey's; now they are in the King's hand.

(19, 2-3 directed to their proper place by transposition signs)

19 *(In WARWICKSHIRE)* 224 a, b

⊕2 The Count of Meulan also holds BERKSWELL in lordship. 4 hides.
He has 3 of these hides in lordship. Land for 8 ploughs.
In lordship 1; 4 slaves.
7 villagers with 3 smallholders have 1 plough.
Meadow, 5 acres; woodland 1 league long and 1 league wide.
Value 40s.

3 The Count also holds ½ hide, waste, in WHITACRE.
Value 12d.

Leofnoth held these lands freely before 1066.

3[23] LAND OF HUGH OF GRANDMESNIL 224 c

·X· *(Chs.22 and 23 are transposed)*

[In WARDEN Hundred]

1 Hugh of Grandmesnil holds 1½ virgates of land in (West) FARNDON.
Land for 1 plough.
2 villagers have it there.
The value was and is 5s.

In STOTFOLD Hundred

2 Hugh holds 2 hides, 1 virgate of land and the third part of 1 virgate from Hugh in MARSTON (Trussell) and THORPE (Lubenham).
Land for 4½ ploughs. In lordship 2; 2 slaves.
23 villagers and 17 smallholders have 7 ploughs.
Meadow, 10 acres.
The value was 20s; now 60s.
Oslac held it freely.

In GRAVESEND Hundred

3 He also holds 3½ hides in WEEDON (Bec) in exchange for Watford.

Tra.ē.VIII.car 7 dim. In dn̄io.ē una 7 dim.7 II.uilli
cū pb̄ro 7 III.bord hn̄t dim car. Ibi.III.milit cū.VI.uill
7 III.bord hn̄t.IIII.car 7 dim.Ibi.XVII.ac p̄ti.7 XII.ac
siluæ.7 molin̄ de.XL.den. Valuit.XL.sol.Modo.L.sol.

Idē ten.IIII.hid in *ASCEBI*.Tra.ē.X.car.
In dn̄io st̄.III.car 7 VI.serui.7 XV.uilli 7 III.bord cū.V.
car.Ibi.VIII.ac p̄ti. Valuit.XL.sol.Modo.LX.solid.

OSBERN ten de Hug.III.hid una v min in *WELINTONE*.
Tra.ē.VII.car.In dn̄io sunt.II.7 III.serui.7 V.uilli
cū.IIII.car.Ibi molin̄ de.XII.den.7 VIII.ac p̄ti.
Valuit.XX.solid.Modo XL.solid.Balduin libe tenuit.

Idē ten.I.hid in *STAVERTONE*.Tra.ē.II.car 7 dimid.
Ibi st̄.II.car cū.I.uillo 7 V.bord. Valuit.XV.solid.
Modo.XX.sol.Leuric tenuit de Balduino

Idē ten.IIII.partes dimid hidæ in *TORP*.Tra.ē.I.car.
Hæc ibi.ē in dn̄io cū.I.bord.7 II.ac p̄ti. Valuit.XII.den.
Modo.X.solid. Aluuin tenuit de Balduino

HVGO ten de.H.in *MERDEFORD*.II.hid *IN FOXELEA HD̄*.
7 q̄ntā partē.I.hidæ.Tra.ē.V.car.In dn̄io.ē una.
7 IIII.serui.7 IX.uilli cū pb̄ro 7 IIII.bord hn̄t.III.car.
Ibi silua.IIII.q̄rent lḡ.7 una q̄z lat. Valuit.XX.sol.
Modo.L.solid.Willa libe tenuit. *IN SVTONE HD̄*.

IVO ten de.H.in *NIWEBOTLE*.VI.hid cū append suis.
Tra.ē.XV.car.In dn̄io sunt.III.car 7 dimid.7 VIII.serui.
Ibi un miles 7 XII.uilli 7 IIII.bord hn̄t.IIII.car.
Ibi.VII.ancillæ 7 VII.ac p̄ti. Valuit.IIII.lib.m̄.VI.lib.
Balduin tenuit cū soca 7 saca.

Land for 8½ ploughs. In lordship 1½.
2 villagers with a priest and 3 smallholders have ½ plough.
3 men-at-arms with 6 villagers and 3 smallholders have 4½ ploughs.
Meadow, 17 acres; woodland, 12 acres; a mill at 40d.
The value was 40s; now 50s.

4 He also holds 4 hides in ASHBY (St. Ledgers). Land for 10 ploughs.
In lordship 3 ploughs; 6 slaves;
15 villagers and 3 smallholders with 5 ploughs.
Meadow, 8 acres.
The value was 40s; now 60s.

5 Osbern holds 3 hides, less 1 virgate, from Hugh in WELTON.
Land for 7 ploughs. In lordship 2; 3 slaves;
5 villagers with 4 ploughs.
A mill at 12d; meadow, 8 acres.
The value was 20s; now 40s.
Baldwin held it freely.

6 He also holds 1 hide in STAVERTON. Land for 2½ ploughs.
2 ploughs there, with
1 villager and 5 smallholders.
The value was 15s; now 20s.
Leofric held it from Baldwin.

7 He also holds 4 parts of ½ hide in THRUPP (Grounds).
Land for 1 plough; it is there, in lordship, with
1 smallholder.
Meadow, 2 acres.
The value was 12d; now 10s.
Alwin held it from Baldwin.

In FOXLEY Hundred

8 Hugh holds 2 hides and the fifth part of 1 hide from Hugh
in MAIDFORD. Land for 5 ploughs. In lordship 1; 4 slaves.
9 villagers with a priest and 4 smallholders have 3 ploughs.
Woodland 4 furlongs long and 1 furlong wide.
The value was 20s; now 50s.
Willa held it freely.

In SUTTON Hundred

9 Ivo holds 6 hides with their dependencies from Hugh in NEWBOTTLE.
Land for 15 ploughs. In lordship 3½ ploughs; 8 slaves.
A man-at-arms, 12 villagers and 4 smallholders have 4 ploughs.
7 female slaves; meadow, 7 acres.
The value was £4; now £6.
Baldwin held it, with full jurisdiction.

HVGO ten̄ de.H.in *MIDELTONE* .II.hid̄.Tra.ē.v.car̄.
In dn̄io.ē una.7 IX.uill̄i cū p̄bro hn̄t.III.car̄.Ibi
XII.ac̄ p̄ti.Valuit 7 ual.XL.solid̄.Godric̄ lib̄e tenuit.
HVGO ten̄ de.H.in *SVTONE*.I.hid̄ 7 dim̄.7 decimā
partē.I.hidæ.Tra.ē.IIII.car̄.In dn̄io.ē una.7 II.serui.
7 II.bord̄ hn̄t dimid̄ car̄.Ibi molin̄ de.II.sol̄. tenuer̄.
Valuit.x.solid̄.Modo.xxx.solid̄.Willa 7 Turbern̄
IVO ten̄ de.H.in *BIVELDE*.II.hid̄. *IN WARADONE HD̄.*
Tra.ē.v.car̄.In dn̄io.ē una.cū.I.uill̄o 7 uno bord̄.
Valuit.II.solid̄.Modo.x.sol̄.Tres taini lib̄e tenuer̄.
RICARD̄ ten̄ de.H.in *WODEFORD*.II.hid̄.Tra.ē.v.car̄.
In dn̄io sunt.II.æ 7 IIII.serui.7 una ancilla.7 XI.uill̄i
hn̄t.III.car̄.Ibi.II.ac̄ p̄ti.7 molin̄ de.VIII.solid̄.
Valuit.XL.solid̄.Modo.LX.solid̄.Balduin̄ lib̄e tenuit.
HVGO ten̄ in *EGEDONE*.II.hid̄ de Hugone.Tra.ē.v.car̄.
In dn̄io sunt.II.æ 7 II.serui.7 XII.uill̄i cū.III.car̄.
Ibi molin̄ de.II.solid̄.7 II.ac̄ p̄ti.Valuit.XL.sol̄.M̊.L.sol̄.
WALTERI ten̄ unā v̄ træ de.H.in *CERVELTONE*.
Tra.ē dim̄ car̄.Valuit 7 ual.v.sol̄. Aluuin̄ lib̄e tenuit.
.XXII.[II] HVGO [Luri] ten̄ de rege dim̄ hid̄ in parua *WELEDONE*.Tra.ē.III.car̄. *IN CORBEI HD̄.*
In dn̄io.ē una.cū.I.seruo.7 XI.uill̄i hn̄t.II.car̄.Silua ibi.VI.q̃z lḡ.7 II.q̃z lat̄.
Vluric̄ lib̄e tenuit. Valuit x.sol̄.Modo.xx.sol̄.

10 Hugh holds 2 hides from Hugh in MIDDLETON (Cheney).
Land for 5 ploughs. In lordship 1.
9 villagers with a priest have 3 ploughs.
Meadow, 12 acres.
The value was and is 40s.
Godric held it freely.

11 Hugh holds 1½ hides and the tenth part of 1 hide from Hugh in (Kings) SUTTON. Land for 4 ploughs. In lordship 1; 2 slaves.
2 smallholders have ½ plough.
A mill at 2s.
The value was 10s; now 30s.
Willa and Thorbern held it.

In WARDEN Hundred

12 Ivo holds 2 hides from Hugh in BYFIELD. Land for 5 ploughs.
In lordship 1, with
1 villager and 1 smallholder.
The value was 2s; now 10s.
Three thanes held it freely.

13 Richard holds 2 hides from Hugh in WOODFORD (Halse).
Land for 5 ploughs. In lordship 2; 4 male slaves, 1 female.
11 villagers have 3 ploughs.
Meadow, 2 acres; a mill at 8s.
The value was 40s; now 60s.
Baldwin held it freely.

14 Hugh holds 2 hides from Hugh in EYDON. Land for 5 ploughs.
In lordship 2; 2 slaves;
12 villagers with 3 ploughs.
A mill at 2s; meadow, 2 acres.
The value was 40s; now 50s.

[In GRAVESEND Hundred]

15 Walter holds 1 virgate of land from Hugh in CHARWELTON.
Land for ½ plough.
The value was and is 5s.
Alwin held it freely.

(Ch. 24 added at foot of col. 224 c, interrupts ch. 23 which is continued at head of col. 224 d)

24 [LAND OF HUGH OF IVRY]

In CORBY Hundred

1 Hugh (of) Ivry holds ½ hide from the King in LITTLE WELDON.
Land for 3 ploughs. In lordship 1, with 1 slave.
11 villagers have 2 ploughs.
Woodland 6 furlongs long and 2 furlongs wide.
The value was 10s; now 20s.
Wulfric held it freely.

de Luri
ROGERIVS ten de. H. *COTESFORDE*. Ibi sunt. VI. hidæ.
Tra. ē. X. car. In dnio sunt. III. 7 IIII. possēt. ēē.
Ibi sunt. X. uitti 7 V. bord. 7 XL. ac pasturæ.
Valuit. C. solid. Modo. VIII. lib.
Idē Rog ten de. H. *CERLENTONE*. Ibi sunt. X. hidæ.
Tra. ē. XV. car. In dnio sunt. IIII. car. 7 VI. serui.
7 XV. uitti 7 XI. bord hnt. XI. car. Pratū. IIII. qz
lg. 7 II. qz lat. Pasturæ. III. qz lg. 7 II. qz lat.
Valuit. VIII. lib. Modo. X. lib. Balduin libe tenuit.
Huj træ sunt. IIII. hidæ in dnio.
HVGO ten. II. hid 7 dim in *SCIPTVNE*.
Tra. ē. IIII. car. In dnio sunt. II. 7 IIII. serui. 7 II. uitti
7 III. bord hnt. I. car. Ibi molin de. XI. sol. 7 IIII. ac
pti. 7 III. qrent pasturæ. Valuit. XL. sol. Modo. IIII.
lib 7 X. solid. Aluric libe tenuit.
In *SCIPFORD* ten Aba XI. hid de Hugone. Tra. ē
VIII. car. In dnio sunt. II. 7 IIII. ac pti. 7 molin
redd. XXXII. denar. 7 XIII. qrent pasturæ.
Valuit 7 uat. IIII. lib 7 X. solid. Balduin tenuit.

.XXII. TERRA HVGONIS COMITIS. *IN WAREDON HD.*

※ HVGO Comes ten de rege in *BIFELDE*. VIII. hid. 7 Robt
de eo. Tra. ē. XX. car. In dnio sunt. II. 7 V. serui. 7 VIII.
uitti 7 III. bord hnt. III. car. Ibi un miles cū. II. uittis
ht. I. car. 7 II. libi hoēs manent ibi. ptū. I. leuu lg.
7 VII. qz lat. Valuit 7 uat. VIII. lib. Aschil libe tenuit.
Idē. R. ten de comite. I. hid in *BOTENDONE*. Tra. ē
II. car 7 dimid. In dnio. ē una. 7 VI. uitti cū pbro
7 IIII. bord hnt. I. car. 7 un miles ht dim car. Ibi. V.
ac pti. Valuit XXX. solid. Modo. XL. sol. Aschil tenuit.

(Ch. 23 continued)

(In OXFORDSHIRE)

16 Roger of Ivry holds COTTISFORD from Hugh. 6 hides. 224 d
Land for 10 ploughs. In lordship 3; a fourth possible.
10 villagers and 5 smallholders.
Pasture, 40 acres.
The value was 100s; now £8.

17 Roger also holds CHARLTON (on Otmoor) from Hugh. 10 hides.
Land for 15 ploughs. In lordship 4 ploughs; 6 slaves.
15 villagers and 11 smallholders have 11 ploughs.
Meadow 4 furlongs long and 2 furlongs wide;
pastures 3 furlongs long and 2 furlongs wide.
The value was £8; now £10.
Baldwin held it freely.
Of this land 4 hides are in lordship.

18 Hugh holds 2½ hides in SHIPTON (on Cherwell). Land for 4 ploughs.
In lordship 2; 4 slaves.
2 villagers and 3 smallholders have 1 plough.
A mill at 11s; meadow, 4 acres; pasture, 3 furlongs.
The value was 40s; now £4 10s.
Aelfric held it freely.

19 Abba holds 11 hides from Hugh in SIBFORD. Land for 8 ploughs.
In lordship 2.
Meadow, 4 acres; a mill which pays 32d; pasture, 13 furlongs.
The value was and is £4 10s.
Baldwin held it.

22 LAND OF EARL HUGH

In WARDEN Hundred

1 Earl Hugh holds 8 hides from the King in BYFIELD, and Robert from him. Land for 20 ploughs. In lordship 2; 5 slaves.
8 villagers and 3 smallholders have 3 ploughs. A man-at-arms with 2 villagers has 1 plough. 2 free men live there.
Meadow 1 league long and 7 furlongs wide.
The value was and is £8.
Askell held it freely.

2 Robert also holds 1 hide from the Earl in BODDINGTON.
Land for 2½ ploughs. In lordship 1.
6 villagers with a priest and 4 smallholders have 1 plough.
A man-at-arms has ½ plough.
Meadow, 5 acres.
The value was 30s; now 40s.
Askell held it.

Idē ten̄ de com̄ .i. hid̄ 7 unā v̄ træ IN
in *KAPEFORD*. Tra. ē. ii. car̄ 7 dim̄. In dn̄io. ē una.
7 iii. serui. 7 iii. uitti cū. i. car̄. Ibi molin̄ de. vi. solid̄
7 viii. den̄. 7 iii. ac̄ p̄ti. Valuit 7 ual. xxx. solid̄.
Idē ten̄. iiii. hid̄ in *MERESTONE*. *IN EDBOLDESTOV HD̄.*
Tra. ē. x. car̄. In dn̄io sunt. iiii. 7 ix. serui. 7 xxvi. uitti
7 x. bord̄ cū. vi. car̄. Ibi molin̄ de. viii. sol. 7 xxiiii. ac̄
p̄ti. Valuit 7 ual. x. lib̄.
Idē ten̄. ii. hid̄ in *RODESTONE*. Tra. ē. v. car̄. In dn̄io
sunt. ii. 7 vi. serui. 7 x. uitti 7 v. bord̄ cū. iii. car̄. Ibi. xii.
ac̄ p̄ti. 7 vi. ac̄ siluæ. Valuit 7 ual. c. sol. *IN SVTONE HD̄.*
Idē ten̄ in *MIDELTONE*. iiii. partes. ii. hidar̄. Tra. ē. iiii.
car̄. In dn̄io sunt. ii. 7 viii. uitti hn̄t. i. car̄. Ibi. viii. ac̄
p̄ti. Valuit 7 ual. iii. lib̄. Soca p̄tin̄ ad Sutone.
Idē ten̄ dim̄ hid̄ in *BLACVLVESLEA*. *IN FOXHELA HD̄.*
Tra. ē. i. car̄ 7 dim̄. Ibi hn̄t. ii. uitti dim̄ car̄. Valuit
7 ual. viii. solid̄. Ketel tenuit. Soca p̄tin̄ ad Nortone.
Idē ten̄. ii. hid̄ 7 unā v̄ træ *IN GISLEBVRG HD̄ 7 DIM̄.*
in *GIVERTOST*. Tra. ē. iiii. car̄. In dn̄io. ē dim̄ car̄. 7 viii.
uitti cū p̄bro 7 ix. bord̄ 7 ii. sochis hn̄t. i. car̄ 7 dimid̄.
Ibi. viii. ac̄ p̄ti. Valuit 7 ual. xx. solid̄. Godric libe tenuit.
GOZELIN ten̄ de comite. iiii. hid̄ *IN FOXESLAV HVND̄.*
in *SLAPTONE*. Tra. ē. x. car̄. In dn̄io sunt. ii. 7 iii. serui.
7 vi. uitti cū. i. bord̄ hn̄t. ii. car̄. Ibi. viii. ac̄ p̄ti.
Valuit 7 ual. iii. lib̄.
Has tras tenuit Aschil cū saca 7 soca. Modo ten̄ hoēs comit̄.

He also holds

3 in TRAFFORD 1 hide and 1 virgate of land from the Earl.
Land for 2½ ploughs. In lordship 1; 3 slaves;
3 villagers with 1 plough.
A mill at 6s 8d; meadow, 3 acres.
The value was and is 30s.

in ALBOLDSTOW Hundred

4 in MARSTON (St. Lawrence) 4 hides. Land for 10 ploughs.
In lordship 4; 9 slaves;
26 villagers and 10 smallholders with 6 ploughs.
A mill at 8s; meadow, 24 acres.
The value was and is £10.

5 in RADSTONE 2 hides. Land for 5 ploughs. In lordship 2; 6 slaves;
10 villagers and 5 smallholders with 3 ploughs.
Meadow, 12 acres; woodland, 6 acres.
The value was and is 100s.

in SUTTON Hundred

6 in MIDDLETON (Cheney) 4 parts of 2 hides.
Land for 4 ploughs. In lordship 2.
8 villagers have 1 plough.
Meadow, 8 acres.
The value was and is £3.
The jurisdiction belongs to (Kings) Sutton.

in FOXLEY Hundred

7 in BLAKESLEY ½ hide. Land for 1½ ploughs.
2 villagers have ½ plough.
The value was and is 8s.
Ketel held it. The jurisdiction belongs to (Greens) Norton.

in GUILSBOROUGH Hundred and a half

8 in YELVERTOFT 2 hides and 1 virgate of land.
Land for 4 ploughs. In lordship ½ plough.
8 villagers with a priest, 9 smallholders and 2 Freemen
have 1½ ploughs.
Meadow, 8 acres.
The value was and is 20s.
Godric held it freely.

In FOXLEY Hundred

9 Jocelyn holds 4 hides from the Earl in SLAPTON. Land for 10
ploughs. In lordship 2; 3 slaves.
6 villagers with 1 smallholder have 2 ploughs.
Meadow, 8 acres.
The value was and is £3.
Askell held these lands, with full jurisdiction. Now Earl Hugh's
men hold them.

XXV. TERRA HENRICI DE FERIERES. *IN CLAILEA HD.*

HENRICVS DE FEREIRES ten.III.hid 7 qntā partē uni9 hidæ in *PERIE*.Tra.ē.x.car.In dnio sunt.III.car. 7 III.serui.7 xx.uitti 7 VII.bord cū pbro hnt.VII.car. Ibi molin de.XVIII.sol.7 IIII.den.7 XVI.ac pti.Silua VI.qrent 7 XIIII.ptic lg.7 II.qz 7 dim lat. Valuit 7 uali.VI.lib.Tosti com tenuit.

IN TICEMERSE. SASWALO ten de Henrico.x.hid *IN NARRESFORD HD.* 7 II.partes dim hidæ una v min.Tra.ē.xv.car.In dnio sunt.IIII.car.7 VIII.serui.7 XVI.uitti 7 v.bord hnt VI.car 7 dim.7 VII.sochi cū.IIII.car 7 dim.Ibi molin de.XXI.solid 7 IIII.den.7 xxx.ac pti.Silua.IIII.qz lg.7 una lat.Valuit.III.lib.Modo.VII.lib. Bundi libe tenuit. *IN ANDFERDESHO HD.*

RADVLFVS ten de.H.in *ECHENTONE*.IIII.hid.Tra.ē VIII.car.In dnio.I.hida 7 dim de hac tra.7 ibi.II.car. 7 IIII.serui.7 VIII.uitti 7 IX.bord 7 XII.sochi cū.VIII. bord.hnt.VI.car.Ibi.II.molini de.XIIII.sol.7 XXXII. ac pti.Valuit.III.lib.Modo.c.solid.Bundi tenuit,

XXVI. TERRA ROBERTI DE TODENI.

ROTBERTVS DE TODENI.III.hid in *STOCHE*.Tra.ē VI.car.In dnio sunt.II.7 III.serui.7 IX.uitti 7 II.bord cū.I.socho hnt.III.car.Ibi molin de.XII.den.Silua .v.qrent lg.7 III.qz lat.Valuit.LX.sol.modo.XL.sol. Osulfus libe tenuit.T.R.E.

Idem ten.III.hid 7 unā v træ in *WILBERDESTONE*. Tra.ē.VI.car.De hac tra.ē.I.hida in dnio.7 ibi.II.car cū.I.seruo.7 XII.uitti 7 VII.bord hnt.III.car.Silua IX.qrent lg.7 v.qz lat.Valuit.XL.sol.Modo.xxx.sol.

25 LAND OF HENRY OF FERRERS

In CLEYLEY Hundred 225 a

1 Henry of Ferrers holds 3 hides and the fifth part of 1 hide in POTTERSPURY. Land for 10 ploughs. In lordship 3 ploughs; 3 slaves.
20 villagers and 7 smallholders with a priest have 7 ploughs.
A mill at 18s 4d; meadow, 16 acres; woodland 6 furlongs and 14 perches long and 2½ furlongs wide.
The value was and is £6.
Earl Tosti held it.

In NAVISFORD Hundred

2 In TITCHMARSH Saswalo holds from Henry 10 hides and 2 parts of ½ hide, less 1 virgate. Land for 15 ploughs. In lordship 4 ploughs; 8 slaves.
16 villagers and 5 smallholders have 6½ ploughs; 7 Freemen with 4½ ploughs.
A mill at 21s 4d; meadow, 30 acres; woodland 4 furlongs long and 1 wide.
The value was £3; now £7.
Bondi held it freely.

In HAMFORDSHOE Hundred

3 Ralph holds 4 hides from Henry in ECTON. Land for 8 ploughs. In lordship 1½ hides of this land; 2 ploughs there; 4 slaves.
8 villagers, 9 smallholders and 12 Freemen with 8 smallholders have 6 ploughs.
2 mills at 14s; meadow, 32 acres.
The value was £3; now 100s.
Bondi held it.

26 LAND OF ROBERT OF TOSNY

[In STOKE Hundred]

1 Robert of Tosny (holds) 3 hides in STOKE (Albany).
Land for 6 ploughs. In lordship 2; 3 slaves.
9 villagers and 2 smallholders with 1 Freeman have 3 ploughs.
A mill at 12d; woodland 5 furlongs long and 3 furlongs wide.
The value was 60s; now 40s.
Oswulf held it freely before 1066.

2 He also holds 3 hides and 1 virgate of land in WILBARSTON.
Land for 6 ploughs. 1 hide of this land is in lordship; 2 ploughs there, with 1 slave.
12 villagers and 7 smallholders have 3 ploughs.
Woodland 9 furlongs long and 5 furlongs wide.
The value was 40s; now 30s.

Idẽ ten̄ .I.hid̄ 7 unã bouatã t̄ræ *IN WICESLEA WAPENT.*
in *SEGENTONE*.T̄ra.ẽ.IIII.car̄. In dn̄io ſunt.IIe.7 II.
ſerui.7 VIII.uiłłi 7 II.bord̄ cũ pb̄ro hn̄t.I.car̄ 7 dim̄.
Ibi.III.ac̄ p̄ti. Silua.I.q̄z lḡ.7 altera lat̄. Rob̄tus
n̄ hť niſi.III.partẽ ſiluæ. Similit̄ de t̄ra arabili.
Ad hanc t̄rã ptin̄ una v̄ t̄ræ in *BERCHEDONE*. Ibi sť
IIII.uiłłi cũ dimid̄ car̄.
Valuit.XL.ſol. Modo.XX.ſol. *IN FOXESLEA HD̄.*
Idẽ ten̄.III.hid̄ in *SEWELLE* 7 IIII.partes uni9 v̄.T̄ra.ẽ.VII.
car̄. In dn̄io.ẽ una 7 dim̄.7 II.ſerui.7 VIII.uiłłi 7 III.bord̄
hn̄t.III.car̄ 7 dim̄. Ibi molin̄ de.XII.den̄.7 VII.ac̄ p̄ti.
Silua.II.q̄rent̄ 7 dim̄ lḡ.7 II.q̄rent̄ lat̄. Valuit.X.ſol
modo.LX.ſolid̄. *IN RODEWELLE HD̄.*
HVGO ten̄ de Ro.I.hid̄ 7 dim̄ in *RISTONE*.T̄ra.ẽ.IIII.car̄.
In dn̄io.ẽ una.7 II.ſerui.7 IIII.uiłłi 7 III.bord̄ 7 III.ſocħi
cũ.II.car̄ 7 dimid̄ int̄ om̄s. Ibi.IIII.ac̄ p̄ti.7 XV.ac̄ ſiluæ.
Valuit X.ſol. Modo.XXX.ſolid̄.Soca ptin̄ ad Waleſdone.
Idẽ ten̄ in *DEISBVRG* dimid̄ hid̄.T̄ra.ẽ.II.car̄. Eduin9 tenuit.
In dn̄io.ẽ una.7 II.ſerui.7 III.bord̄. Ibi dimid̄ ac̄ ſiluæ.
Valuit.V.ſolid̄.Modo.XX.ſolid̄. Oſulf9 lib̄e tenuit.
Roger9 ten̄ dimid̄ hid̄ de Rob̄to in *PIPEWELLE*.T̄ra.ẽ.II.car̄.
Ibi.ẽ una 7 dim̄ car̄ cũ.IIII.bord̄.7 V.ac̄ ſiluæ. Valuit.V.
ſol. Modo.VI.ſol. Eduin9 lib̄e tenuit.
ILDVIN9 ten̄ de.Ro.II.hid̄ in *BRANTONE*.T̄ra.ẽ.V.car̄.
In dn̄io ſunt.IIe.7 VI.ſerui.7 V.uiłłi 7 IIII.bord̄ cũ.II.car̄
7 dimid̄. Ibi.XXII.ac̄ p̄ti. Silua.V.q̄rent̄ lḡ.7 III.q̄z lat̄.
Valuit X.ſol. Modo.XL.ſolid̄. Oſulf9 tenuit

In WITCHLEY Wapentake

3 He also holds 1 hide and 1 bovate of land in SEATON.
Land for 4 ploughs. In lordship 2; 2 slaves.
8 villagers and 2 smallholders with a priest have 1½ ploughs.
Meadow, 3 acres; woodland 1 furlong long and another wide.
Robert has only the third part of the woodland; the same with the arable land.

1 virgate of land in BARROWDEN belongs to this land.
4 villagers there with ½ plough.
The value was 40s; now 20s.

In FOXLEY Hundred

4 He also holds 3 hides and 4 parts of 1 virgate in SEAWELL.
Land for 7 ploughs. In lordship 1½; 2 slaves.
8 villagers and 3 smallholders have 3½ ploughs.
A mill at 12d; meadow, 7 acres;
woodland 2½ furlongs long and 2 furlongs wide.
The value was 10s; now 60s.

In ROTHWELL Hundred

5 Hugh holds 1½ hides from Robert in RUSHTON. Land for 4 ploughs.
In lordship 1; 2 slaves;
4 villagers, 3 smallholders and 3 Freemen with 2½ ploughs between them.
Meadow, 4 acres; woodland, 15 acres.
The value was 10s; now 30s.
The jurisdiction belongs to Weldon. Edwin held it.

6 He also holds ½ hide in DESBOROUGH. Land for 2 ploughs.
In lordship 1; 2 slaves;
3 smallholders.
Woodland, ½ acre.
The value was 5s; now 20s.
Oswulf held it freely.

7 Roger holds ½ hide from Robert in PIPEWELL. Land for 2 ploughs.
1½ ploughs there, with
4 smallholders.
Woodland, 5 acres.
The value was 5s; now 6s.
Edwin held it freely.

[In STOKE Hundred]

8 Hildwin holds 2 hides from Robert in BRAMPTON (Ash).
Land for 5 ploughs. In lordship 2; 6 slaves;
5 villagers and 4 smallholders with 2½ ploughs.
Meadow, 22 acres; woodland 5 furlongs long and 3 furlongs wide.
The value was 10s; now 40s.
Oswulf held it.

ILDVIN9 ten de.Ro.I.hid.una bouata 7 dim min9 in *DINGLE*.

225 b Tra.ẽ.II.car.In dnio.ẽ una 7 dim.7 II.uilli 7 v.bord cu dim car.Ibi.III.ac pti.7 III.ac siluæ.Valuit.x.sol.Modo.xx.sol.

Gvnfrid9 7 Walchelin9 ten de.Ro.III.hid in *ASCELE*.
Tra.ẽ.VI.car.In dnio sunt.II.7 VII.uilli 7 IX.bord hnt III.car.Ibi molin de.XXXII.den.7 IX.ac pti.7 II.ac spineti. Silua.III.qrent lg.7 VIII.pticas lat.7 in alio loco IIII.ac siluæ.ptin ad hanc tram.Valuit xx.sol.Modo. xxx.solid.Frano 7 Algar libe tenuer.

Wibert9 ten de.Ro.tciã partẽ uni9 hidæ in ead uilla
Tra.ẽ.I.car.quæ ibi.ẽ cu.II.bord 7 uno seruo.Valuit xvI.den.Modo.v.solid.Algar libe tenuit.

.XXVII. TERRA ROBERTI DE STADFORD *IN WAREDONE HD*.

ROTBERTVS de STATFORD ten in *STANTONE*.III.v træ 7 Hugo de eo.Tra.ẽ.III.car.In dnio.ẽ una.7 III.serui. 7 VI.uilli 7 v.bord cu.II.car.Ibi.III.ac pti.
Valuit.x.solid.Modo.xxx.solid.Æileua libe tenuit.T.R.E.

XXVIII. TERRA ROBERTI DE OILGI. *IN CLAILEA HVND*.

ROTBERTVS de OILGI.I.hid 7 unã v træ in *WICHA*.7 Roger9 de eo.Tra.ẽ.x.car.In dnio sunt.III.car.7 VII.serui.7 VII. uilli 7 III.bord cu.IIII.car.Ibi.x.ac pti.Silua.XI.qrent lg.7 VI.qrent lat.Valuit.XL.sol.Modo.c.solid.
Azor libe tenuit.T.R.E. *IN SVTONE HVND*.

Idẽ ten de.Ro.I.hid in *TEWORDE*.Tra.ẽ.III.car 7 dimid. In dnio.ẽ una.7 II.serui.7 VII.uilli hnt.II.car 7 dimid. Ibi molin de.xxx.den.Valuit.x.sol.Modo.xxx.solid.

* Idẽ.Ro.ẽn dimid hid 7 v.tam partẽ.I.hidæ in *PRESTONE*.Tra.ẽ.I.car 7 dimid.7 tant ibi.ẽ cu.IIII.

9 Hildwin holds 1 hide, less 1½ bovates, from Robert in DINGLEY.
Land for 2 ploughs. In lordship 1½; 225 b
2 villagers and 5 smallholders with ½ plough.
Meadow, 3 acres; woodland, 3 acres.
The value was 10s; now 20s.

10 Gunfrid and Walkelin hold 3 hides from Robert in ASHLEY.
Land for 6 ploughs. In lordship 2.
7 villagers and 9 smallholders have 3 ploughs.
A mill at 32d; meadow, 9 acres; spinney, 2 acres;
woodland 3 furlongs long and 8 perches wide;
4 acres of woodland elsewhere belong to this land.
The value was 20s; now 30s.
Fran and Algar held it freely.

11 Wibert holds the third part of 1 hide from Robert in the same village.
Land for 1 plough which is there, with
2 smallholders and 1 slave.
The value was 16d; now 5s.
Algar held it freely.

27 LAND OF ROBERT OF STAFFORD

In WARDEN Hundred

1 Robert of Stafford holds 3 virgates of land in STONETON, and
Hugh from him. Land for 3 ploughs. In lordship 1; 3 slaves;
6 villagers and 5 smallholders with 2 ploughs.
Meadow, 3 acres.
The value was 10s; now 30s.
Aeleva held it freely before 1066.

28 LAND OF ROBERT D'OILLY

In CLEYLEY Hundred

1 Robert d'Oilly (holds) 1 hide and 1 virgate of land in WICKEN,
and Roger from him. Land for 10 ploughs. In lordship 3 ploughs;
7 slaves;
7 villagers and 3 smallholders with 4 ploughs.
Meadow, 10 acres; woodland 11 furlongs long and 6 furlongs wide.
The value was 40s; now 100s.
Azor held it freely before 1066.

In SUTTON Hundred

2 He also holds 1 hide from Robert in THENFORD. Land for 3½ ploughs.
In lordship 1; 2 slaves.
7 villagers have 2½ ploughs.
A mill at 30d.
The value was 10s; now 30s.

3 Robert also holds ½ hide and the fifth part of 1 hide in PURSTON.
Land for 1½ ploughs; as many there, with

uillis 7 II. bord. Ibi. VIII. ac̄ p̄ti. Valuit. x. sol̄. Modo. XII. sol̄.
Leuuin tenuit. 7 q̄libet ire potuit. Sed inde rex soca habeb̄.

.XXVII. TERRA ROBERTI DE VECI. *IN RODEWELLE HD̄.*

ROTBERT9 de VECI ten̄. I. hid̄ in *BADEBROC*. Tra. ē. II. car.
Vna. ē in dn̄io. 7 IIII. bord̄ hn̄t alia car. Valuit. v. solid̄.
Modo. x. solid̄. Ailric libe tenuit. T.R.E.

.XXX. TERRA ROBERTI DE BVCI. *IN STOCH HVND̄.*

ROTBERT9 de BVCI ten̄. II. partes uni9 hidæ in *ASCE*. Tra. ē. I.
car. Hanc hn̄t ibi. VI. sochi. Valuit 7 ual. x. sol̄. 7 VIII. den̄.
Idē ten̄. II. hid̄ 7 II. partes uni9 hidæ in *WESTONE*. Tra. ē. VI. car.
Ibi. x. sochi hn̄t. III. car 7 dim̄. Valuit. x. sol̄. Modo. XL. II. sol̄
Idē ten̄. I. hid̄ 7 II. partes dimid̄ hidæ in *SVTONE*. 7 VIII. den̄.
Tra. ē. II. car 7 dim̄. Has hn̄t ibi. VIII. sochi. Valuit. v. solid̄.
Modo. XXI. solid̄ 7 IIII. denar.
Idem ten̄ in *DINGLEI*. II. partes uni9 hidæ. 7 II. partes duar
★ partiū uni9 hidæ. Tra. ē. IIII. car. Ibi. XI. sochi hn̄t. II. car 7 dim̄.
Valuit. x. solid̄. Modo. XIII. solid̄ 7 IIII. den̄.
Idē ten̄. II. hid̄ in *BRANTONE*. Tra. ē. IIII. car. Ibi. VIII. sochi
hn̄t. III. car. Valuit. x. sol̄. Modo. VIII. denar plus. *IN CORBEI*
Idē ten̄. I. hid̄ 7 III. v̄ træ in *WELEDENE*. Tra. ē. v. car. *HVND̄.*
In dn̄io sunt. II. car. 7 VIII. uilli 7 II. bord̄ cū. I. socho hn̄t. IIII.
car. Silua. I. leuū lḡ. 7 III. q̄rent lat. Valuit. v. sol̄. m̄. XXX. sol̄.
Has tras tenuit Norman9 7 quo uoluit ire potuit.

4 villagers and 2 smallholders.
Meadow, 8 acres.
The value was 10s; now 12s.
Leofwin held it; he could go wherever he would, but the King had its jurisdiction.

29 LAND OF ROBERT OF VESSEY

In ROTHWELL Hundred

1 Robert of Vessey holds 1 hide in BRAYBROOKE. Land for 2 ploughs.
In lordship 1.
4 smallholders have another plough.
The value was 5s; now 10s.
Alric held it freely before 1066.

30 LAND OF ROBERT OF BUCY

In STOKE Hundred

1 Robert of Bucy holds 2 parts of 1 hide in ASHLEY.
Land for 1 plough.
6 Freemen have it there.
The value was and is 10s 8d.

He also holds

2 in WESTON (by Welland) 2 hides and 2 parts of 1 hide.
Land for 6 ploughs.
10 Freemen have 3½ ploughs.
The value was 10s; now 42s 8d.

3 in SUTTON (Bassett) 1 hide and 2 parts of ½ hide.
Land for 2½ ploughs.
8 Freemen have them there.
The value was 5s; now 21s 4d.

4 in DINGLEY 2 parts of 1 hide and 2 parts of 2 parts of 1 hide.
Land for 4 ploughs.
11 Freemen have 2½ ploughs.
The value was 10s; now 13s 4d.

5 in BRAMPTON (Ash) 2 hides. Land for 4 ploughs.
8 Freemen have 3 ploughs.
The value was 10s; now 8d more.

in CORBY Hundred

6 in WELDON 1 hide and 3 virgates of land. Land for 5 ploughs.
In lordship 2 ploughs.
8 villagers and 4 smallholders with 1 Freeman have 4 ploughs.
Woodland 1 league long and 3 furlongs wide.
The value was 5s; now 30s.
Norman held these lands; he could go where he would.

Idē Robt ten unā v træ in *WELEDENE*. Rex calūniat eā.

WALTERI ten de Robto in *ASCELEI* *IN STOCH HVND*.

tciā partē uni hidæ. Soca. ē de Weledene. Tra. ē dimid.

car. Ibi. II. sochi hnt. I. car. 7 II. acs pti. Valuit. v. sol. m. III. sol.

HVGO ten de Ro. I. hid in *BRANTONE*. Tra. ē. I. car. Norman tenuit.

Tam st in dnio. II. car. 7 II. serui cū. I. bord. Valuit. II. sol. m. xx. sol.

225 c

Normann ten de. Ro. II. hid in *BLAREWICHE*. Tra. ē. VI.

car. Hugo 7 Wills ten de eo. In dnio st. II. car. 7 XII. uilli

7 v. bord hnt. IIII. car. Ibi molin de. xxx. den. 7 VI. ac

pti. Silua. I. leuu lg. 7 III. qrent lat. Valet. XVIII. sol.

HVGO ten dim hid in *BADEBROC* de. Ro. *IN RODEWEL HD*.

Tra. ē. I. car. Valuit 7 ual. XVI. den. Norman tenuit

Idē. H. ten de Ro. tciā partē uni hidæ in ead uilla.

Tra. ē dim car. Ibi. ē tam. I. car cū. I. bord.

Valuit. XII. den. Modo. III. solid. Vlchet tenuit.

WIlls ten de. Ro. dim hid in *RISTONE*. Tra. ē. I.

car. Vna tam 7 dim car est ibi cū. IIII. uillis 7 II. bord.

Ibi dim molin de. XII. den. 7 VI. ac siluæ. Vlchet tenuit.

Valuit. XII. den. Modo. VI. sol. Soca. ē in Waledone.

In ead uilla ht dim v træ vastā. *IN SPEREHOV HD*

Idē. W. ten de. Ro. II. hid 7 unā v træ 7 dimid. in

MOLTONE. Tra. ē. v. car. In dnio sunt. III. car cū. I. seruo.

7 Robert also holds 1 virgate of land in WELDON.
The King claims it.

In STOKE Hundred

8 Walter holds the third part of 1 hide from Robert in ASHLEY.
The jurisdiction is WELDON'S. Land for ½ plough.
2 Freemen have 1 plough, and
meadow, 2 acres.
The value was 5s; now 3s.

9 Hugh holds 1 hide from Robert in BRAMPTON (Ash). Land for 1 plough. However, 2 ploughs in lordship; 2 slaves, with
1 smallholder.
The value was 2s; now 20s.
Norman held it.

[In CORBY Hundred]

10 Norman holds 2 hides from Robert in BLATHERWYCKE. Land for 225 c
6 ploughs. Hugh and William hold from him. In lordship 2 ploughs.
12 villagers and 5 smallholders have 4 ploughs.
A mill at 30d; meadow, 6 acres; woodland 1 league long and 3 furlongs wide.
Value 18s.

In ROTHWELL Hundred

11 Hugh holds ½ hide in BRAYBROOKE from Robert. Land for 1 plough.
The value was and is 16d.
Norman held it.

12 Hugh also holds the third part of 1 hide from Robert in the same village. Land for ½ plough. 1 plough there, however, with
1 smallholder.
The value was 12d; now 3s.
Ulfketel held it.

13 William holds ½ hide from Robert in RUSHTON. Land for 1 plough.
1½ ploughs there, however, with
4 villagers and 2 smallholders.
½ mill at 12d; woodland, 6 acres.
Ulfketel held it.
The value was 12d; now 6s.
The jurisdiction is in Weldon.
In the same village he has ½ virgate of land, waste.

In SPELHOE Hundred

14 William also holds 2 hides and 1½ virgates of land from Robert in MOULTON. Land for 5 ploughs. In lordship 3 ploughs, with 1 slave.

7 VII . uilli 7 IIII . bord hnt . II . car . Ibi molin de . VIII . denar . Valuit . XX . solid . Modo . L . sol . Thori tenuit.

Robt ten de . Ro . III . v træ una bouata min in *BOCHETONE* . Tra . e . I . car 7 dim . Vna hnt ibi . IIII . bord cu . I . uillo . 7 I . seruo . 7 IIII . ac pti . Valuit . V . sol . m . X . sol.

Radulf ten de . Ro . una v tre 7 una bouata in *SPRETONE* . Tra . e dim car . Vna tam . e ibi cu . VI . bord . Valuit 7 ual . V . solid . Vlmar libe tenuit.

Wills ten de . Ro . I . hid 7 IIII . partes *IN FOXLEV HD.* dim hidæ in *BRADENE* . Tra . e . III . car 7 dimid. In dnio sunt . II . 7 IIII . uilli hnt . I . car . Ibi una ac pti. Valuit . LX . solid . Modo . XL . sol. *IN GISLEBVRG HD 7 DIM.*

Rotbt ten de Ro . una v træ in *CRETONE* . Tra . e . II . bou. Ibi . e un francig cu . II . bob . Valet . II . solid. Vlmar libe tenuit. / Bradene tenuit Chenric . de rege . E.

.XXX. TERRA RADVLFI PAGENEL.

RADVLFVS Pagenel ten de rege . II . hid *IN STOC HD.* 7 Roger de eo . Tra . e . IIII . car . In dnio . e una . 7 IIII . uilli 7 III . bord hnt . I . car 7 dimid . Ibi . II . serui . Valuit . V . sol. Modo . X . solid . Turchil libe tenuit.

.XXXI TERRA RADVLFI DE LIMESI. *IN WILEBROC HD.*

RADVLFVS De Limesi ten de rege . II . hid in *WESTONE*. 7 Herluin de eo . Tra . e . VI . car . In dnio sunt . II . 7 III . serui.

7 villagers and 4 smallholders have 2 ploughs.
A mill at 8d.
The value was 20s; now 50s.
Thori held it.

15 Robert holds 3 virgates of land, less 1 bovate, from Robert in BOUGHTON. Land for 1½ ploughs.
4 smallholders have 1 there, with 1 villager and 1 slave.
Meadow, 4 acres.
The value was 5s; now 10s.

16 Ralph holds 1 virgate of land and 1 bovate from Robert in SPRATTON. Land for ½ plough; 1 there, however, with 6 smallholders.
The value was and is 5s.
Wulfmer held it freely.

In FOXLEY Hundred

17 William holds 1 hide and 4 parts of ½ hide from Robert in BRADDEN. Land for 3½ ploughs. In lordship 2.
4 villagers have 1 plough.
Meadow, 1 acre.
The value was 60s; now 40s.

In GUILSBOROUGH Hundred and a half

18 Robert holds 1 virgate of land from Robert in CREATON. Land for 2 oxen.
1 Frenchman with 2 oxen.
Value 2s.
Wulfmer held it freely.

19 Kenric held BRADDEN from King Edward.

31] LAND OF RALPH PAGNELL

In STOKE Hundred

1 Ralph Pagnell holds 2 hides from the King, and Roger from him. Land for 4 ploughs. In lordship 1.
4 villagers and 3 smallholders have 1½ ploughs.
2 slaves.
The value was 5s; now 10s.
Thorkell held it freely.

32] LAND OF RALPH OF LIMESY

In WILLYBROOK Hundred

1 Ralph of Limesy holds 2 hides from the King in COLLYWESTON, and Herlwin from him. Land for 6 ploughs. In lordship 2; 3 slaves.

7 xvi . uitti 7 III . bord hnt . v . car . Ibi molin de . xx . sol.
7 XII . ac pti . Silua . III . qrent lg . 7 II . qz lat . Valuit . c.
solid . Modo . vi . lib . Morcar tenuit. (comes)

.XXXII. TERRA ROBERTI ALBI. *IN NEVESLVND HD.*

ROTBERTVS albz ten de rege . III . hid in *GRASTONE*.
7 Roger de eo . Tra . e . VIII . car . In dnio . e una . cu . I . seruo.
7 XII . uitti cu pbro 7 VI . bord hnt . v . car . Ibi . II . ac pti.
Silua . I . leuu lg . 7 IIII . qrent lat . Valuit 7 ual . XL . sol.
Achi libe tenuit . T.R.E.

.XXXIII. TERRA WILLI DE CAHAINGES.

WILLS de CAHAINGES . ten de rege . I . hid in *FLORA* . Tra . e . III . car.
In dnio . e . I . car . 7 II . serui . 7 IIII . uitti 7 III . bord hnt . I . car . Ibi molin
de . v . sol . 7 IIII . ac pti . Valet . xx . sol . Ernui libe tenuit T.R.E.

225 d

.XXX. TERRA WILLELMI PEVREL.

WILLELM PEVREL ten de rege *HECHAM* . Ibi sunt.
VI . hidæ . Tra . e . XII . car 7 dim . In dnio st . II . hidæ de hac tra.
7 ibi . IIII . car . 7 IIII . serui . 7 XVI . uitti 7 IX . bord cu pbro
hnt . VIII . car 7 dim . Ibi . e mercat redd . xx . sol p ann.
7 molin de . xx . sol . 7 x . ac pti . Silua . I . qz lg . 7 alia lat.
Ad hoc m ptin H MEBRA.
In *RISDENE* . VI . hidæ . Tra . e . XII . car . Has hnt ibi XIX.
sochi . 7 molin de . x . sol . 7 XXX . ac pti.
In Celuestone 7 Caldecote . I . hida 7 III . v træ Tra . e . III . car.
Has hnt ibi . VI . sochi . 7 III . ac pti.
In Cnutestone . I . hida 7 una v træ 7 dim . Tra . e . II . car.
Has hnt ibi . v . sochi . 7 molin de xx . sol . 7 VI . ac pti.

16 villagers and 3 smallholders have 5 ploughs.
A mill at 20s; meadow, 12 acres; woodland 3 furlongs long and 2 furlongs wide.
The value was 100s; now £6.
Earl Morcar held it.

[33] LAND OF ROBERT BLUNT

In NAVISLAND Hundred

1 Robert Blunt holds 3 hides from the King in GRAFTON (Underwood), and Roger from him. Land for 8 ploughs. In lordship 1, with 1 slave.
12 villagers with a priest and 6 smallholders have 5 ploughs.
Meadow, 2 acres; woodland 1 league long and 4 furlongs wide.
The value was and is 40s.
Aki held it freely before 1066.

[34] LAND OF WILLIAM OF KEYNES

[In NOBOTTLE Hundred]

1 William of Keynes holds 1 hide from the King in FLORE.
Land for 3 ploughs. In lordship 1 plough; 2 slaves.
4 villagers and 3 smallholders have 1 plough.
A mill at 5s; meadow, 4 acres.
Value 20s.
Ernwy held it freely before 1066.

[35] LAND OF WILLIAM PEVEREL 225 d

[In HIGHAM Hundred]

1a William Peverel holds HIGHAM (Ferrers) from the King. 6 hides.
Land for 12½ ploughs. In lordship 2 hides of this land; 4 ploughs there; 4 slaves.
16 villagers and 9 smallholders with a priest have 8½ ploughs.
A market which pays 20s a year; a mill at 20s; meadow, 10 acres; woodland 1 furlong long and another wide.

To this manor belong these members:-

b In RUSHDEN 6 hides. Land for 12 ploughs.
19 Freemen have them there.
A mill at 10s; meadow, 30 acres.

c In CHELVESTON and CALDECOTT 1 hide and 3 virgates of land.
Land for 3 ploughs.
6 Freemen have them there.
Meadow, 3 acres.

d In KNUSTON 1 hide and 1½ virgates of land. Land for 2 ploughs.
5 Freemen have them there.
A mill at 20s; meadow, 6 acres.

In Irencestre . I . hida 7 III . v træ de soca . Tra . e . II . car.
Has hnt ibi . III . sochi 7 X . acs pti . Ibi est un francig cu . I . car
7 molin ibi de . XVI . sol . caluniosu int rege 7 Willmu.
In Farnedis . III . v træ de soca . Tra . e . I . car . Hanc hnt ibi
In Potintone dim hida de soca . Ibi sunt ⁊ II . sochi.
IIII . uitti cu . I . car.
In Estone . una v træ 7 dimid . Vasta . e
In Rande . VII . hidæ 7 dim . 7 dim v træ de soca . cu append.
Tra . e . XIIII . car . Ibi sunt . XX . uitti cu . XV . car . 7 XX . ac pti.
Tot M cu append ualuit X . lib . qdo recep . Modo . XVIII . lib.
Gitda tenuit cu saca 7 soca.
Sochi de Risdene 7 Irencestre 7 Rande fuer hoes Burred
7 iccirco . G . eps clamat hominatione eoz.
Ide . W . ten . III . hid 7 dim . 7 qrta parte uni v In CLIPESTVNE de soca Na
uesberiæ . Tra . e . VII . car . Ibi un miles cu . I . car . 7 XIX . sochi
cu . VII . uittis 7 III . bord hnt . VI . car . Valuit . XL . sol . Modo . XX . sol.
Ide ten *NEVBOTE* . Ibi . I . hida . 7 dim v træ . Tra . e . III . car.
Has ht in dnio cu . I . seruo . 7 IIII . uitti 7 IIII . bord hnt . I . car.
Ibi molin de . VII . sol . 7 VI . ac siluæ.
In *OLLETORP* ht ide W . tcia parte . I . hidæ 7 d virgat . Soca
ptin ad Neubote . Tra . e . I . car . Hanc hnt ibi . III . sochi.
In *BRININTONE* ht id . W . una hid 7 dim . Tra . e . II . car.
Has hnt ibi . VI . sochi cu pbro . q ten dim hid ejd træ.
In *HEROLVESTONE* . e una hida 7 dim . Tra . e . III . car . Has
hnt ibi . III . sochi cu pbro. ⁊ un sochs.
In *CLACHESTORP* . e dim hida . Tra . e . I . car . Hanc ht ibi

e In IRCHESTER 1 hide and 3 virgates of land of the jurisdiction.
Land for 2 ploughs.
3 Freemen have them there, and
meadow, 10 acres
A Frenchman with 1 plough.
A mill at 16s; it is in dispute between the King and William.

f In FARNDISH 3 virgates of land of the jurisdiction.
Land for 1 plough;
2 Freemen have it there.

g In PODINGTON ½ hide of the jurisdiction.
4 villagers with 1 plough.

h In EASTON (Maudit) 1½ virgates of land. Waste.

i In RAUNDS 7½ hides and ½ virgate of land of the jurisdiction
with dependencies. Land for 14 ploughs.
20 villagers with 15 ploughs.
Meadow, 20 acres.

j Value of the whole manor with dependencies, £10 when
acquired; now £18.
Gytha held it, with full jurisdiction.
The Freemen of Rushden, Irchester and Raunds were Burgred's
men; for this reason Bishop Geoffrey claims their homage.

[In STOTFOLD Hundred]

2 William also holds 3½ hides and the fourth part of 1 virgate in
CLIPSTON of the jurisdiction of Naseby. Land for 7 ploughs.
1 man-at-arms with 1 plough; 19 Freemen with 7 villagers
and 3 smallholders have 6 ploughs.
The value was 40s; now 20s.

[In NOBOTTLE Hundred]

3 a He also holds NOBOTTLE. 1 hide and ½ virgate of land.
Land for 3 ploughs. He has them, in lordship, with 1 slave.
4 villagers and 4 smallholders have 1 plough.
A mill at 7s; woodland, 6 acres.
[To this manor belong these members:-]

b In ALTHORP William also has the third part of 1 hide and ½ virgate.
The jurisdiction belongs to Nobottle. Land for 1 plough.
3 Freemen have it there.

c In BRINGTON William also has 1½ hides. Land for 2 ploughs.
6 Freemen have them there, with a priest who holds ½
hide of this land.

d In HARLESTONE 1½ hides. Land for 3 ploughs.
3 Freemen with a priest have them there.

e In GLASSTHORPE(HILL) ½ hide. Land for 1 plough.
1 Freeman has it there.

In *FLORE* . ē dimid hida. Tra. ē. I. car. Hanc hnt ibi. III. sochi.
Quando Wills has tras recep: ualb. IIII. lib. Modo. VII. lib.
Idem. W. ten. IIII. hid in *DVSTONE*. 7 Gitda libe tenuit.
Tra. ē. VIII. car. In dnio st. II. 7 II. serui. 7 XIII. uitti 7 III. bord
cu. III. sochis hnt. VI. car. Ibi molin de. XX. sot. 7 XXX. ac
pti. 7 XI. ac siluæ. Valuit. XL. sot. Modo. C. solid.
Idem. W. ten. VII. hid in *NAVESBERIE*. Tra. ē. XIIII. car.
In dnio sunt. II. 7 VIII. uitti cu pbro 7 II. sochis 7 XI. bord
hnt. III. car. Ibi. VIII. ac pti. Valuit. XX. sot. Modo. LX. sot.
Idē. W. ten. III. hid 7 dim in *CORTENHALE*. *IN COLESTREV HD.*
De hac tra st. II. hidæ in dnio una v min. Tra. ē. IX. car.
In dnio sunt. II. car cu. I. seruo. 7 XII. uitti cu. I. bord 7 pbro
hnt. VII. car. Ibi molin de. XII. den. 7 IIII. ac pti. Silua. II.
qrent lg. 7 II. qz lat. Valuit. IIII. lib. Modo. V. lib.
Idem. W. ten. III. hid 7 dim in *BLIDESWORDE*. Tra. ē. IX. car.
De hac tra st in dnio. II. hidæ una v min. 7 ibi st. II. car. 7 XII.
uitti. 7 VI. bord hnt. VII. car. Ibi molin de. II. sot. 7 IIII. ac pti.
Silua. XII. qrent lg. 7 VIII. qz lat. Valuit. III. lib. M. IIII. lib.
Oms has tras tenuit Gitda T.R.E. cu saca 7 soca.

226 a

Pagen ten de. W. II. hid in *BERCHEBI*. *IN ALWARDESLEA HD.*
Tra. ē. V. car. In dnio sunt. II. cu. I. seruo. 7 X. uitti 7 VIII.
bord cu. III. car. Ibi. VI. ac pti. Silua. VI. pticas lg. 7 IIII.
Wap lat. Valuit. XXX. solid. Modo. LX. solid. *IN WICESLEA HD.*
Sasfrid ten de. W. II. hid 7 dimid in *EPINGEHA*.
Tra. ē. IIII. car. In dnio. ē una. cu. I. seruo. 7 VIII. uitti
7 IIII. bord cu. II. car. Ibi molin 7 dim de. XII. solid.

f In FLORE ½ hide. Land for 1 plough.
3 Freemen have it there.

g When William acquired these lands the value was £4; now £7.
Gytha held them freely.

4 William also holds 4 hides in DUSTON. Land for 8 ploughs.
In lordship 2; 2 slaves.
13 villagers and 3 smallholders with 3 Freemen have 6 ploughs.
A mill at 20s; meadow, 30 acres; woodland, 11 acres.
The value was 40s; now 100s.

[? In GUILSBOROUGH Hundred and a half]

5 William also holds 7 hides in NASEBY. Land for 14 ploughs.
In lordship 2.
8 villagers with a priest, 2 Freemen and 11 smallholders have 3 ploughs.
Meadow, 8 acres.
The value was 20s; now 60s.

In COLLINGTREE Hundred

William also holds 3½ hides in COURTEENHALL. In lordship 2 hides of this land, less 1 virgate. Land for 9 ploughs.
In lordship 2 ploughs, with 1 slave.
12 villagers with 1 smallholder and a priest have 7 ploughs.
A mill at 12d; meadow, 4 acres; woodland 2 furlongs long and 2 furlongs wide.
The value was £4; now £5.

William also holds 3½ hides in BLISWORTH. Land for 9 ploughs.
In lordship 2 hides of this land, less 1 virgate. 2 ploughs there.
12 villagers and 6 smallholders have 7 ploughs.
A mill at 2s; meadow, 4 acres; woodland 12 furlongs long and 8 furlongs wide.
The value was £3; now £4.

Gytha held all these lands before 1066, with full jurisdiction.

In ALWARDSLEY Hundred 226 a

Payne holds 2 hides from William in BARBY. Land for 5 ploughs.
In lordship 2, with 1 slave;
10 villagers and 8 smallholders with 3 ploughs.
Meadow, 6 acres; woodland 6 perches long and 4 wide.
The value was 30s; now 60s.

In WITCHLEY Hundred

Sasfrid holds 2½ hides from William in EMPINGHAM. Land for 4 ploughs. In lordship 1, with 1 slave;
8 villagers and 4 smallholders with 2 ploughs.
1½ mills at 12s; meadow, 4 acres; woodland, 6 acres.

7 IIII. ac̄ p̄ti. 7 VI. ac̄ siluæ. Valuit 7 uał. XX. solid. / HD.
Eduuard 7 Fredgis tenuer̄ cū saca 7 soca. *IN GRAVESEND*
Idē ten̄. IIII. hid in *CATESBI*. Tra. ē. VIII. car. In dn̄io
sunt. II. 7 II. serui 7 una ancilla. 7 XVII. uilli cū pbro
7 IIII. bord hn̄t. VI. car. Ibi. II. molini de. XVI. denar.
7 IIII. ac̄ p̄ti. De hac tra ten̄ un miles. I. hid. 7 ht̄. II. car.
Tot̄ ualuit. XL. solid. Modo. IIII. lib. Gitda libe tenuit.
Idē ten̄ dim hid qnta parte min *IN CLAISLEA HD.*
in *ACESHILLE*. Vasta. ē. *IN RODEWELLE HVND.*
Ambrosius ten̄ de. W. unā hid 7 unā v̄ træ in *DEISBVRG*.
Tra. ē. III. car. In dn̄io sunt. II. 7 III. serui. 7 una ancilla.
7 XI. uilli 7 VIII. bord cū. I. car 7 dim. Ibi molin̄ de. II. soł.
Silua. II. qrent lḡ. 7 II. q̄z lat̄. Valuit 7 uał. XL. solid.
Idē ten̄. I. hid 7 dimid 7 tciā partē uni v̄ in *CAILMARC*.
Tra. ē. IIII. car. In dn̄io sunt. II. 7 VII. uilli 7 II. bord hn̄t
II. car. In ead uilla ten̄ unā v̄ træ quæ Vasta. ē. H̄ reddit
geld in *NARNINWORDE*. Valuit. V. soł. Modo. XL. solid.
Osmund libe tenuit.
Turstin ten̄ de. W. unā v̄ træ 7 dim in *BOSIETE*. Soca ptin
ad *HECHA*. Tra. ē dim car̄. 7 tant ibi. ē. Valet. V. solid.
Eustachi ten̄ de. W. dimid hid in *HAREGRAVE*. Soca
ptin ad *HECHĀ*. Tra. ē. I. car̄. Hæc ibi. ē cū. II. bord.
Valet. LXVIII. denar. Ailric libe tenuit
Biscop ten̄ de. W. in *HORPOL*. II. hid 7 dim. Tra. ē. VI. car.
In dn̄io sunt. II. 7 VII. serui. 7 XIIII. uilli cū pbro 7 V. bord hn̄t
IIII. car 7 dimid. Ibi. X. ac̄ p̄ti. 7 X. ac̄ siluæ. Valuit. XXX. soł.
Modo. XL. solid. Idem tenuit libe T.R.E.

The value was and is 20s.
Edward and Fredegis held it with full jurisdiction.

In GRAVESEND Hundred

0 He also holds 4 hides in CATESBY. Land for 8 ploughs.
In lordship 2; 2 male slaves, 1 female.
17 villagers with a priest and 4 smallholders have 6 ploughs.
2 mills at 16d; meadow, 4 acres.
1 man-at-arms holds 1 hide of this land. He has 2 ploughs.
The value of the whole was 40s; now £4.
Gytha held it freely.

In CLEYLEY Hundred

1 He also holds ½ hide, less a fifth part, in *ACESHILLE*. Waste.

In ROTHWELL Hundred

2 Ambrose holds 1 hide and 1 virgate of land from William in DESBOROUGH. Land for 3 ploughs. In lordship 2; 3 male slaves, 1 female;
11 villagers and 8 smallholders with 1½ ploughs.
A mill at 2s; woodland 2 furlongs long and 2 furlongs wide.
The value was and is 40s.

3 He also holds 1½ hides and the third part of 1 virgate in KELMARSH. Land for 4 ploughs. In lordship 2.
7 villagers and 2 smallholders have 2 ploughs.
In the same village he holds 1 virgate of land which is waste.
It pays tax in Arthingworth.
The value was 5s; now 40s.
Osmund held it freely.

[In HIGHAM Hundred]

4 Thurstan holds 1½ virgates of land from William in BOZEAT. The jurisdiction belongs to Higham (Ferrers). Land for ½ plough.
As much there.
Value 5s.

5 Eustace holds ½ hide from William in HARGRAVE. The jurisdiction belongs to Higham (Ferrers). Land for 1 plough; it is there, with
2 smallholders.
Value 68d.
Alric held it freely.

[In NOBOTTLE Hundred]

6 Bishop holds 2½ hides from William in HARPOLE. Land for 6 ploughs.
In lordship 2; 7 slaves.
14 villagers with a priest and 5 smallholders have 4½ ploughs.
Meadow, 10 acres; woodland, 10 acres.
The value was 30s; now 40s.
He also held it freely before 1066.

226 a

Drogo ten unā hid 7 unā v træ in *RAVENESTORP*. Tra. ē
III. car. Has hnt ibi. III. sochi 7 III. uilli 7 v. bord. Ibi. III. ac
pti. Valuit. x. sol. Modo. xx. solid.

Idē ten. II. hid in *TECHE*. Tra. ē. IIII. car. Has hnt ibi. IIII.
sochi 7 II. uilli 7 IIII. bord. Ibi. I. ac pti. Valuit. x. sol. M. xx. sol.

Idē ten. III. v træ 7 dim in *COTA*. Tra. ē. III. car. In dnio
sunt. II. 7 III. seru 7 I. ancill. 7 un uills 7 IIII. bord hnt
dimid car. Ibi molin de. IIII. sol. 7 IIII. ac pti.

Huic ... ptin in *TORNEBERIE*. I. hida de soca. Tra. ē. II.
car. Ibi. ē una car. 7 IIII. ac pti. In *WINEWIC*. st. III.
virg tre. Tra. ē. I. car. Hanc ht ibi. I. sochs.

In *ECDONE*. ē una v træ 7 dim. Tra. ē. I. car. Ibi. ē un
sochs hns dim car. In *ESSEBI*. ē una v træ 7 dim.
Tra. ē. I. car. Ibi. ē. I. sochs cū dim car. In *NORTOT*
ē dimid hida. Tra. ē. I. car. Hanc ht ibi. I. sochs. 7 II. acs
pti. In *HOLEWELLE*. ē una v træ. Tra. ē dim car.
Hanc ht ibi. I. sochs. xxx. solid.

Tot ... *COTE* cū append ualb qdo recep. xv. sol. Modo

Rotbt ten de. W. dim hid in *TORNEBERIE*. Soca
ptin ad Nauesberie. Tra. ē dimid car. Vasta. ē.

Rotbt ten de. W. in *HOHTONE*. *IN WIMERESLEA HD*.
unā hid 7 dim virg 7 II. caruc tre. Tra. ē. IIII. car.
In dnio sunt. II. 7 IIII. serui. 7 xv. uilli 7 VI. bord hnt
. II. car. Ibi. x. ac pti. Silua. III. qz lg. 7 II. qz lat.
Valuit 7 ual. XL. sol. Osmund libe tenuit.

17 Drogo holds 1 hide and 1 virgate of land in RAVENSTHORPE.
Land for 3 ploughs.
3 Freemen, 3 villagers and 5 smallholders have them there.
Meadow, 3 acres.
The value was 10s; now 20s.

18 He also holds 2 hides in TEETON. Land for 4 ploughs.
4 Freemen, 2 villagers and 4 smallholders have them there.
Meadow, 1 acre.
The value was 10s; now 20s.

[In GUILSBOROUGH Hundred and a half]

19 a He also holds 3½ virgates of land in COTON. Land for 3 ploughs.
In lordship 2; 3 male slaves, 1 female.
1 villager and 4 smallholders have ½ plough.
A mill at 4s; meadow, 4 acres.

To this manor belong:-

b In THORNBY 1 hide of the jurisdiction. Land for 2 ploughs;
1 plough there.
Meadow, 4 acres.

c In WINWICK 3 virgates of land. Land for 1 plough.
1 Freeman has it there.

d In (West) HADDON 1½ virgates of land. Land for 1 plough.
1 Freeman who has ½ plough.

e In (Cold) ASHBY 1½ virgates of land. Land for 1 plough.
1 Freeman with ½ plough.

f In NORTOFT ½ hide. Land for 1 plough.
1 Freeman has it there and
meadow, 2 acres.

g In HOLLOWELL 1 virgate of land. Land for ½ plough.
1 Freeman has it there.

h Value of the whole manor of COTON with its dependencies,
when acquired 15s; now 30s.

20 Robert holds ½ hide from William in THORNBY. The jurisdiction
belongs to Naseby. Land for ½ plough. Waste.

In WYMERSLEY Hundred

21 Robert holds 1 hide, ½ virgate and 2 carucates of land from
William in HOUGHTON. Land for 4 ploughs.
In lordship 2; 4 slaves.
15 villagers and 6 smallholders have 2 ploughs.
Meadow, 10 acres; woodland 3 furlong long and 2 furlongs wide.
The value was and is 40s.
Osmund held it freely.

Rotbt ten de.W.III.hid 7 dim hid *IN CLAIESLEA HD.*
7 qnta parte dim hidæ in *PIRIE*.Tra.e.IX.car.In dnio
sunt.II.7 VII.serui.7 XVIII.uitti 7 VII.bord cu pbro
hnt.VII.car.Ibi molin de.XXVI.solid 7 VIII.denar.
7 X.ac pti.Silua.VI.qz lg.7 IIII.qz 7 II.pticas lat.
Valuit 7 ual.IIII.lib.Gitda libe tenuit.
Alured ten.III.v træ 7 dim in *GISLEBVRG* de.W.
Tra.e.I.car 7 dim.Ibi.e ipsa in dnio.7 II.serui.7 II.uitti
7 III.bord cu dim car.Ibi.IIII.ac pti.Valuit.VI.sol.
Modo.XXX.solid.Gitda libe tenuit. *IN FOXLEA HD.*
Walter ten de.W.II.hid in *BACVLVESLEA*.Tra.e
.V.car.In dnio sunt.II.7 II.serui.7 V.uitti cu.II.car.
Ibi molin de.V.sol.7 una ac pti.Silua.III.qz lg.
7 una qz lat.Valuit.X.sol.Modo.XL.solid.
Turstin ten de.W.dim hid 7 dim v træ in *CORTENHALO*.
7 e Soca de alio Cortenhalo com Witti.Tra.e.I.car.
Dimid car ibi.e.7 ualet.VI.sol.
Ambrosius ten de.W.IIII.hid.in *MOLITONE*.Tra.e.IIII.
car.In dnio sunt.II.7 III.serui.7 IIII.uitti 7 V.bord
cu.II.car.Ibi.XVI.ac pti.Valuit 7 ual.IIII.lib.
Has tras libe tenuit Gitda.T.R.E.

.XXXV. TERRA WILLI FILIJ ANSCVLF *IN WICESLEA WAP.*

Wills fili Ansculfi 7 Robt de eo ten dim hid
in *TOLTORP*.Tra.e.IIII.car.Rex inde ht soca.
In dnio.e una.7 XII.uitti 7 XV.bord hnt.III.car.
Ibi.IIII.molini de.XL.solid.7 XX.ac pti.VIII.sochi tenuer.
Valuit.XL.sol.Modo.C.solid.

In CLEYLEY Hundred 226 b

22 Robert holds 3½ hides and the fifth part of ½ hide from William in PAULERSPURY. Land for 9 ploughs. In lordship 2; 7 slaves.
18 villagers and 7 smallholders with a priest have 7 ploughs.
A mill at 26s 8d; meadow, 10 acres; woodland 6 furlongs long and 4 furlongs and 2 perches wide.
The value was and is £4.
Gytha held it freely.

[In GUILSBOROUGH Hundred and a half]

23 Alfred holds 3½ virgates of land in GUILSBOROUGH from William. Land for 1½ ploughs; they are there, in lordship; 2 slaves;
2 villagers and 3 smallholders with ½ plough.
Meadow, 4 acres.
The value was 6s; now 30s.
Gytha held it freely.

In FOXLEY Hundred

24 Walter holds 2 hides from William in BLAKESLEY. Land for 5 ploughs. In lordship 2; 2 slaves;
5 villagers with 2 ploughs.
A mill at 5s; meadow, 1 acre; woodland 3 furlongs long and 1 furlong wide.
The value was 10s; now 40s.

[In COLLINGTREE Hundred]

25 Thurstan holds ½ hide and ½ virgate of land from William in COURTEENHALL. It is a jurisdiction of another Courteenhall, William's manor. Land for 1 plough. ½ plough there.
Value 6s.

[? In WARDEN Hundred]

26 Ambrose holds 4 hides from William in MOLLINGTON. Land for 4 ploughs. In lordship 2; 3 slaves;
4 villagers and 5 smallholders with 2 ploughs.
Meadow, 16 acres.
The value was and is £4.

Gytha held these lands freely before 1066.

[36] LAND OF WILLIAM SON OF ANSCULF

In WITCHLEY Wapentake

1 William son of Ansculf holds ½ hide in TOLETHORPE, and Robert from him. Land for 4 ploughs. The King has the jurisdiction from it. In lordship 1 [plough].
12 villagers and 15 smallholders have 3 ploughs.
4 mills at 40s; meadow, 20 acres.
8 Freemen held it.
The value was 40s; now 100s.

Otbert ten de. W.III.hid in *Bernac*. Tra. ē. v. car.
In dnio.ē una.7 II.serui.7 xv.uitti 7 II.bord cū.I.socho
hnt.IIII.car.Ibi.XII.ac pti.Silua.II.qz lg.7 una lat.
Valuit.xx.sol.Modo.IIII.lib.Bundi libe tenuit.

Radulf ten de.W.III.hid in *Bromwic*. Tra.ē.III.
car.In dnio.ē una.7 x.uitti 7 III.bord hnt.III.car.
Silua ibi.I.leu lg.7 dim leu lat.Valuit 7 ual.XL.sol.

Witts.F.malger ten de.W.I.hid.in *Wavre*. tenuit Brictuin.
Tra.ē.II.car.In dnio.ē una.cū.I.uitto.Ibi.IIII.ac
pti.Silua.I.qz lg.7 dim qz lat.Valuit 7 ual.x.sol.
Vluuin libe tenuit.T.R.E.sic 7 alii.

.XXXVI. Terra Willi Lovet. *In Stotfald Hund.*

Witts Luueth ten de rege tciā partē uni virgate træ
Vasta fuit 7 est.

XXXVII. Terra Walterij De Ainc. *In Grvesend hd.*

Walterivs De Aincurt ten de rege.III.hid 7 dim
in *Brandestone*. Tra.ē.IX.car.In dnio st.III.car.
7 XIII.uitti 7 IIII.bord hnt.IIII.car.Ibi molin de.II.
solid.7 VIII.ac pti.7 una ac silue.Valuit xx.solid.
Modo.IIII.lib 7 x.solid.Tori libe tenuit.

226 c

.XXXIX. Terra Walterij Flandrens. *In Rodewelle hd.*

Walterivs Flandrensis ten de rege dim hid in *Pipe
welle*. Tra.ē.I.car.Dodin ten de Waltio.Ibi.ē una car
cū.II.bord.7 v.ac siluæ.Valuit 7 ual.IIII.sol.Leuenot tenuit.

In UPTON Wapentake

2 Odbert holds 3 hides from William in BARNACK. Land for 5 ploughs. In lordship 1; 2 slaves.
15 villagers and 2 smallholders with 1 Freeman have 4 ploughs.
Meadow, 12 acres; woodland 2 furlongs long and 1 wide.
The value was 20s; now £4.
Bondi held it freely.

(In STAFFORDSHIRE)

3 Ralph holds 3 hides from William in (West) BROMWICH.
Land for 3 ploughs. In lordship 1.
10 villagers and 3 smallholders have 3 ploughs.
Woodland 1 league long and ½ league wide.
The value was and is 40s.
Brictwin held it.

(In WARWICKSHIRE)

4 William son of Mauger holds 1 hide from William in OVER.
Land for 2 ploughs. In lordship 1, with
1 villager.
Meadow, 4 acres; woodland 1 furlong long and ½ furlong wide.
The value was and is 10s.
Wulfwin held it freely before 1066, as did others.

37] LAND OF WILLIAM LOVETT

In STOTFOLD Hundred

1 William Lovett holds the third part of 1 virgate of land from the King.
It was and is waste.

38] LAND OF WALTER OF AINCOURT

In GRAVESEND Hundred

1 Walter of Aincourt holds 3½ hides from the King in BRAUNSTON.
Land for 9 ploughs. In lordship 3 ploughs.
13 villagers and 4 smallholders have 4 ploughs.
A mill at 2s; meadow, 8 acres; woodland, 1 acre.
The value was 20s; now £4 10s.
Thori held it freely.

39 LAND OF WALTER THE FLEMING 226 c

In ROTHWELL Hundred

1 Walter the Fleming holds ½ hide from the King in PIPEWELL.
Land for 1 plough. Dodin holds from Walter. 1 plough there, with
2 smallholders.
Woodland, 5 acres.
The value was and is 4s.
Leofnoth held it.

Idē ten̄ de.W.unā hid̄ 7 unā v̄ træ in *Cotesbroc*. *In Gislebvrg Hd̄*.
Tra.ē.ii.car̄ 7 dim̄.In dn̄io.ē una 7 iiii.serui.7 i.ancilla.
7 pbr 7 x.uilli 7 v.bord̄ cū.i.car̄ 7 dim̄.Ibi molin̄ de.xii.den̄.
Valuit.x.sol.Modo.xxx.solid̄. / iiii.sol.
Idē ten̄ de.W.ii.v̄ træ 7 unā bouatā træ in *Hohtone*.Val
Fulcher ten̄ de.W.iiii.hid̄ 7 unā v̄ træ in *Langeport*.
Tra.ē.ii.car̄.Has hn̄t ibi xii.uilli 7 vii.bord̄.Ibi.iiii.ac̄
pti 7 fraxinetū.i.q̄z lḡ.7 i.q̄z lat̄.Valet.iiii.lib̄.
Idem ten̄ de.W.ii.hid̄ 7 dim̄ in *Widmale*.Tra.ē.ii.car̄.
Has hr̄ ibi.7 x.uilli 7 v.bord̄ cū pbro hn̄t.iii.car̄.Ibi.i.seru̇
7 una ancilla.7 vi.ac̄ pti.Silua.ii.q̄z lḡ.7 una 7 dim̄ lat̄.
Valuit 7 ual.xl.solid̄. *In Spelehot Hd̄*.
Idē ten̄ de.W.iii.hid̄ 7 una v̄ træ in *Pitesford*.Tra.ē
vii.car̄.In dn̄io.ē una.7 ii.serui.7 xvi.uilli 7 ix.bord̄ hn̄t
vi.car̄.Ibi molin̄ de.xii.den̄.Valuit 7 ual.lxx.solid̄.
Otbtus ten̄ de.W.ii.hid̄ in *Hortone*.Tra.ē.iiii.car
In dn̄io sunt.ii.7 vi.uilli 7 iiii.bord̄ hn̄t.ii.car̄.Ibi.ii.serui.
7 molin̄ de.xii.den̄.7 xii.ac̄ pti.Silua.iii.q̄z lḡ.7 ii.q̄z lat
Valuit.x.sol.Modo.xxx.solid̄. *In Tovecestre Hd̄*.
Idē ten̄ de.W.iiii.hid̄ in *Evelai*.Tra.ē.x.car̄.In dn̄io
sunt.iiii.cū.i.seruo.7 xi.uilli 7 v.bord̄ hn̄t.iiii.car̄.Ibi
ii.molini de.xx.solid̄.7 v.ac̄ pti.Valuit.xl.sol.m̊.iiii.lib̄.

In GUILSBOROUGH Hundred

2 He also holds 1 hide and 1 virgate of land from Walter in COTTESBROOKE. Land for 2½ ploughs. In lordship 1; 4 male slaves, 1 female.

A priest, 10 villagers and 5 smallholders with 1½ ploughs.

A mill at 12d.

The value was 10s; now 30s.

[In MAWSLEY Hundred]

3 He also holds 2 virgates of land and 1 bovate of land from Walter in (Hanging) HOUGHTON.

Value 4s.

4 Fulchere holds 4 hides and 1 virgate of land from Walter in LAMPORT. Land for 2 ploughs.

12 villagers and 7 smallholders have them there.

Meadow, 4 acres; an ash-wood 1 furlong long and 1 furlong wide.

Value £4.

[In ORLINGBURY Hundred]

5 He also holds 2½ hides from Walter in WYTHEMAIL. Land for 2 ploughs. He has them there.

10 villagers and 5 smallholders with a priest have 3 ploughs.

1 male and 1 female slave.

Meadow, 6 acres; woodland 2 furlongs long and 1½ wide.

The value was and is 40s.

In SPELHOE Hundred

6 He also holds 3 hides and 1 virgate of land from Walter in PITSFORD. Land for 7 ploughs. In lordship 1; 2 slaves.

16 villagers and 9 smallholders have 6 ploughs.

A mill at 12d.

The value was and is 70s.

[In WYMERSLEY Hundred]

7 Odbert holds 2 hides from Walter in HORTON. Land for 4 ploughs. In lordship 2.

6 villagers and 4 smallholders have 2 ploughs. 2 slaves.

A mill at 12d; meadow, 12 acres; woodland 3 furlongs long and 2 furlongs wide.

The value was 10s; now 30s.

In TOWCESTER Hundred

8 He also holds 4 hides from Walter in EVENLEY. Land for 10 ploughs. In lordship 4, with 1 slave.

11 villagers and 5 smallholders have 4 ploughs.

2 mills at 20s; meadow, 5 acres.

The value was 40s; now £4.

HVGO teñ de . W . II . hid 7 dim in *ASCEBI* . Tra . ē . VI . car.
In dñio . ē una car . 7 IIII . serui . 7 IX . uitti 7 III . bord hñt
III . car . 7 XII . ac pti . Valuit . XL . sol . Modo . IIII . lib.
Otbtus teñ de . W . II . hid in *EVELAI*. *IN OTBOLDESTOV HD.*
Tra . ē . V . car . Ibi st . IIII . car cū . X . uittis 7 V . bord.
Valuit . XXX . sol . Modo . XL . solid. *IN SVTONE HVND*
Idē teñ . I . hid 7 dim . 7 qntā partē dim hidæ de . W.
Tra . ē . IIII . car . In dñio . ē una 7 dim . cū . I . seruo . 7 V . uitti 7 III .
bord hñtes . I . car 7 dim . Ibi molin de . II . sol.
Valuit . XX . sol . Modo . XL . sol . H tra ptin ad *EVELAI*. *T HD.*
Goduin teñ de . W . II . hid ad æcctam de Pascelle. *IN TOVECESTRE*
in *HECHA* . Tra . ē . V . car . In dñio . ē una car . 7 IX . uitti cū pbro
7 III . bord hñt . II . car . Valuit . XL . sol . Modo . XX . solid
IN PLVNTVNE
Leuenot teñ de . W . unā hid Tra . ē . IIII . car . In dñio
ē una . 7 II . serui . 7 VI . uitti cū . III . car . Ibi . IIII . ac pti.
Valuit 7 uat . XL . solid. *IN GRAVESEND HVND.*
Hugo teñ de . W . unā hid 7 dim . 7 qntā partē dim hidæ
Tra . ē . IIII . car . In dñio sunt . II . car 7 II . serui . 7 VIII . uitti
7 III . bord hñt . II . car . Ibi . II . ac spineti . Valuit 7 uat . XL . sol.
Gildre teñ de . W . II . hid in *AVIESCOTE* . De dim hida ht
ipse sacā 7 socā . 7 rex de . I . hida 7 dim . Tra . ē . V . car . In dñio
sunt . II . car . 7 VIII . uitti cū . I . bord hñt . II . car.
Valuit XV . sol . Modo . XXX . solid. *IN WIMERESLEA HVND.*
Winemar teñ de . W . II . hid 7 dim in *WITONE* . Tra . ē . VII .

[In FOXLEY Hundred]

9 Hugh holds 2½ hides from Walter in (Canons) ASHBY.
Land for 6 ploughs. In lordship 1 plough; 4 slaves.
9 villagers and 3 smallholders have 3 ploughs.
Meadow, 12 acres.
The value was 40s; now £4.

In ALBOLDSTOW Hundred

0 Odbert holds 2 hides from Walter in EVENLEY.
Land for 5 ploughs. 4 ploughs there, with
10 villagers and 5 smallholders.
The value was 30s; now 40s.

In SUTTON Hundred

1 He also holds 1½ hides and the fifth part of ½ hide from Walter.
Land for 4 ploughs. In lordship 1½, with 1 slave;
5 villagers and 3 smallholders who have 1½ ploughs.
A mill at 2s.
The value was 20s; now 40s.
This land belongs to Evenley.

In TOWCESTER Hundred

2 Godwin holds from Walter 2 hides of (the lands of) Pattishall
Church in (Cold) HIGHAM. Land for 5 ploughs. In lordship 1 plough.
9 villagers with a priest and 3 smallholders have 2 ploughs.
The value was 40s; now 20s.

[In FOXLEY Hundred]

3 Leofnoth holds 1 hide from Walter in PLUMPTON.
Land for 4 ploughs. In lordship 1; 2 slaves;
6 villagers with 3 ploughs.
Meadow, 4 acres.
The value was and is 40s.

In GRAVESEND Hundred

4 Hugh holds 1½ hides and the fifth part of ½ hide from Walter.
Land for 4 ploughs. In lordship 2 ploughs; 2 slaves.
8 villagers and 3 smallholders have 2 ploughs.
Spinney, 2 acres.
The value was and is 40s.

[In TOWCESTER Hundred]

5 Gelder holds 2 hides from Walter in ASTCOTE. He has full
jurisdiction of ½ hide and the King of 1½ hides.
Land for 5 ploughs. In lordship 2 ploughs.
8 villagers with 1 smallholder have 2 ploughs.
The value was 15s; now 30s.

In WYMERSLEY Hundred

6 Winemar holds 2½ hides from Walter in WOOTTON. Land for 7 ploughs.

226 c

car̄. In dn̄io sunt. iiæ. 7 ii. serui. 7 xv. uitti 7 vii. borđ cū. v. car̄.
Ibi. iiii. ac̄ p̄ti. Valuit 7 ual. iiii. lib̄. *In Claile hvnd*.
Hugo ten̄ de. W. iii. hiđ 7 q̄ntā partē uni⁹ hidæ. Tra. ē. viii.
car̄. In dn̄io sunt. iiæ. cū. i. seruo 7 ancilla. 7 xvii. uitti 7 v. borđ
hn̄t. vi. car̄. Ibi. xxxvi. ac̄ p̄ti. Silua. iii. q̄z lḡ. 7 iii. q̄z 7 dim̄
7 x. p̄ticas lat̄. Valuit xl. sol̄. Modo. lx. sol̄.
Has t̄ras om̄s tenuit lib̄e Leuenot. T.R.E. 7 poterat ire q̄ uoleb̄.

226 d

Idē Walteri⁹ ten̄ de rege. viii. hiđ in *Pascelle*. De his ht̄
in dn̄io. ii. hiđ. Tra. ē. xx. car̄. In dn̄io s̄t. iie. 7 iio. serui 7 ancilla.
7 xxii. uitti 7 vi. borđ hn̄t xii. car̄. Ibi. iio. molini de. xxxii.
denar̄. Valuit. x. lib̄ q̄do recep̄. Modo. c. sol̄. Leueno tenuit.

.XL. Terra Winemari.

Winemarvs ten̄ de rege dimiđ hiđ 7 q̄ntā partē
uni⁹ v̄ t̄ræ in *Covesgrave*. Tra. ē. i. car̄ 7 dimiđ
In dn̄io. ē una. cū. iii. borđ. Ibi molin̄ de xiii. soliđ.
7 v. ac̄ p̄ti. Silua. iii. q̄z lḡ. 7 ii. q̄z lat̄. Valuit. x. sol̄.
Modo. xx. sol̄. Alden lib̄e tenuit. *In Hechā hđ*
Idem ten̄. ii. hiđ 7 iii. v̄ t̄ræ. Tra. ē. v. car̄. In dn̄io
sunt. iii. car̄. 7 iiii. serui. 7 x. uitti cū p̄b̄ro 7 i. borđ 7 uno
franciḡ hn̄t. ii. car̄. Ibi molin̄ de. viii. den̄. 7 xx. ac̄
p̄ti. Silua. iiii. q̄z lḡ. 7 ii. q̄z lat̄. Valuit. xxx. sol̄. Modo
lx. soliđ. Sex lib̄i hoēs tenuer̄ T.R.E. Vn⁹ eoz Osgot
uocabat̄. cuj⁹ partē t̄ræ calūniat̄ Judita comitissa.
Idē. W. ten̄. iii. v̄ t̄ræ in *Hantone*. Tra. ē. i. car̄ 7 dim̄.
In dn̄io. ē dim̄ car̄. 7 iiii. uitti cū. v. borđ hn̄t. i. car̄.

In lordship 2; 2 slaves;
15 villagers and 7 smallholders with 5 ploughs.
Meadow, 4 acres.
The value was and is £4.

In CLEYLEY Hundred

.7 Hugh holds 3 hides and the fifth part of 1 hide from Walter.
Land for 8 ploughs. In lordship 2, with 1 male and 1 female slave.
17 villagers and 5 smallholders have 6 ploughs.
Meadow, 36 acres; woodland 3 furlongs long and 3½ furlongs and 10 perches wide.
The value was 40s; now 60s.

Leofnoth held all these lands freely before 1066; he could go where he would.

[? In TOWCESTER Hundred]

18 Walter also holds 8 hides from the King in PATTISHALL 226 d
of which he has 2 hides in lordship. Land for 20 ploughs.
In lordship 2; 2 male slaves, 1 female.
22 villagers and 6 smallholders have 12 ploughs.
2 mills at 32d.
Value when acquired £10; now 100s.
Leofnoth held it.

0 LAND OF WINEMAR

[In CLEYLEY Hundred]

1 Winemar holds ½ hide and the fifth part of 1 virgate of land from the King in COSGROVE. Land for 1½ ploughs. In lordship 1, with 3 smallholders.
A mill at 13s; meadow, 5 acres; woodland 3 furlongs long and 2 furlongs wide.
The value was 10s; now 20s.
Haldane held it freely.

In HIGHAM Hundred

2 He also holds 2 hides and 3 virgates of land. Land for 5 ploughs.
In lordship 3 ploughs; 4 slaves.
10 villagers with a priest, 1 smallholder and 1 Frenchman have 2 ploughs.
A mill at 8d; meadow, 20 acres; woodland 4 furlongs long and 2 furlongs wide.
The value was 30s; now 60s.
Six free men held it before 1066. One of them was called Osgot.
Countess Judith claims his part of the land.

3 Winemar also holds 3 virgates of land in *HANTONE*.
Land for 1½ ploughs. In lordship ½ plough.
4 villagers with 5 smallholders have 1 plough.

Ibi . III . ac p̃ti . Valuit 7 ual . x . sol. *IN CLAISLUND HD̃.*

Dodin ten de Winem . I . hid 7 IIII . partes uni v in *ASCE* . Tra . ẽ . III . car . In dñio . ẽ una . cũ I . seruo . 7 v . uitti 7 v . bord hñt . II . car . Ibi . v . ac p̃ti . Silua . VI . q̃z lg. 7 IIII . q̃z lat . Valuit . VIII . sol . modo . XII . solid.

Alden tenuit libe T.R.E. Dodin ñ ht̃ nisi decimã partẽ

Bondi ten . IIII . partes dim hidæ de Win ‡ huj træ. in ead uilla . Tra . ẽ . I . car . Ibi . ẽ un bord . Valet . IIII . sol.

Idem Alden libe tenuit T.R.E.

Maiulf ten de . W . II . v træ 7 dimid . Tra . ẽ . I . car. Hæc ibi . ẽ in dñio 7 VI . uitti cũ dim car . Valuit . x . solid Modo . xx . solid . Alric 7 Siuerd libe tenuer . T.R.E.

.XLI. TERRA WIDON DE REINBCVRT *IN NEVESLUND HD̃.*

Wido de Reinbuedcurt ten de rege . VIII . hid 7 dim in *BURTONE* . Ibi T.R.E. fuer . XIIII . car . De hac tra sunt in dñio . III . hidæ . 7 ibi . III . car . cũ . I . seruo . 7 XXI . uitts 7 XVIII . bord hñt . IX . car . Ibi . II . molini de . XVI . sol. 7 xx . ac p̃ti . 7 dimid ac siluæ . Valuit . XL . sol . m̃ . VI . lib.

Idem ten . II . hid 7 III . v træ *IN WAREDONE HUND.* Tra . ẽ . VI . car 7 dimid . De hac tra . ẽ in dñio una hida. 7 ibi . III . car . 7 xv . uitti cũ p̃bro 7 II . bord hñt . v . car. Ibi . II . molini de . XXVI . sol . 7 xx . ac p̃ti . Valuit . c . sol. Modo . VIII . lib . Tosti libe tenuit . ‡ Burton tenuit Radulf com'.

Idẽ . W . ten . II . hid dimid v min *IN GISLEBURG HD̃ 7 DIMID̃.* in *STANFORD* . 7 abb Benedict emit ab eo . Tra . ẽ . v . car. Ibi sunt . XVII . uitti cũ p̃bro 7 IIII . bord hñtes . IIII . car.

Meadow, 3 acres.
The value was and is 10s.

In CLEYLEY Hundred

4 Dodin holds 1 hide and 4 parts of 1 virgate from Winemar in ASHTON. Land for 3 ploughs. In lordship 1, with 1 slave.
5 villagers and 5 smallholders have 2 ploughs.
Meadow, 5 acres; woodland 6 furlongs long and 4 furlongs wide.
The value was 8s; now 12s.
Haldane held it freely before 1066. Dodin has only the tenth part of this land.

5 Bondi holds 4 parts of ½ hide from Winemar in the same village. Land for 1 plough.
1 smallholder.
Value 4s.
Haldane also held it freely before 1066.

6 Maiwulf holds 2½ virgates of land from Winemar. Land for 1 plough; it is there, in lordship;
6 villagers with ½ plough.
The value was 10s; now 20s.
Alric and Siward held it freely before 1066.

1 LAND OF GUY OF RAIMBEAUCOURT

In NAVISLAND Hundred

1 Guy of Raimbeaucourt holds 8½ hides from the King in BURTON (Latimer). Before 1066, 14 ploughs. In lordship 3 hides of this land; 3 ploughs there, with 1 slave.
21 villagers and 18 smallholders have 9 ploughs.
2 mills at 16s; meadow, 20 acres; woodland, ½ acre.
The value was 40s; now £6.

In WARDEN Hundred

2 He also holds 2 hides and 3 virgates of land. Land for 6½ ploughs. In lordship 1 hide of this land; 3 ploughs there.
15 villagers with a priest and 2 smallholders have 5 ploughs.
2 mills at 26s; meadow, 20 acres.
The value was 100s; now £8.
Tosti held it freely.

Earl Ralph held Burton (Latimer).

In GUILSBOROUGH Hundred and a half

3 Guy also holds 2 hides, less ½ virgate, in STANFORD (on Avon). Abbot Benedict bought it from him. Land for 5 ploughs.
17 villagers with a priest and 4 smallholders who have 4 ploughs.

226 d

Ibi . VIII . ac̃ p̃ti . Valuit . XX . solid̃ . Modo . XL . sol̃.
Leuric lib̃e tenuit . T.R.E. *IN ORDINBARO HVND̃.*

NORGIOT ten̄ de . W . I . hid̃ in *HARGEDONE* . Tra . ē . II . car̄.
In dñio . ē una . cũ . I . seruo 7 ancilla . 7 IIII . uitti cũ . I . bord̃
hñt . I . car̄ . Ibi molin̄ de . VIII . sol̃ . 7 II . ac̃ p̃ti . Valuit . V .
solid̃ . Modo . XX . sol̃ . Algar lib̃e tenuit.

Radulf⁹ ten̄ de . W . I . hid̃ 7 II . v̄ træ 7 dim̄ in *ISHAM* . Tra . ē
III . car̄ . In dñio . ē una . cũ . I . seruo . 7 VII . uitti cũ . I . bord̃
hñt . II . car̄ . Ibi molin̄ de . X . sol̃ . 7 V . ac̃ p̃ti . Valuit . V . sol̃.
Modo . XL . solid̃ . Eluuin⁹ . f . Vlf lib̃e tenuit T.R.E.
De hac t̄ra unā v̄ 7 dimid̃ 7 III . hortulos calũniat̄ ep̄s constant̄.

227 a

Picot 7 Landric̄ 7 Oger⁹ ten̄ de Widone *IN HOCHESLAV HD̃.*
in *ALDEVINCLE* . V . hid̃ . Tra . ē . IX . car̄ . In dñio st̄ . III . car̄.
7 III . serui . 7 XVI . uitti 7 V . bord̃ hñt . V . car̄ . Ibi molin̄
de . VI . solid̃ . 7 X . ac̃ p̃ti . Silua . XVI . q̃z lḡ . 7 VIII . q̃z lat̄.
Valet . L . solid̃ . int̄ om̄s . Lefsi lib̃e tenuit . T.R.E.

Walteri⁹ ten̄ de . W . II . hid̃ 7 dimid̃ *IN STOTFALD HD̃.*
7 t̄ciā partē uni⁹ v̄ in *SOLEBI* . Soca p̄tin̄ ad Stanford.
Ibi ht̄ . I . car̄ in dñio . 7 VII . soch̄ cũ . VI . bord̃ hñt . II . car̄.
Valuit 7 ual̃ . XL . sol̃ . Leuric lib̃e tenuit.

Odelin⁹ ten̄ de . W . III . v̄ træ in *CRANEFORD* . Tra . ē . III . car̄.
In dñio . ē una . 7 un⁹ uitts 7 V . bord̃ hñt . II . car̄ . Valet . XX . sol̃.

Norgiot ten̄ de . W . III . v̄ træ 7 dim̄ in *CVGENHO* . Tra . ē
III . car̄ . In dñio sunt . II . 7 VIII . uitti hñt . I . car̄ . Ibi molin̄
de . XIII . sol̃ . 7 XII ac̃ p̃ti . Silua dim̄ leuū lḡ . 7 una q̃z lat̄.
Valuit . X . solid̃ . Modo . XXX . sol̃ . Eduin⁹ lib̃e tenuit T.R.E.

Meadow, 8 acres.
The value was 20s; now 40s.
Leofric held it freely before 1066.

In ORLINGBURY Hundred

4 Norigot holds 1 hide from Guy in HARROWDEN. Land for 2 ploughs.
In lordship 1, with 1 male and 1 female slave.
4 villagers with 1 smallholder have 1 plough.
A mill at 8s; meadow, 2 acres.
The value was 5s; now 20s.
Algar held it freely.

5 Ralph holds 1 hide and 2½ virgates of land from Guy in ISHAM.
Land for 3 ploughs. In lordship 1, with 1 slave.
7 villagers with 1 smallholder have 2 ploughs.
A mill at 10s; meadow, 5 acres.
The value was 5s; now 40s.
Alwin son of Ulf held it freely before 1066. Of this land the Bishop of Coutances claims 1½ virgates and 3 little gardens.

In HUXLOE Hundred 227 a

6 Picot, Landric and Oger hold 5 hides from Guy in ALDWINCLE.
Land for 9 ploughs. In lordship 3 ploughs; 3 slaves.
16 villagers and 5 smallholders have 5 ploughs.
A mill at 6s; meadow, 10 acres; woodland 16 furlongs long and 8 furlongs wide.
Value 50s between them.
Leofsi held it freely before 1066.

In STOTFOLD Hundred

7 Walter holds 2½ hides and the third part of 1 virgate from Guy in SULBY. The jurisdiction belongs to Stanford (on Avon).
He has 1 plough in lordship.
7 Freemen with 6 smallholders have 2 ploughs.
The value was and is 40s.
Leofric held it freely.

[In NAVISLAND Hundred]

8 Odelin holds 3 virgates of land from Guy in CRANFORD.
Land for 3 ploughs. In lordship 1.
1 villager and 5 smallholders have 2 ploughs.
Value 20s.

[In WYMERSLEY Hundred]

9 Norigot holds 3½ virgates of land from Guy in COGENHOE.
Land for 3 ploughs. In lordship 2.
8 villagers have 1 plough.
A mill at 13s; meadow, 12 acres; woodland ½ league long and 1 furlong wide.
The value was 10s; now 30s.
Edwin held it freely before 1066.

Turchil teñ de.W.III.partes uni⁹ v̄ *IN GISLEBVRG HD̄* 7 *DIM̄.*
in *ELTETONE*.Tra.ē.III.bou̅.Hos hn̄t ibi.II.borđ arantes
Valuit 7 uał.II.solid̄.

.XLII. TERRA EVDONIS FILIJ HVBERTI. *IN CORBEI HD̄.*
EVDO.f.Hub̄ti teñ de rege.II.hid̄ 7 dim̄ in *WACHERLEI.*
Tra.ē.VI.car.De hac tra.ē in dn̄io.I.hida 7 ibi.II.car.
7 IIII.serui.7 XVI.uitti cū pb̄ro 7 IIII.borđ hn̄t.IIII.car.Ibi
molin̄ de.V.soł.7 XII.ac̄ p̄ti.Silua.I.leu̅ lḡ.7 IIII.q̄z lat
Valuit.XX.soł.Modo.C.solid̄. *IN OPTONEGREN HD̄.*
Rolland teñ de Eud̄.I.hid̄ 7 dim̄ in *ESTONE*.Tra.ē.II.car.
Ibi sochi.V.hn̄t.III.car.7 VIII.ac̄s p̄ti.Silua.III.q̄z lḡ.7 una
lat.Valuit.II.soł.Modo.XXX.soł.H̄ tra.ē S̄ Petri de Burg.
Rolland teñ de Eud̄.I.hid̄ 7 dim̄ in *ESTONE*. *IN WILEBROC HD̄.*
Tra.ē.IIII.car.In dn̄io sunt.III.car.7 IIII.serui.7 XV.uitti
cū.III.borđ hn̄t.III.car.Ibi molin̄ de.XX.soł.7 VIII.ac̄ p̄ti.
Silua.III.q̄z lḡ.7 II.q̄z lat.Valuit.XX.soł.Modo.VI.lib̄.
Drond⁹ lib̄e tenuit.T.R.E.

.XLIII. TERRA GHILONIS FRIS ANCVLFI *IN FOXLEV HVND̄*
GILO teñ de rege.III.hid̄ in *WEDONE*.Tra.ē.VII.car 7 dim̄
In dn̄io st̄.III.car.7 IX.serui 7 VI.ancillæ.Ibi.I.miles 7 XIII.
uitti 7 VI.borđ hn̄t.IIII.car.7 dim̄.Ibi molin̄ de.II.solid̄
7 VI.ac̄ p̄ti.Valuit.XL.soł.7 modo.LX.solid̄.Fregist 7 Siuuard tenuer̄.

In GUILSBOROUGH Hundred and a half

10 Thorkell holds 3 parts of 1 virgate from Guy in ELKINGTON.
Land for 3 oxen.
2 smallholders who plough have them.
The value was and is 2s.

42 LAND OF EUDO SON OF HUBERT

In CORBY Hundred

1 Eudo son of Hubert holds 2½ hides from the King in WAKERLEY.
Land for 6 ploughs. In lordship 1 hide of this land; 2 ploughs there; 4 slaves.
16 villagers with a priest and 4 smallholders have 4 ploughs.
A mill at 5s; meadow, 12 acres; woodland 1 league long and 4 furlongs wide.
The value was 20s; now 100s.

In UPTON Hundred

2 Roland holds 1½ hides from Eudo in EASTON (on-the-Hill).
Land for 2 ploughs.
5 Freemen have 3 ploughs, and
meadow, 8 acres. Woodland 3 furlongs long and 1 wide.
The value was 2s; now 30s.
This land is (part) of St. Peter's (Church) of Peterborough.

In WILLYBROOK Hundred

3 Roland holds 1½ hides from Eudo in EASTON (on the Hill).
Land for 4 ploughs. In lordship 3 ploughs; 4 slaves.
15 villagers with 3 smallholders have 3 ploughs.
A mill at 20s; meadow, 8 acres; woodland 3 furlongs long and 2 furlongs wide.
The value was 20s; now £6.
Thrond held it freely before 1066.

43 LAND OF GILES BROTHER OF ANSCULF

In FOXLEY Hundred

1 Giles holds 3 hides from the King in WEEDON (Lois). Land for 7½ ploughs. In lordship 3 ploughs; 9 male and 6 female slaves.
A man-at-arms, 13 villagers and 6 smallholders have 4½ ploughs.
A mill at 2s; meadow, 6 acres.
The value was 40s; now 60s.
Fredegis and Siward held it.

Goisfrid ten̄ de Gilone . i . hid̄ 7 dim̄ in *Mortone* Tra . ē
vi . car̄ . In dn̄io st̄ . iii . car̄ . 7 v . serui . 7 xiiii . uitti 7 iii . bord̄ .
cū . iii . car̄ . Ibi . xxx . ac̄ p̄ti . Valuit . viii . lib̄ . Modo . iiii . lib̄ .
Goduin ten̄ de . G . dim̄ hid̄ in *Selvestone* . ⁊ Leuric libe tenuit .
Tra . ē . i . car̄ . Ibi sunt . ii . uitti . 7 iii . ac̄ p̄ti . Silua . i . leū 7 dim̄
lḡ . 7 una leū lat̄ . Quarta pars huj siluæ ptin̄ ad hanc tr̄a .
Valuit . ii . sol̄ . Modo . v . sol̄ . Siuuard libe tenuit .
Ipse Gilo ten̄ . ii . hid̄ in *Wapeham* . De *In Tovecestre Hd.*
hac tra st̄ . iii . v̄ in dn̄io . Tra . ē . v . car̄ . In dn̄io st̄ . ii . 7 ix . serui .
7 iii . ancillæ . 7 xvii . uitti 7 viii . bord̄ cū p̄bro hn̄t . iii . car̄ .
Ibi molin̄ de . iiii . sol̄ . 7 v . ac̄ p̄ti . Silua . xi . q̄z lḡ . 7 vi . lat̄ .
Valuit . c . sol̄ . Modo . iiii . lib̄ . Leuric 7 Siuuard libe tenuer̄ .
Ipse Gilo ten̄ . ii . hid̄ in *Stane* . Tra . ē *In Alboldestov Hd.*
. v . car̄ . De hac tra . st̄ . iii . v̄ in dn̄io . 7 ibi . ii . car̄ . 7 iiii . serui .
7 ii . ancillæ . 7 xi . uitti cū bord̄ hn̄t . iii . car̄ . Ibi molin̄ de . ii . sol̄ .

227 b
Ad hoc m̄ jacen̄ . iiii . partes uni hidæ *In Sitton* hd̄ . Tra . ii . car̄ .
Ibi . ē un hō hn̄s . i . car̄ . Tot̄ ualuit . l . sol̄ . Modo . lx . solid̄ .
Landric ten̄ de . G . ii . hid̄ 7 iiii . partes dim̄ hidæ in *Brime* .
Tra . ē . vi . car̄ . In dn̄io st̄ . ii . car̄ . 7 ii . serui . 7 iii . ancillæ .
7 vi . uitti cū p̄bro hn̄t . ii . car̄ . Ibi molin̄ de . xxxii . denar̄ .
7 iiii . ac̄ p̄ti . Valuit . xl . sol̄ . Modo . lx . sol̄ . Leuric libe tenuit
Ingelrann ten̄ de . G . ii . hid̄ in *Torp* . Tra . ē . v . car̄ . In dn̄io
ē una . 7 vi . uitti 7 iii . bord̄ hn̄t . ii . car̄ . Valuit . xl . solid̄ .
Modo . l . sol̄ . Osmund Dan libe tenuit .

2 Geoffrey holds 1½ hides from Giles in MORETON (Pinkney).
Land for 6 ploughs. In lordship 3 ploughs; 5 slaves;
14 villagers and 3 smallholders with 3 ploughs.
Meadow, 30 acres.
The value was £8; now £4.
Leofric held it freely.

3 Godwin holds ½ hide from Giles in SILVERSTONE. Land for 1 plough.
2 villagers.
Meadow, 3 acres; woodland 1½ leagues long and 1 league wide.
The fourth part of this woodland belongs to this land.
The value was 2s; now 5s.
Siward held it freely.

In TOWCESTER Hundred

4 Giles holds 2 hides himself in WAPPENHAM. In lordship 3 virgates of this land. Land for 5 ploughs. In lordship 2; 9 male and 3 female slaves.
17 villagers and 8 smallholders with a priest have 3 ploughs.
A mill at 4s; meadow, 5 acres; woodland 11 furlongs long and 6 wide.
The value was 100s; now £4.
Leofric and Siward held it freely.

In ALBOLDSTOW Hundred

5 Giles holds 2 hides himself in STEANE. Land for 5 ploughs. In lordship 3 virgates of this land. 2 ploughs there; 4 male and 2 female slaves.
11 villagers with a smallholder have 3 ploughs.
A mill at 2s.
In Sutton Hundred 4 parts of 1 hide lie in this manor. 227 b
Land for 2 ploughs. A man who has 1 plough.
The value of the whole was 50s; now 60s.

6 Landric holds 2 hides and 4 parts of ½ hide from Giles in *BRIME*. Land for 6 ploughs. In lordship 2 ploughs; 2 male and 3 female slaves.
6 villagers with a priest have 2 ploughs.
A mill at 32d; meadow, 4 acres.
The value was 40s; now 60s.
Leofric held it freely.

7 Ingelrann holds 2 hides from Giles in THORPE (Mandeville).
Land for 5 ploughs. In lordship 1.
6 villagers and 3 smallholders have 2 ploughs.
The value was 40s; now 50s.
Osmund the Dane held it freely.

Hugo 7 Landric' ten de . G . II . hid in *STOTEBERIE* . Tra . ē . v . car . In dnio . ē una . 7 II . serui . 7 v . uilli 7 III . bord . 7 alij . III . hoēs cū . I . car . Silua . III . qz lg . 7 II . qz lat. Valuit . xxx . sol . Modo . XL . solid . Osmund libe tenuit.

Goisfrid' 7 Robt' ten . II . hid de . G . in *ESTWELLE* . Tra . ē . v . car . In dnio sunt . II . cū . I . seruo . 7 VIII . uilli 7 VIII . bord hnt . III . car . Ibi molin de . XII . den . 7 x . ac pti . Silua VI . qz lg . 7 una qz 7 v . ptic lat . Valuit 7 uat . XL . sol.

Goisfrid' ten de . G . dimid hid . 7 Leuric 7 Aluric tenuer . in *SIGRESHĀ* . Tra . I . car 7 II . boū . In dnio . ē car . 7 III . uilli. Valuit 7 uat . x . sol . Leuric libe tenuit. *IN WAREDON HD.*

Ipse Gilo ten . IIII . hid in *SVLGRAVE* . 7 Hugo 7 Landric' 7 Otbt' de eo . Tra . ē . x . car . In dnio st . III . car . cū . I . seruo. 7 XX . uilli 7 VI . bord hnt . v . car . Ibi . VIII . ac pti. Valuit . IX . lib . Modo . VII . lib . Quattuor hoēs tenuer . sed discede n potuer . qa Soca huj' træ ptin ad Waredone.

.XLIIII. TERRA GOISFRIDI ALSELIN. *IN COLESTREV HD.*

GOISFRID' Alselin ten de rege . III . hid 7 dim in *MIDELTONE*. 7 Witts ten de eo . Tra . ē . IX . car . In dnio . ē una . 7 XVI . uilli cū pbro 7 v . bord hnt . VII . car . Ibi molin de . XXX . den . 7 x . ac pti . Silua . III . qz lg . 7 II . qz 7 dim lat. Huic ₥ ptin . II . hid in *COLENTREV* . una . v min' . Tra . ē . IIII . car . Has hnt ibi . II . sochi 7 v . uilli . Ibi . III . ac pti.

8 Hugh and Landric hold 2 hides from Giles in STUCHBURY.
Land for 5 ploughs. In lordship 1; 2 slaves;
5 villagers, 3 smallholders and 3 other men with 1 plough.
Woodland 3 furlongs long and 2 furlongs wide.
The value was 30s; now 40s.
Osmund held it freely.

9 Geoffrey and Robert hold 2 hides from Giles in ASTWELL.
Land for 5 ploughs. In lordship 2, with 1 slave.
8 villagers and 8 smallholders have 3 ploughs.
A mill at 12d; meadow, 10 acres; woodland 6 furlongs long and 1 furlong and 5 perches wide.
The value was and is 40s.
Leofric and Aelfric held it.

10 Geoffrey holds ½ hide from Giles in SYRESHAM. Land for 1 plough and 2 oxen. The plough is in lordship.
3 villagers.
The value was and is 10s.
Leofric held it freely.

In WARDEN Hundred

11 Giles holds 4 hides himself in SULGRAVE, and Hugh, Landric and Odbert from him. Land for 10 ploughs. In lordship 3 ploughs, with 1 slave.
20 villagers and 6 smallholders have 5 ploughs.
Meadow, 8 acres.
The value was £9; now £7.
Four men held it, but they could not leave because the jurisdiction of this land belongs to (Chipping) Warden.

44 LAND OF GEOFFREY ALSELIN

In COLLINGTREE Hundred

1a Geoffrey Alselin holds 3½ hides from the King in MILTON (Malsor), and William holds from him. Land for 9 ploughs. In lordship 1.
16 villagers with a priest and 5 smallholders have 7 ploughs.
A mill at 30d; meadow, 10 acres; woodland 3 furlongs long and 2½ furlongs wide.

b To this manor belong 2 hides, less 1 virgate, in COLLINGTREE.
Land for 4 ploughs.
2 Freemen and 5 villagers have them there.
Meadow, 3 acres.

In *Torp*. ẽ dim̃ hida ptin ad Mildetone. Tra. ẽ. i. car̃. quæ ibi. ẽ cũ. i. uitto. Tot valuit. iiii. lib. Modo. vi. lib.
Winemar ten dimid hid de. G. in ead uilla. Tra. ẽ. i. car. Ipsa ibi. ẽ. Valuit. v. sol. Modo. viii. sol. De hac dimid hida tantm̃ ht. W. socã. Totã hanc trã. tenuit Tochi cũ saca 7 soca.

.XLV. TERRA GOISFRIDI DE MANNEVILE *IN SVTONE HVND.*

GOISFRID de Manneuile ten de rege *Aienho*. Ibi sunt. iii. hidæ 7 qntã partẽ. i. hidæ. Tra. ẽ. viii. car. De hac trã. ẽ hida 7 v. pars uni hidæ in dñio. 7 ibi. iii. car. 7 viii. serui. 7 xxiii. uitti 7 ix. bord cũ. v. car. Ibi molin de. x. solid. 7 xx. ac pti. Valuit. vi. lib. m̃. viii. lib. Asgar tenuit T.R.E.
Osbn ten de. Go. i. hid 7 ii. partes uni v in *Cliwetone*. Tra. ẽ. iii. car. In dñio. ẽ una. 7 iii. serui. 7 x. uitti cũ. i. car 7 dim. 7 molin de. ii. sol. Valuit 7 ual. xxx. solid. Suartlin tenuit. 7 discede n̄ potuit.
Suetman ten de. Go. v. partẽ dimid hidæ in *Creveltone*. Tra. ẽ ii. bou. Ibi. ẽ un uitts cũ dim car. Val. iii. sol. Asgar libe tenuit.
Vltbert ten de. Go. *Hintone*. Ibi st. ii. hidæ. *IN WAREDONE HD.* Tra. ẽ. v. car. In dñio st. ii. car. 7 ii. serui. 7 x. uitti 7 iii. bord cũ. iii. car. Ibi molin de. ii. sol. 7 iii. ac pti. Valuit. xl. sol. Modo. lx. sol.
Malger ten de. Go. vi. hid in *Estone*. Tra. ẽ. x. car. In dñio st. iii. car.

c In ROTHERSTHORPE is ½ hide which belongs to Milton (Malsor).
Land for 1 plough; it is there, with
1 villager.
The value of the whole was £4; now £6.

2 Winemar holds ½ hide from Geoffrey in the same village.
Land for 1 plough; it is there.
The value was 5s; now 8s.
Winemar only has the jurisdiction of this ½ hide.
Toki held all this land, with full jurisdiction.

45 LAND OF GEOFFREY DE MANDEVILLE

In SUTTON Hundred

1 Geoffrey de Mandeville holds AYNHO from the King. 3 hides and the fifth part of 1 hide. Land for 8 ploughs. In lordship 1 hide and the fifth part of 1 hide of this land. 3 ploughs there; 8 slaves;
23 villagers and 9 smallholders with 5 ploughs.
A mill at 10s; meadow, 20 acres.
The value was £6; now £8.
Asgar held it before 1066.

2 Osbern holds 1 hide and 2 parts of 1 virgate from Geoffrey in CROUGHTON. Land for 3 ploughs. In lordship 1; 3 slaves;
10 villagers with 1½ ploughs.
A mill at 2s.
The value was and is 30s.
Swartling held it; he could not leave.

3 Sweetman holds the fifth part of ½ hide from Geoffrey in CROUGHTON.
Land for 2 oxen.
1 villager with ½ plough.
Value 3s.
Asgar held it freely.

In WARDEN Hundred

4 Wihtbert holds HINTON from Geoffrey. 2 hides. Land for 5 ploughs.
In lordship 2 ploughs; 2 slaves;
10 villagers and 3 smallholders with 3 ploughs.
A mill at 2s; meadow, 3 acres.
The value was 40s; now 60s.

5 Mauger holds 6 hides from Geoffrey in ASTON (le Walls).
Land for 10 ploughs. In lordship 3 ploughs; 5 slaves.

7 v.serui.7 xv.uilli 7 v.bord hnt.vi.car. Ibi.xii.ac pti.
Valuit.c.solid.Modo.vi.lib. *In Niwebotlagrave hd.*
Balduin ten de.Go.dimid hida in *Flora*.Tra.e.i.car.Hæc
ibi.e cu.i.uillo.7 ii.seruis.7 iiii.ac pti.7 de parte molini
ht.v.solid.Valuit tot.v.sol.Modo.xv.sol. *In Foxesle hd.*
Ernald ten de Go.dim hida in *Silvestone*.Tra.e.i.car.
Hec ibi.e cu.ii.seruis 7.i.uillo 7 i.bord.Valuit.x.sol.M.xx.sol.
Ide ten de.Go.ii.hid in *Hintone*.Tra.e.v.car.In dnio
sunt.ii.car.7 ii.serui.7 xi.uilli 7 v.bord hnt.iii.car.Ibi
molin de.ii.sol.7 xvi.ac pti.Silua.ii.qz lg.7 dim qrent
lat.Valuit.xxx.sol.Modo.lxx.solid. *In Edboldeston hd.*
Osbn ten de.Go.i.hid 7 dim.7 ii.partes uni v In *Culeorde*.
Tra.e.iiii.car.In dnio sunt.ii.7 iiii.serui.7 x.uilli cu.i.
bord hnt.ii.car.Ibi molin de.xl.den.Valuit 7 ual.iii.lib.
Has tras oms Goisfridi tenuit Asgar T.R.E.

XLVI. Terra Gislebti De gand. *In Nevbotlagrave hd.*

Gislebert De Gand ten de rege.iii.hid 7 dim in *Cese lingeberie*.7 Goisfrid ten de eo.Tra.e.x.car.In dnio st
.iii.car.7 de ipsa tra.i.hida 7 dim.7 x.serui.7 xxii.uilli 7 vii.
bord cu.iiii.car.Ibi.ii.molini de.xl.sol.7 xiiii.ac pti.
7 x.ac siluæ.Valuit.iiii.lib.Modo.vi.lib.
Sasgar ten de.Gi.i.hid 7 una v tre 7 dim in *Haiforde*.
Tra.e.ii.car.In dnio.e dim car.7 iii.uilli cu.i.bord hnt
.i.car.Ibi.iiii.ac pti.Valuit.x.sol.Modo.xx.sol.

15 villagers and 5 smallholders have 6 ploughs. 227 c
Meadow, 12 acres.
The value was 100s; now £6.

In NOBOTTLE Hundred

6 Baldwin holds ½ hide from Geoffrey in FLORE.
Land for 1 plough; it is there, with
1 villager and 2 slaves.
Meadow, 4 acres; he has 5s from part of a mill.
The value of the whole was 5s; now 15s.

In FOXLEY Hundred

7 Arnold holds ½ hide from Geoffrey in SILVERSTONE.
Land for 1 plough; it is there, with 2 slaves,
1 villager and 1 smallholder.
The value was 10s; now 20s.

[? In TOWCESTER Hundred]

8 He also holds 2 hides from Geoffrey in HINTON (in the Hedges).
Land for 5 ploughs. In lordship 2 ploughs; 2 slaves.
11 villagers and 5 smallholders have 3 ploughs.
A mill at 2s; meadow, 16 acres; woodland 2 furlongs long and ½ furlong wide.
The value was 30s; now 70s.

In ALBOLDSTOW Hundred

9 Osbern holds 1½ hides and 2 parts of 1 virgate from Geoffrey in CULWORTH. Land for 4 ploughs. In lordship 2; 4 slaves.
10 villagers with 1 smallholder have 2 ploughs.
A mill at 40d.
The value was and is £3.

Asgar held all these lands of Geoffrey's before 1066.

6 LAND OF GILBERT OF GHENT

In NOBOTTLE Hundred

1 Gilbert of Ghent holds 3½ hides from the King in KISLINGBURY, and Geoffrey holds from him. Land for 10 ploughs. In lordship 3 ploughs and 1½ hides of this land; 10 slaves;
22 villagers and 7 smallholders with 4 ploughs.
2 mills at 40s; meadow, 14 acres; woodland, 10 acres.
The value was £4; now £6.

2 Sasgar holds 1 hide and 1½ virgates of land from Gilbert in HEYFORD. Land for 2 ploughs. In lordship ½ plough.
3 villagers with 1 smallholder have 1 plough.
Meadow, 4 acres.
The value was 10s; now 20s.

ꝑ HD̃.

Ipſe. Gi. ten̄. IIII. hid̄ in *STOWE*. Tra. ē. x. car̄. *IN GRAVESEND*
In dn̄io ſunt. III. car̄. 7 VII. ſerui. 7 XIIII. uilli 7 VI. bord̄ hn̄t
VII. car̄. Ibi molin̄ de. LXIIII. den̄. Silua. VII. q̄z lḡ. 7 III.
q̄rent̄ lat̄. Valuit. LX. ſol̄. Modo. C. ſolid̄.

Ipſe. Gi. ten̄ *EPINGEHA͞M* Ibi ſt̄. IIII. hidæ. De his. III. in dn̄io.
Tra. ē. VIII. car̄. In dn̄io ſt̄. IIII. car̄. 7 VIII. ſerui. 7 XV. uilli
cū. IIII. car̄. Ibi. V. molini de. XLII. ſol̄ 7 VIII. den̄. 7 X. ac̄
p̄ti. Silua. I. q̄z lḡ. 7 X. ꝑtic̄ lat̄. Valuit. C. ſol̄. M̊. X. lib̄.

Ipſe ten̄ in ead̄ uilla. VII. hid̄ 7 dimid̄ 7 unā bouatā træ
de ſoca regis de Roteland. 7 dicit regē ſuū aduocat̄ eſſe.
Tra. ē. XV. car̄. Has hn̄t ibi. XIIII. ſochi cū. L. 7 uno uillo.
Ibi. V. molini de. XXIIII. ſol̄. 7 X. ac̄ p̄ti. 7 X. ac̄ ſiluæ.
Valuit 7 ual̄. VIII. lib̄. *IN WILEBROC HD̃.*

Ipſe. Gi. ded̄ S̄ Petro ſup̄ diuā dim̄ hid̄ in *ESTONE*. Tra. ē
. II. car̄. In dn̄io. ē una. 7 IIII. uilli hn̄t aliā. Ibi. IIII. ac̄ p̄ti.
Valuit. V. ſol̄. Modo. X. ſol̄. Om̄s has t̄ras tenuit Tonna

Rotb̄t ten̄ de. Gi. *WICFORD*. Ibi. XV. hidæ. ꝑ cū ſaca 7 ſoca.
Tra. ē. XIX. car̄. In dn̄io ſt̄. IIII. 7 X. ſerui. 7 XXXIII. uilli
7 XXI. bord̄ hn̄t. XV. car̄. Ibi. II. molini de. XV. ſol̄. 7 III. q̄z
p̄ti. in lḡ. 7 tn̄td̄ in lat̄. Silua. I. q̄z lḡ. 7 tn̄td̄ lat̄.
Valuit. X. lib̄. Modo. XX. lib̄. Wlf libe tenuit. T.R.E.

.XLVII. TERRA GOISFR̄ DE WIRCE. *IN GISLEBVRG HD̃ 7 DIMID̄.*

GOISFRID DE WIRCE ten̄ de rege. IIII. hid̄ in *WELLESFORD*
7 Alfrid de eo. Tra. ē. VIII. car̄. In dn̄io ſt̄. II. 7 II. ſerui. 7 I. ancila.
7 XII. uilli cū p̄b̄ro 7 II. bord̄ hn̄t. IIII. car̄. Ibi. XX. ac̄ p̄ti.

In GRAVESEND Hundred

3 Gilbert holds 4 hides himself in STOWE. Land for 10 ploughs. In lordship 3 ploughs; 7 slaves.
14 villagers and 6 smallholders have 7 ploughs.
A mill at 64d; woodland 7 furlongs long and 3 furlongs wide.
The value was 60s; now 100s.

[In WITCHLEY Wapentake]

4 Gilbert holds EMPINGHAM himself. 4 hides. 3 of them in lordship. Land for 8 ploughs. In lordship 4 ploughs; 8 slaves;
15 villagers with 4 ploughs.
5 mills at 42s 8d; meadow, 10 acres; woodland 1 furlong long and 10 perches wide.
The value was 100s; now £10.

5 In the same village he holds 7½ hides and 1 bovate of land himself of the King's Jurisdiction of Rutland and he states that the King is his patron. Land for 15 ploughs.
14 Freemen with 51 villagers have them there.
5 mills at 24s; meadow, 10 acres; woodland, 10 acres.
The value was and is £8.

In WILLYBROOK Hundred

6 Gilbert himself gave to Saint-Pierre-sur-Dives ½ hide in EASTON (on the Hill). Land for 2 ploughs. In lordship 1.
4 villagers have another.
Meadow, 4 acres.
The value was 5s; now 10s.

Tonna held all these lands, with full jurisdiction.

(In WARWICKSHIRE)

7 Robert holds WHICHFORD from Gilbert. 15 hides. Land for 19 ploughs. In lordship 4; 10 slaves.
33 villagers and 21 smallholders have 15 ploughs.
2 mills at 15s; meadow, 3 furlongs in length and as much in width; woodland 1 furlong long and as wide.
The value was £10; now £20.
Ulf held it freely before 1066.

47 LAND OF GEOFFREY OF LA GUERCHE

In GUILSBOROUGH Hundred and a half

1 a Geoffrey of La Guerche holds 4 hides from the King in WELFORD, and Alfred from him. Land for 8 ploughs. In lordship 2; 2 male slaves, 1 female.
12 villagers with a priest and 2 smallholders have 4 ploughs.
Meadow, 20 acres.

Huic ϖ ptin.ii.v tre 7 dim in *Essebi*.Tra.ē.i.car.7 qrta pars uni v træ in *Etendone*. Ibi st.ii.bord redd.xxii.den. Eid ϖ ptin.ii.hidæ 7 dim in *Solebi*.Tra.ē.v.car. *In Stofald Hd.* Vasta.ē.Tot T.R.E.ualuit.xx.sol.Modo.lx.solid.Leuric libe

Idē.Go.ten in *Crec*.iiii.hid.una v træ min.Tra.ē.viii.car.Γ tenuit T.R.E. In dnio st.iii.car.7 iiii.serui.7 xvii.uilli cū pbro 7 vi.bord hnt.v.car.Ibi.xii.ac pti Valuit.xxx.sol.Modo.iiii.lib 7 x.solid.Huic træ adjacēt.iiii.sochi q reddt x.den.

227 d

XLVIII. TERRA GVNFRIDI DE CIOCHES. *In Corbei Hvnd*.

Gvnfrid de Cioches ten de rege dim hid in *Boctone*. Tra.ē.i.car. Hanc hnt ibi.ii.uilli cū.i.bord. Valuit 7 ual

Idē.G.ten in *Nevtone*.iii.v træ 7 unā bouatā Γ vi.sol. 7 tciā partē uni bouate.Tra.ē.ii.car.In dnio.ē una.7 iiii. uilli cū.iiii.bord hnt aliā.Silua ibi dim qz lg.7 .ptic lat. Valuit 7 ual.x.solid. Azur libe tenuit has.ii.tras.

Idē ten.iii.hid 7 unā v træ 7 dim *In Spereholt Hd.* in *Belinge*.Tra.ē.vii.car.In dnio st.ii.7 iiii.serui.7 xvi. uilli cū pbro hnt.v.car.Ibi molin de.ii.sol.7 l.ac pti. Valuit.xl.sol.Modo.lxx.sol.Suain libe tenuit.

Idē ten.v.hid in *Wilavestone*.Tra.ē.x.car.In dnio sunt.iiii.7 viii.serui.7 xxii.uilli cū pbro 7 iiii.bord hnt vi.car.Ibi molin de.v.sol.7 xlviii.ac pti.Valuit.iii.lib. Modo.x.lib.Quattuor teini tenuer cū saca 7 soca.

b To this manor belong 2½ virgates of land in (Cold) ASHBY. Land for 1 plough. The fourth part of 1 virgate of land in ELKINGTON.

2 smallholders who pay 22d.

In STOTFOLD Hundred

c To the same manor belong 2½ hides in SULBY. Land for 5 ploughs. It is waste.

The value of the whole before 1066, 20s; now 60s.

Leofric held it freely before 1066.

2 Geoffrey also holds 4 hides, less 1 virgate of land, in CRICK. Land for 8 ploughs. In lordship 3 ploughs; 4 slaves.

17 villagers with a priest and 6 smallholders have 5 ploughs. Meadow, 12 acres.

The value was 30s; now £4 10s.

4 Freemen who pay 10d are attached to this land.

8 LAND OF GUNFRID OF CHOCQUES 227 d

In CORBY Hundred

1 Gunfrid of Chocques holds ½ hide from the King in BOUGHTON. Land for 1 plough.

2 villagers with 1 smallholder have it there.

The value was and is 6s.

2 Gunfrid also holds 3 virgates of land, 1 bovate and the third part of 1 bovate in NEWTON. Land for 2 ploughs. In lordship 1.

4 villagers with 4 smallholders have another.

Woodland ½ furlong long and 5 perches wide.

The value was and is 10s.

Azor held these two lands freely.

He also holds

in SPELHOE Hundred

3 in BILLING 3 hides and 1½ virgates of land. Land for 7 ploughs. In lordship 2; 4 slaves.

16 villagers with a priest have 5 ploughs.

A mill at 2s; meadow, 50 acres.

The value was 40s; now 70s.

Swein held it freely.

[in HIGHAM Hundred]

4 in WOLLASTON 5 hides. Land for 10 ploughs. In lordship 4; 8 slaves.

22 villagers with a priest and 4 smallholders have 6 ploughs.

A mill at 5s; meadow, 48 acres.

The value was £3; now £10.

Four thanes held it, with full jurisdiction.

Idē teñ. I. hid 7 dim̄ in *CRANESLEA*. *IN ORDINBARO HD̄*.
Tra. ē. III. car̄. In dn̄io. ē una. 7 II. serui. 7 IIII. uilli cū pbro
7 x. bord hn̄t. II. car̄. Ibi. v. ac̄ p̄ti. Valuit 7 uat xxx solid.
Idē teñ. II. hid 7 unā v̄ træ 7 dim̄ hid de soca *IN GISLEBVRG HD̄*.
Tra. ē. v. car̄ 7 dim̄. In dn̄io st̄. III. car̄. 7 VII. serui. 7 XIII. uilli
7 v. bord 7 v. sochi hn̄t. II. car̄ 7 dim̄. Ibi. VIII. ac̄ p̄ti.
Valuit 7 uat. IIII. lib. ⌐ Valet. IIII. sol.
Idē teñ unā v̄ træ in *EDONE*. Tra. ē dim̄ car̄. 7 h ibi. ē cū. I. seruo.
Idē teñ. I. hid in *CRAPTONE*. Tra. ē. II. car̄. In dn̄io. ē una.
7 IIII. serui. 7 III. uilli cū. II. bord hn̄t. I. car̄. Valuit. xx. sol.
Modo. xxx. solid. *IN COLENTREV HVND*.
Idē teñ. II. hid 7 dim̄ in *TORP*. Tra. ē. VII. car̄. In dn̄io st̄. II.
7 VII. serui. 7 XIIII. uilli 7 v. bord hn̄t. v. car̄. Ibi molin̄ de
XXXII. den. Silua. v. q̄z 7 dim̄ lḡ. 7 una q̄z 7 dim̄ lat.
Valuit. IIII. lib. Modo. c. solid. *IN GRAVESEND HVND*.
Idē teñ dim̄ hid 7 v. partē dim̄ hidæ in *WESTORP*.
Tra. ē. I. car̄. Hec ibi. ē cū. II. bord. Valuit. II. sol. m̄. VI. sol.
Has t̄ras om̄s sup̄dictas tenuit Suain cū saca 7 soca. ⌐ *HD̄*.
Idē teñ. II. hid 7 v. partē. II. hidar̄ in *GRIMBERIE*. *IN SVTONE*
Tra. ē. VI. car̄. In dn̄io st̄. II. 7 IIII. serui. 7 XV. uilli cū. III. bord
hn̄t. IIII. car̄. Ibi molin̄ de. x. sol. 7 xxx. ac̄ p̄ti. Valuit. IIII.
lib. Modo. VI. lib. Triū dn̄ioz. ē h t̄ra. Leuenot tenuit cū sac̄ 7 soc̄.
Winemar̄ teñ de. G. I. hid 7 III. v̄ træ in *CNVTESTONE*.
Tra. ē. II. car̄. In dn̄io. ē una 7 dim̄ cū. I. seruo. 7 VI. uilli
hn̄t. I. car̄. Ibi molin̄ de. VIII. den. 7 VII. ac̄ p̄ti. Valuit. v. sol
Modo. xx. sol. Vluiet libe tenuit T.R.E Eustachi calūniat̄.

in ORLINGBURY Hundred

5 in CRANSLEY 1½ hides. Land for 3 ploughs. In lordship 1; 2 slaves.
4 villagers with a priest and 10 smallholders have 2 ploughs.
Meadow, 5 acres.
The value was and is 30s.

in GUILSBOROUGH Hundred

6 2 hides, 1 virgate of land and ½ hide of the jurisdiction.
Land for 5½ ploughs. In lordship 3 ploughs; 7 slaves.
13 villagers, 5 smallholders and 5 Freemen have 2½ ploughs.
Meadow, 8 acres.
The value was and is £4.

7 in (West) HADDON 1 virgate of land. Land for ½ plough;
it is there, with 1 slave.
Value 4s.

8 in CREATON 1 hide. Land for 2 ploughs. In lordship 1; 4 slaves.
3 villagers with 2 smallholders have 1 plough.
The value was 20s; now 30s.

in COLLINGTREE Hundred

9 in ROTHERSTHORPE 2½ hides. Land for 7 ploughs. In lordship 2;
7 slaves.
14 villagers and 5 smallholders have 5 ploughs.
A mill at 32d; woodland 5½ furlongs long and 1½ furlongs wide.
The value was £4; now 100s.

in GRAVESEND Hundred

10 in THRUPP (Grounds) ½ hide and the fifth part of ½ hide. Land
for 1 plough; it is there, with
2 smallholders.
The value was 2s; now 6s.

Swein held all the above lands, with full jurisdiction.

in SUTTON Hundred

11 in GRIMSBURY 2 hides and the fifth part of 2 hides. Land for 6 ploughs.
In lordship 2; 4 slaves.
15 villagers with 3 smallholders have 4 ploughs.
A mill at 10s; meadow, 30 acres.
The value was £4; now £6.
This land is in 3 lordships. Leofnoth held it, with full jurisdiction.

[In HIGHAM Hundred]

12 Winemar holds 1 hide and 3 virgates of land from Gunfrid in KNUSTON.
Land for 2 ploughs. In lordship 1½, with 1 slave.
6 villagers have 1 plough.
A mill at 8d; meadow, 7 acres.
The value was 5s; now 20s.
Wulfgeat held it freely before 1066. Eustace claims it.

Johs ten de.G.dimid v træ in *WESTONE*. *IN SPELEHOV HD.*
Ibi.ē un uitts hns.III.animalia. *IN NIWEBOTLAGRAVE HD.*
Olbald ten de.G.I.hid 7 unā v træ in *FLORA*.Tra.ē.III.car.
In dnio st.II.7 IIII.serui.7 V.uitti cū.IIII.bord hnt.I.car.
Ibi.VI.ac pti.Valuit.X.sol.Modo.XXV.sol.Duo taini tenuer.
Tetbald ten de.G.III.v træ 7 IIII.partē *IN CLAIESLEA HD.*
uni v in *HVLECOTE*.Tra.ē.II.car.In dnio.ē una.7 VII.uitti
hnt aliā.Ibi.V.ac pti.Valuit.XII.sol.Modo.XV.solid.
Bondi ten de.G.III.v træ 7 IIII.partē uni v in *ADESTANESTONE*.
Tra.ē.II.car.In dnio.ē una.7 VI.uitti hnt aliā.Ibi.III.ac pti
7 de parte molini.IIII.solid.Silua.V.qz lg 7 in lat.Duo dni
eā tenent.Valet.XII.solid.Idē Bondi libe tenuit.
Dodin ten de.G.IIII.partes dimid hidæ in *RODE*.Tra.ē.I.car.
H ibi.ē cū.II.bord.Silua dim qz lg.7 IIII.ptic lat.
Valuit.XII.den.Modo.IIII.solid.Suain libe tenuit T.R.E.

228 a

.XLIX TERRA SIGAR DE CIOCHES.

SIGAR de Cioches ten de rege.IIII.hid *IN TOVECESTRE HD.*
7 IIII.partes dim hidæ.Tra.ē.X.car.De hac tra.I.hida
ē in dnio.7 ibi.III.car.7 V.serui.7 III.ancillæ.7 XXI.uitts
cū pbro 7 XI.bord hnt.VIII.car.Ibi.VIII.ac pti.Silua
IIII.qz lg.7 III.qz lat.Valuit 7 ual.VI.lib.Tosti com tenuit.

In SPELHOE Hundred

13 John holds ½ virgate of land from Gunfrid in WESTON (Favell).
1 villager who has 3 cattle.

In NOBOTTLE Hundred

14 Wulfbald holds 1 hide and 1 virgate of land from Gunfrid in FLORE.
Land for 3 ploughs. In lordship 2; 4 slaves.
5 villagers with 4 smallholders have 1 plough.
Meadow, 6 acres.
The value was 10s; now 25s.
Two thanes held it.

In CLEYLEY Hundred

15 Theobald holds 3 virgates of land and the fourth part of 1 virgate from Gunfrid in HULCOTE. Land for 2 ploughs. In lordship 1.
7 villagers have another.
Meadow, 5 acres.
The value was 12s; now 15s.

16 Bondi holds 3 virgates of land and the fourth part of 1 virgate from Gunfrid in EASTON NESTON. Land for 2 ploughs. In lordship 1.
6 villagers have another.
Meadow, 3 acres; from part of a mill, 4s; woodland 5 furlongs long and in width; two lords hold it.
Value 12s.
Bondi also held it freely.

17 Dodin holds 4 parts of ½ hide from Gunfrid in ROADE.
Land for 1 plough; it is there, with
2 smallholders.
Woodland ½ furlong long and 4 perches wide.
The value was 12d; now 4s.
Swein held it freely before 1066.

49 LAND OF SIGAR OF CHOCQUES 228 a

In TOWCESTER Hundred

1 Sigar of Chocques holds 4 hides and 4 parts of ½ hide from the King.
Land for 10 ploughs. In lordship 1 hide of this land. 3 ploughs there; 5 male and 3 female slaves.
21 villagers with a priest and 11 smallholders have 8 ploughs.
Meadow, 8 acres; woodland 4 furlongs long and 3 furlongs wide.
The value was and is £6.
Earl Tosti held it.

.L. TERRA SVAIN. *IN CLAIESLEA HD̃.*

SVAIN ten̄ de rege . IIII . hid̄ in *STOCHE* . Tra . ē . x . car̄. In d̄nio . ē una . 7 XIIII . uilłi cū p̄bro 7 VII . bord̄ hn̄t . v . car̄. Ibi molin̄ de . XIII . sold̄ . 7 IIII . den̄ . 7 XXX . ac̄ p̄ti . Silua . III . q̄z lḡ . 7 II . q̄z 7 dim̄ lat̄ . Valuit 7 ual̄ . III . lib̄.

.LI. TERRA SIBOLDI. *IN HOCHESLAV HD̃.*

SIBOLD̄ ten̄ de rege unā v̄ træ 7 dim̄ in *LVDEWIC* . Tra . ē . I . car̄ 7 dim̄ . De hac tra . ē una v̄ in d̄nio . 7 ibi . I . car̄ . 7 II . uilłi 7 II . bord̄ . cū dim̄ car̄ . Valuit . IIII . sol̄ . Modo . x . solid. Lefsi lib̄e tenuit T.R.E.

.LII. TERRA OGERII. *IN NARRESFORD HD̃.*

OGERVS ten̄ de rege . II . hid̄ 7 dim̄ in *KAPESTONE* . Tra . ē . v . car̄ . In d̄nio s̄t . II . car̄ cū . I . seruo . 7 VII . uilłi 7 v . bord̄ hn̄t . I . car̄ . 7 IIII . sochi cū . I . car̄ . Ibi molin̄ de . XX . sol̄ . 7 XII . ac̄ p̄ti . Silua VI . q̄z lḡ . 7 totid̄ lat̄ . Valuit 7 ual̄ . III . lib̄.

.LIII. TERRA DROGON̄ DE BEVREIRE *IN WINEMERESLEA HD̃.*

DROGO de Beureire ten̄ de rege . I . hid̄ 7 III . v̄ træ in *CEDESTONE* . Tra . ē . v . car̄ . In d̄nio . ē . I . car̄ . cū . I . seruo . 7 IX . uilłi 7 IIII . bord cū . III . car̄ . Silua . I . q̄rent̄ lḡ . 7 tn̄td̄ lat̄ . Valuit . XX . sol̄ . Modo . XL . sol̄ . Vlf tenuit hō Wallef comit̄. Judita comitissa calūniat̄.

.LIIII. TERRA MANNONIS *IN SVTONE HD̃.*

MAINO ten̄ de rege . I . hid̄ in *TANEFORD* . Tra . ē . II . car̄ 7 dim̄. In dnio . ē una . 7 III . serui . 7 VI . uilłi hn̄t . I . car̄ 7 dimid̄.

50 ## LAND OF SWEIN

In CLEYLEY Hundred

1 Swein holds 4 hides from the King in STOKE (Bruerne).
Land for 10 ploughs. In lordship 1.
14 villagers with a priest and 7 smallholders have 5 ploughs.
A mill at 13s 4d; meadow, 30 acres; woodland 3 furlongs long and 2½ furlongs wide.
The value was and is £3.

51 ## LAND OF SIBOLD

In HUXLOE Hundred

1 Sibold holds 1½ virgates of land from the King in LOWICK.
Land for 1½ ploughs. In lordship 1 virgate of this land.
1 plough there;
2 villagers and 2 smallholders with ½ plough.
The value was 4s; now 10s.
Leofsi held it freely before 1066.

52 ## LAND OF OGER [THE BRETON]

In NAVISFORD Hundred

1 Oger holds 2½ hides from the King in THRAPSTON. Land for 5 ploughs.
In lordship 2 ploughs, with 1 slave.
7 villagers and 5 smallholders have 1 plough; 4 Freemen with 1 plough.
A mill at 20s; meadow, 12 acres; woodland 6 furlongs long and as many wide.
The value was and is £3.

53 ## LAND OF DROGO OF BEUVRIÈRE

In WYMERSLEY Hundred

1 Drogo of Beuvrière holds 1 hide and 3 virgates of land from the King in CHADSTONE. Land for 5 ploughs. In lordship 1 plough, with 1 slave;
9 villagers and 4 smallholders with 3 ploughs.
Woodland 1 furlong long and as wide.
The value was 20s; now 40s.
Ulf, Earl Waltheof's man, held it. Countess Judith claims it.

54 ## LAND OF MAINOU [THE BRETON]

In SUTTON Hundred

1 Mainou holds 1 hide from the King in THENFORD. Land for 2½ ploughs. In lordship 1; 3 slaves.
6 villagers have 1½ ploughs.

7 de parte molini . xxx . den . Valuit 7 uat . xl . solid . Algar libe tenuit . T.R.E. *In Claiesle hd.*

Idẽ ten . iii . v tre . in *Wiche* . Tra . ẽ . iii . car . In dñio st . ii . car cũ . i . seruo . 7 v . uitti cũ . i . bord hñt . ii . car . Ibi . vi . ac pti . Silua x . qrent lg . 7 iii . qz lat . Valuit 7 uat . xl . sot . Siuuard libe tenuit.

Berner ten de . M . iiii . hid . 7 ii . partes uni v in *Medewelle* . Tra . ẽ . viii . car . In dñio . ẽ una . cũ . i . seruo . 7 viii . uitti 7 iiii . bord 7 vi . sochi hñt . vi . car . Ibi . viii . ac pti . Valuit . v . sot . Modo . xl . solid . Leuric libe tenuit. *In Stotfald hd.*

Huic ᴍ ptin una v træ in *Dractone* . H cũ ᴍ appicat *In Rodewelle Hund.*

.LV. TERRA EVSTACHIJ.

Evstachivs ten de rege . i . hid 7 ii.as v træ 7 dim in *Isham*. Tra . ẽ . iii . car . In dñio . ẽ una . 7 vii . uitti 7 iii . bord cũ . ii . car . Ibi molin de . x . sot . 7 v . ac pti . Valuit 7 uat . xl . solid . Hanc trã occupauit ui Eustachi sup æcctam de Ramesy.

Rainald ten de . E . iii . hid in *Niwetone* . Tra . ẽ . v . car . In dñio . ẽ una . 7 viii . uitti 7 v . bord cũ . iii . car 7 dim . Ibi molin de . lxiiii . den . 7 viii . ac pti . Silua . iiii . qz lg . 7 ii . qz lat . Valuit . x . solid . Modo . xxx . solid . Norman tenuit has . ii . tras.

Alured ten de . E . in *Pochebroc* . i hid 7 unã v træ . Tra . ẽ . ii . car . In dñio . ẽ una . 7 iiii . uitti cũ pbro 7 iiii . bord hñt car 7 dim . Valuit . ii . sot . Modo . xx . solid . Ormar libe tenuit.

From part of a mill, 30d.
The value was and is 40s.
Algar held it freely before 1066.

In CLEYLEY Hundred

2 He also holds 3 virgates of land in WICKEN. Land for 3 ploughs.
In lordship 2 ploughs, with 1 slave.
5 villagers with 1 smallholder have 2 ploughs.
Meadow, 6 acres; woodland 10 furlongs long and 3 furlongs wide.
The value was and is 40s.
Siward held it freely.

In STOTFOLD Hundred

3 Berner holds 4 hides and 2 parts of 1 virgate from Mainou in MAIDWELL.
Land for 8 ploughs. In lordship 1, with 1 slave.
8 villagers, 4 smallholders and 6 Freemen have 6 ploughs.
Meadow, 8 acres.
The value was 5s; now 40s.
Leofric held it freely.

In ROTHWELL Hundred

To this manor belongs 1 virgate of land in DRAUGHTON. It is assessed with this manor.

55 LAND OF EUSTACE [OF HUNTINGDON]

[In ORLINGBURY Hundred]

1 Eustace holds 1 hide and 2½ virgates of land from the King in ISHAM. Land for 3 ploughs. In lordship 1;
7 villagers and 3 smallholders with 2 ploughs.
A mill at 10s; meadow, 5 acres.
The value was and is 40s.
Eustace appropriated this land by force from Ramsey Church.

[In WILLYBROOK Hundred]

2 Reginald holds 3 hides from Eustace in (WOOD)NEWTON.
Land for 5 ploughs. In lordship 1;
8 villagers and 5 smallholders with 3½ ploughs.
A mill at 64d; meadow, 8 acres; woodland 4 furlongs long and 2 furlongs wide.
The value was 10s; now 30s.
Norman held these two lands.

[In POLEBROOK Hundred]

3 Alfred holds 1 hide and 1 virgate of land from Eustace in POLEBROOK. Land for 2 ploughs. In lordship 1.
4 villagers with a priest and 4 smallholders have 1½ ploughs.
The value was 2s; now 20s.
Ordmer held it freely.

Widelard ten de.E.dim hid in *WINEWINCLE*.Tra.ē.II.car.
In dn̄io.ē una.cū.I.seruo.7 III.uilli cū.II.car.Ibi.III.ac pti.
Valuit.x.sol.Modo.XL.solid.Achi tenuit. *IN NEVESLVND HD.*

Agemund ten de.E.dim hid in *GRASTONE*.Tra.ē.I.car.
Ipsa ibi.ē cū qbzdā hōibz.Valuit 7 ual.v.solid. *IN NARESFORD HD.*

Alured ten de.E.I.hid 7 unā v træ in *DOTONE*.Tra.ē.II.car.
In dn̄io.ē una.7 un uills cū.III.bord ht dim car.Valuit.III.sol.
Modo.x.solid.

228 b

.LVI. TERRA JVDITÆ COMITISSÆ. *IN WICELEA WAPENT.*

JVDITA Comitissa ten de rege.I.hid 7 dim in *RIEHALE*.
Tra.ē.VIII.car cū appendic.In dn̄io.ē una.7 IIII.serui.7 x.
uilli 7 IIII.sochi hn̄t.IIII.car.Ibi.II.molini de.XXXVI.solid.
Silua.IIII.q̄rent lḡ.7 II.q̄z lat.
Huic m̄ ptin *BELMESTORP*.Ibi.I.hida 7 dimid.7 in dn̄io.II.
car.7 XIIII.uilli 7 VI.bord hn̄t.IIII.car.Ibi molin de.x.sol.
7 VIII.den.7 XVI.ac pti.Tot ualuit 7 ual.VI.lib.

Ipsa ten.tciā partē uni hidæ in *ASCE*.Ibi sť.III.sochi reddt
p ann.v.sol 7 IIII.den.

In *SVTONE*.ē dim hida.7 tcia pars dim hidæ.7 ibi.IIII.sochi hn̄t
.I.car 7 dim.7 reddt p ann.x.sol 7 VIII.den.

In *WESTONE*.ē.I.hida 7 tcia pars.I.hidæ.7 ibi.v.sochi
hn̄t.I.car 7 dim.7 reddt p ann.XXI.sol 7 IIII.den.

In *TINGLEA*.ē tcia pars uni hidæ.7 III.partes.II.partiū
uni hidæ.7 ibi.v.sochi cū.I.car 7 dimid.reddt VI.sol 7 VIII.
denar.

In *BRANTONE*.ē.I.hida.7 ibi.IIII.sochi hn̄t.II.car.
7 reddt p ann.v.sol.7 IIII.den.
Totā hanc trā tenuit Wallef com.7 tntd ualuit qtū nc ualet.

Ipsa comit ten.VI.hid in *FODRINGEIA*. *IN WILEBROC HD.*
Tra.ē.XII.car.De hac tra.II.hidæ sť in dn̄io.7 ibi.III.car.
7 III.serui.7 XIX.uilli cū pbro 7 VI.bord hn̄t.IX.car.Ibi

4 Oidelard holds ½ hide from Eustace in WINWICK.
Land for 2 ploughs. In lordship 1, with 1 slave;
3 villagers with 2 ploughs.
Meadow, 3 acres.
The value was 10s; now 40s.
Aki held it.

In NAVISLAND Hundred

5 Agemund holds ½ hide from Eustace in GRAFTON (Underwood).
Land for 1 plough; it is there, with some men.
The value was and is 5s.

In NAVISFORD Hundred

6 Alfred holds 1 hide and 1 virgate of land from Eustace in CLOPTON.
Land for 2 ploughs. In lordship 1.
1 villager with 3 smallholders has ½ plough.
The value was 3s; now 10s.

56 LAND OF COUNTESS JUDITH 228 b

In WITCHLEY Wapentake

1 Countess Judith holds 1½ hides from the King in RYHALL.
Land for 8 ploughs, with dependencies. In lordship 1; 4 slaves.
10 villagers and 4 Freemen have 4 ploughs.
2 mills at 36s; woodland 4 furlongs long and 2 furlongs wide.
BELMESTHORPE belongs to this manor. 1½ hides. In lordship 2 ploughs.
14 villagers and 6 smallholders have 4 ploughs.
A mill at 10s 8d; meadow, 16 acres.
The value of the whole was and is £6.

[In STOKE Hundred]

2 She holds the third part of 1 hide herself in ASHLEY.
3 Freemen; they pay 5s 4d a year.

3 In SUTTON (Bassett) ½ hide and the third part of ½ hide.
4 Freemen have 1½ ploughs; they pay 10s 8d a year.

4 In WESTON (By Welland) 1 hide and the third part of 1 hide.
5 Freemen have 1½ ploughs; they pay 21s 4d a year.

5 In DINGLEY the third part of 1 hide and 3 parts of 2 parts of 1 hide.
5 Freemen with 1½ ploughs; they pay 6s 8d.

6 In BRAMPTON (Ash) 1 hide.
4 Freemen have 2 ploughs; they pay 5s 4d a year.
Earl Waltheof held the whole of this land. The value was as much then as now.

In WILLYBROOK Hundred

7 The Countess holds 6 hides herself in FOTHERINGHAY. Land for 12 ploughs. In lordship 2 hides of this land; 3 ploughs there; 3 slaves.
19 villagers with a priest and 6 smallholders have 9 ploughs.

molin̄ de . VIII . sol̄ . 7 XL . ac̄ p̄ti . Silua . I . leu̇ lḡ . 7 IX . q̄z lat̄ . cū onerat̄ 7 rex in ea n̄ uenat̄ : uał . x . solid̄.

Valuit . VIII . lib̄ . Modo . XII . lib̄ . Turchil lib̄e tenuit . T.R.E.

Ipsa . Co . ten̄ . v . hid̄ in *HARINGEWORDE* . Tra . ē . XVI . car̄ . In d̄nio st̄ . III . car̄ . 7 VI . serui 7 una ancilla . 7 XXVI . uill̄i 7 VIII . bord̄ 7 VI . soch̄i hn̄t . x . car̄ . Ibi molin̄ de . v . sol̄ . 7 v . q̄rent̄ p̄ti in lḡ . 7 II . q̄z lat̄ . Silua . VIII . q̄z lḡ . 7 I . leuu̇ . 7 III . q̄z lat̄ . Valuit 7 uał . x . lib̄ . Turchil lib̄e tenuit.

In *LANGEPORT* . ē una bouata t̄ræ cū . I . bord̄ . redd̄ . XVI . denar̄.

In *BRADEBROC* . ē dimid̄ v̄ t̄ræ de soca . Ibi un̄ uill̄s h̄t dim̄ car̄ . Valuit 7 uał . IIII . solid̄.

In *BRACSTONE* st̄ . II . v̄ t̄ræ 7 dimid̄ . Ibi . III . soch̄i hn̄t . II . car̄ . Valuit 7 uał . x . solid̄.

In *BVRTONE* . ē una hida 7 dim̄ de soca . Tra . ē . III . car̄ . Has hn̄t ibi . III . soch̄i cū . IIII . uill̄is 7 v . bord̄ . 7 VIII . ac̄s p̄ti.

In *CRANESLEA* . ē una hida . 7 ibi . VI . soch̄i cū . v . bord̄ hn̄t II . car̄ . 7 VIII . ac̄s p̄ti.

In *HANINTONE* st̄ . III . v̄ t̄ræ . 7 ibi . IIII . soch̄i hn̄t . I . car̄ 7 dim̄ . 7 II . ac̄s p̄ti . He . III . t̄ræ ualb̄ . XL . sol̄ . m̄ . XVI . denar̄ plus.

Ipsa . co . ten̄ . IIII . hid̄ in *BARTONE* . Tra . ē . VIII . car̄ . In d̄nio st̄ . II . 7 III . serui . 7 VIII . uill̄i 7 VI . bord̄ 7 XI . soch̄i hn̄t . VI . car̄ . Ibi . III . molini de . XXVIII . sol̄ 7 VIII . den̄ . 7 XXXIIII . ac̄ p̄ti . Valuit 7 uał . IIII . lib̄ . Bondi tenuit cū saca 7 soca.

Ipsa . Co . ten̄ . IIII . hid̄ in *DODINTONE* . Tra . ē . VIII . car̄ . In d̄nio st̄ . II . car̄ . 7 II . serui . 7 XII . uill̄i 7 v . bord̄ cū . IIII . soch̄is hn̄t . VI .

A mill at 8s; meadow, 40 acres; woodland 1 league long and 9 furlongs wide; value when stocked and the King is not hunting in it, 10s.

The value was £8; now £12.

Thorkell held it freely before 1066.

[In CORBY Hundred]

8 The Countess holds 5 hides herself in HARRINGWORTH. Land for 16 ploughs. In lordship 3 ploughs; 6 male slaves, 1 female.

26 villagers, 8 smallholders and 6 Freemen have 10 ploughs.

A mill at 5s; meadow, 5 furlongs in length and 2 furlongs wide; woodland 8 furlongs long and 1 league and 3 furlongs wide.

The value was and is £10.

Thorkell held it freely.

[In MAWSLEY Hundred]

9 In LAMPORT 1 bovate of land, with

1 smallholder who pays 16d.

[In ROTHWELL Hundred]

10 In BRAYBROOKE ½ virgate of land of the jurisdiction.

1 villager has ½ plough.

The value was and is 4s.

11 In DRAUGHTON 2½ virgates of land.

3 Freemen have 2 ploughs.

The value was and is 10s.

[In ORLINGBURY Hundred]

12 In BROUGHTON 1½ hides of the jurisdiction. Land for 3 ploughs.

3 Freemen with 4 villagers and 5 smallholders have them there, and meadow, 8 acres.

13 In CRANSLEY 1 hide.

6 Freemen with 5 smallholders have 2 ploughs, and meadow, 8 acres.

14 In HANNINGTON 3 virgates of land.

4 Freemen have 1½ ploughs, and meadow, 2 acres.

The value of these three lands was 40s; now 16d more.

[In HAMFORDSHOE Hundred]

15 The Countess holds 4 hides herself in (Earls) BARTON.

Land for 8 ploughs. In lordship 2; 3 slaves.

8 villagers, 6 smallholders and 11 Freemen have 6 ploughs.

3 mills at 28s 8d; meadow, 34 acres.

The value was and is £4.

Bondi held it, with full jurisdiction.

16 The Countess holds 4 hides herself in (Great) DODDINGTON.

Land for 8 ploughs. In lordship 2 ploughs; 2 slaves.

12 villagers and 5 smallholders with 4 Freemen have 6 ploughs.

car̃. Ibi. xii. ac̃ p̃ti. Valuit 7 ual̃. iiii. lib̃. Bondi tenuit.
Ipsa. Co. ten̄. iiii. hid̃ in *Wilebi*. Tra. ē. vii. car̃. In dnio. ē
una. 7 vii. sochi hnt. vi. car̃. Valuit 7 ual̃. iiii. lib̃. Bondi tenuit.
Ipsa. Co. ten̄. iiii. hid̃ in *Asbi*. Tra. ē. vii. car̃. In dnio. ē una.
7 ii. serui. 7 vi. uilli 7 vi. bord̃ cū. viii. sochis hnt. vi. car̃.
Valuit 7 ual̃. iiii. lib̃. Bundi tenuit. Hæ. iii. træ ptin̄ ad *Burtone*.
In *Buchetone* st̃. iii. v̄ træ de soca. Tra. ē. i. car̃ 7 dimid̃.
Has hnt ibi. iiii. sochi cū. iii. bord̃. *In Wimaresleà hd̃ 7 dimid̃.*
Ipsa. Co. ten̄. iii. hid̃ 7 dim̄ in *Gerdelai*. Tra. ē. ix. car̃. De
hac tra. ē in dnio. i. hida. 7 ibi. iii. car̃. 7 xvi. uilli cū. xii. bord̃
hnt. vi. car̃.

228 c
Silua ibi. xiii. q̃rent̃ lḡ. 7 viii. q̃z lat̃. h tra T.R.E 7 m̄
se desd̃ p. iii. hid̃ 7 dimid̃. Huic ptin̄ h sequentia mēbra.
In *Grendone* st̃. iii. hidæ 7 una v̄ træ. Tra. ē. ix. car̃.
Has hnt ibi. xii. sochi. 7 iii. molin̄ de. iii. sol̃. 7 xxx. ac̃s p̃ti.
In *Wicentone*. ē una v̄ træ de soca. Tra. ē dim̄ car̃. Hanc
hnt ibi. ii. bord̃. sochi.
In *Dodintone*. ē una hida. Tra. ē. ii. car̃. Has hnt ibi. vi.
In *Bachelintone* st̃. ii. hidæ de soca. Tra. ē. vi. car̃. has hnt
ibi. viii. sochi 7 iiii. bord̃. 7 x. ac̃s p̃ti. Vasta. ē.
In *Hortone*. ē una v̄ træ 7 de soca. i. hida. Tra. ē dim̄ car̃.
In *Wilavestone*. ht̃ comitissa. i. hidæ socam.
In *Bragefelde* st̃. iii. v̄ træ. Tra. ē. ii. car̃. has hnt ibi
iii. sochi cū. iii. bord̃. 7 ii. ac̃s siluæ.
In *Quintone*. ē dim̄ hida. Tra. ē. i. car̃. Hanc hnt ibi. ii. sochi
cū. ii. uillis 7 v. bord̃. 7 iiii. ac̃s p̃ti.

Meadow, 12 acres.
The value was and is £4.
Bondi held it.

17 The Countess holds 4 hides herself in WILBY. Land for 7 ploughs.
In lordship 1.
7 Freemen have 6 ploughs.
The value was and is £4.
Bondi held it.

18 The Countess holds 4 hides herself in (Mears) ASHBY.
Land for 7 ploughs. In lordship 1; 2 slaves.
6 villagers and 6 smallholders with 8 Freemen have 6 ploughs.
The value was and is £4.
Bondi held it.

These three lands belong to (Earl's) Barton.

[In SPELHOE Hundred]

9 In BOUGHTON 3 virgates of land of the jurisdiction. Land for 1½ ploughs.
4 Freemen with 3 smallholders have them there.

In WYMERSLEY Hundred and a half

a The Countess holds 3½ hides herself in YARDLEY (Hastings).
Land for 9 ploughs. In lordship 1 hide of this land. 3 ploughs there.
16 villagers with 12 smallholders have 6 ploughs.
Woodland 13 furlongs long and 8 furlongs wide. 228 c
Before 1066 and now this land answered for 3½ hides.
The following members belong to it:-

b In GRENDON 3 hides and 1 virgate of land. Land for 9 ploughs.
12 Freemen have them there, and
3 mills at 3s; meadow, 30 acres.

c In WHISTON 1 virgate of land of the jurisdiction. Land for ½ plough.
2 smallholders have it there.

d In DENTON 1 hide. Land for 2 ploughs.
6 Freemen have them there.

e In HACKLETON 2 hides of the jurisdiction. Land for 6 ploughs.
8 Freemen and 4 smallholders have them there, and
meadow, 10 acres.

f In HORTON 1 virgate of land and 1 hide of the jurisdiction.
Land for ½ plough. Waste.

g In WOLLASTON the Countess has the jurisdiction of 1 hide.

h In BRAFIELD (on the Green) 3 virgates of land. Land for 2 ploughs.
3 Freemen with 3 smallholders have them there, and
woodland, 2 acres.

i In QUINTON ½ hide. Land for 1 plough.
2 Freemen with 2 villagers and 5 smallholders have it there, and
meadow, 4 acres.

In *HARDINGESTONE* st̃ . ii . hidæ . Tra . ẽ . iiii . car̃ . Ibi . vi . sochi 7 vi . bord hñt . iii . car̃ . 7 iii . acs p̃ti. Tot̃ m̃ cũ append ualuit . xii . lib̃ . Modo . xv . lib̃ . Wallef com tenuit.

Ipsa . Co . ten̄ . viii . hid in *DAVENTREI* . Tra . ẽ . xvi . car. In dñio st̃ . iii . car . 7 iii . serui . 7 xx . uitti cũ pbro 7 x . bord hñt . vii . car . Ibi . xii . ac p̃ti . Valuit . iii . lib̃ . Modo . viii . lib̃.

In *TEOWELLE* ten̄ . co . i . hid 7 dim . Tra . ẽ . ii . car̃ . In dñio . ẽ una car cũ . ii . bord . Valuit 7 ual . x . solid . Wallef comes tenuit

Hugo ten̄ de Comitissa dim hid in *WEDLINGEBERIE* . 7 p tanto se desd T . R . E . Tra . ẽ . i . car 7 dim . In dñio . ẽ una cũ . i . seruo . 7 ii . uitti 7 ii . bord hñt dim car . Ibi molin̄ de . v . solid. Valuit . x . solid . Modo . xx . solid . Goduin libe tenuit T . R . E.

Idẽ ten̄ de . Co . dim hid in *WALETONE* . Tra . ẽ . i . car . Hanc hñt ibi . iii . sochi . Valuit . ii . sol . Modo . v . solid.

Robt ten̄ de . Co . ii . hid 7 unã v træ in *BITLESBROCH*. Tra . ẽ . iii . car 7 dim . In dñio . ẽ una 7 ii . serui . 7 xii . uitti cũ . iiii . bord hñt . ii . car̃ 7 dim . Ibi . xx . ac p̃ti . Silua minuta . i . q̃z 7 dim in lg̃ . 7 tntd in lat . Valuit . xx ti . sol. Modo . xxx . solid . Eduuard tenuit cũ saca 7 soca.

Grimbald ten̄ de . Co . iii . hid una bouata min in *TICHECOTE*. Tra . ẽ . vi . car̃ . In dñio . ẽ una . 7 viii . sochi cũ . xii . uittis 7 uno bord hñt . v . car̃ . Ibi molin̄ de . xxiiii . solid . 7 xii . ac p̃ti. Valuit . xxx . solid . Modo . l . solid . Eduuard tenuit . 7 hanc

j In HARDINGSTONE 2 hides. Land for 4 ploughs.
6 Freemen and 6 smallholders have 3 ploughs, and meadow, 3 acres.

k The value of the whole manor with dependencies was £12; now £15.
Earl Waltheof held it.

[In GRAVESEND Hundred]

1 The Countess holds 8 hides herself in DAVENTRY. Land for 16 ploughs.
In lordship 3 ploughs; 3 slaves.
20 villagers with a priest and 10 smallholders have 7 ploughs.
Meadow, 12 acres.
The value was £3; now £8.

[In HUXLOE Hundred]

2 In TWYWELL the Countess holds 1½ hides. Land for 2 ploughs.
In lordship 1 plough, with
2 smallholders.
The value was and is 10s.
Earl Waltheof held it.

From the Countess

[in HAMFORDSHOE Hundred]

3 Hugh holds ½ hide in WELLINGBOROUGH. It answered for as much before 1066. Land for 1½ ploughs. In lordship 1, with 1 slave.
2 villagers and 2 smallholders have ½ plough.
A mill at 5s.
The value was 10s; now 20s.
Godwin held it freely before 1066.

4 he also holds ½ hide in *WALETONE*. Land for 1 plough.
3 Freemen have it there.
The value was 2s; now 5s.

[in WITCHLEY Wapentake]

5 Robert holds 2 hides and 1 virgate of land in BISBROOKE.
Land for 3½ ploughs. In lordship 1; 2 slaves.
12 villagers with 4 smallholders have 2½ ploughs.
Meadow, 20 acres; underwood 1½ furlongs in length and as much in width.
The value was 20s; now 30s.
Edward held it, with full jurisdiction.

6 Grimbald holds 3 hides, less 1 bovate, in TICKENCOTE.
Land for 6 ploughs. In lordship 1.
8 Freemen with 12 villagers and 1 smallholder have 5 ploughs.
A mill at 24s; meadow, 12 acres.
The value was 30s; now 50s.
Edward held it also.

Idē ten̄ de . Co . i . hidā in *Horne* . Tra . ē . ii . car̄ . In dn̄io . ē una . 7 ii . serui . 7 ii . ancillæ . 7 ix . uilli cū . iiii . bord̄ hn̄t . ii . car̄ . Ibi molin̄ de . iiii . sol̄ 7 viii . den̄ . Valuit . xx . sol̄ . m̄ . xxx . solid̄ .

Idē ten̄ unā v̄ træ de . Co . in *Ferendone* . Tra . ē . ii . bou̅ . Valuit 7 ual̄ . xxxii . denar̄ . Turchill liƀe tenuit . T.R.E.

Idē ten̄ de . co . iii . hid̄ 7 unā v̄ træ in *Multone* . Tra . ē . vi . car̄ 7 dim̄ . In dn̄io . ē una . 7 xii . uilli cū . iiii . bord̄ hn̄t . v . car̄ 7 dimid̄ . Valuit 7 ual̄ . xl . solid̄ . Ailric liƀe tenuit T.R.E.

Turgar ten̄ de . Co . in *Newetone* . iii . v̄ træ *In Corbi hd̄.* 7 unā bouatā . 7 tciā partem uni9 bouatæ . Tra . ē . ii . car̄ . In dn̄io . ē una . 7 iiii . uilli cū . iiii . bord̄ hn̄t aliā . Ibi dim̄ molin̄ de . xvi . den̄ . Silua . i . q̄z 7 dim̄ lḡ . 7 tntd̄ lat̄ . Valet . vi . sol̄ . Idē liƀe tenuit .

Chetelbert ten̄ de . Co . i . hid̄ 7 unā v̄ træ . *In Rodewelle hd̄.* in *Bradebroc* . Tra . ē . ii . car̄ . Hæ sunt ibi cū . ii . uillis 7 iiii . bord̄ . Valuit 7 ual̄ . xv . solid̄ . Idē liƀe tenuit T.R.E.

228 d

Vlf ten̄ de Comitissa . i . hid̄ de Soca in *Ocedone* . *In Stotfald hd̄.* Tra . ē . ii . car̄ . Ipse sunt ibi cū . v . sochis 7 vi . bord̄ . Valet . xx . solid̄ . Idē liƀe tenuit T.R.E.

Biscop ten̄ de . Co . dimid̄ hidā in *Muletone* . Tra . ē . i . car̄ . Ipsa ibi . ē cū . ii . uillis 7 ii . bord̄ . Valet . x . sol̄ .

Turbern ten̄ de . Co . dimid̄ hidā in *Hortone* . Tra . ē . i . car̄ . Ibi . ē dim̄ car̄ cū . ii . bord̄ . Valuit . viii . sol̄ . m̄ . x . sol̄ .

7 he also holds 1 hide in HORN. Land for 2 ploughs.
In lordship 1; 2 male and 2 female slaves.
9 villagers with 4 smallholders have 2 ploughs.
A mill at 4s 8d.
The value was 20s; now 30s.

[in STOTFOLD Hundred]

8 he also holds 1 virgate of land in (East) FARNDON. Land for 2 oxen.
The value was and is 32d.
Thorkell held it freely before 1066.

[in SPELHOE Hundred]

9 he also holds 3 hides and 1 virgate of land in MOULTON.
Land for 6½ ploughs. In lordship 1.
12 villagers with 4 smallholders have 5½ ploughs.
The value was and is 40s.
Alric held it freely before 1066.

in CORBY Hundred

0 Thorgar holds 3 virgates of land and 1 bovate and the third part of 1 bovate in NEWTON. Land for 2 ploughs. In lordship 1.
4 villagers with 4 smallholders have another.
½ mill at 16d; woodland 1½ furlongs long and as wide.
Value 6s.
He also held it freely.

in ROTHWELL Hundred

1 Ketelbert holds 1 hide and 1 virgate of land in BRAYBROOKE.
Land for 2 ploughs; they are there, with
2 villagers and 4 smallholders.
The value was and is 15s.
He also held it freely before 1066.

in STOTFOLD Hundred 228 d

2 Ulf holds 1 hide of the jurisdiction in OXENDON. Land for 2 ploughs; they are there, with
5 Freemen and 6 smallholders.
Value 20s.
He also held it freely before 1066.

[in SPELHOE Hundred]

3 Bishop holds ½ hide in MOULTON. Land for 1 plough;
it is there, with
2 villagers and 2 smallholders.
Value 10s.

[in WYMERSLEY Hundred]

4 Thorbern holds ½ hide in HORTON. Land for 1 plough.
½ plough there, with
2 smallholders.
The value was 8s; now 10s.

Leuric ten de . Co : in *WELETONE* 7 in *TORP* dimid hidā
7 unā v træ . qnta parte dim hidæ min . Tra . ē . I . car.
In dn̄io . ē dimid car cū . II . bord . Valet . VIII . solid.
Idē Leuric tenuit T.R.E. Rex ht inde socā.
Willelm ten de . Co : IIII . hid in *GLADESTONE* . Tra . ē
VIII . car . In dn̄io . ē : I . car 7 dim . 7 II . serui . 7 V . uilti
7 III . sochi cū . II : bord hn̄t . V . car . Ibi : X . ac p̄ti.
Valuit 7 ual : XL . solid . Eduuard tenuit cū saca 7 soca.
Huic m̄ ptin . VI . sochi in *LVFENHAM* regis . 7 un in
SEGESTONE . 7 un in *TORP* . quoz pecunia sup notata . ē.
Lanzelin ten de . Co . in *NEWETONE* *IN CORBEI HD.*
III . v træ 7 unā bouatā 7 tciā partē uni bouatæ . Tra . ē
II . car : In dn̄io . ē una . 7 VIII . uilti cū . IIII . bord hn̄t aliā.
Ibi molin de . VII . sol . 7 VIII . den : Silua . I . qz lg . 7 dim
qrent lat . Valuit . V . sol . Modo . XVI . solid.
Idē . L . ten de . Co . I : hid 7 dimid . 7 dim v tre in *ACHELAV.*
Tra . ē . V : car . In dn̄io . ē una 7 II . serui : 7 XIX . uilti hn̄t
III . car . p̄tū . IIII . qrent lg . 7 III . ptic lat . Silua . I . leu
lg . 7 dim leu lat . Valuit . XX . sol . Modo . XXX . solid.
Bondi libe tenuit has tras . T.R.E.
Idē ten de . Co . II . hid una v min in *BOSIETA* . Tra . ē
IIII . car . In dn̄io . ē una . 7 II . serui . 7 VI . uilti cū . II . bord
hn̄t . III . car . Ibi . X . ac p̄ti . Silua . II . qz lg . 7 I . qz lat.
Valuit 7 ual . XL . sol . Stric tenuit de Wallef comite.
Fulcher ten de . Co . III . hid *IN MALESLEA HD.*
7 III . v tre in *WOLDGRAVE* Tra . ē . VII . car . In dn̄io st . II.
7 XIIII . uilti cū . IX . bord hn̄t . IIII . car . 7 IIII . sochi cū.
VIII . bord hn̄t . I . car 7 dim . Ibi . XII . ac p̄ti. 7 saca.
Valuit 7 ual . III . lib . Comitissa ht socā . Alsi tenuit cū soca

[in GRAVESEND Hundred]

35 Leofric holds [hide and 1 virgate of land, less the fifth part of ½ hide, in WELTON and THRUPP (Grounds). Land for 1 plough.
In lordship ½ plough, with
2 smallholders.
Value 8s.
Leofric also held it before 1066. The King has jurisdiction from it.

[in WITCHLEY Wapentake]

36 William holds 4 hides in GLASTON. Land for 8 ploughs.
In lordship 1½ ploughs; 2 slaves.
5 villagers and 3 Freemen with 2 smallholders have 5 ploughs.
Meadow, 10 acres.
The value was and is 40s.
Edward held it, with full jurisdiction.
To this manor belong 6 Freemen in LUFFENHAM, a manor of the King's, 1 in SEATON and 1 in THORPE (by Water), whose resources are noted above.

in CORBY Hundred

37 Lancelin holds 3 virgates of land and 1 bovate and the third part of 1 bovate in NEWTON. Land for 2 ploughs. In lordship 1.
8 villagers with 4 smallholders have another.
A mill at 7s 8d; woodland 1 furlong long and ½ furlong wide.
The value was 5s; now 16s.

38 Lancelin also holds 1½ hides and ½ virgate of land in OAKLEY.
Land for 5 ploughs. In lordship 1; 2 slaves.
19 villagers have 3 ploughs.
Meadow 4 furlongs long and 3 perches wide; woodland 1 league long and ½ league wide.
The value was 20s; now 30s.
Bondi held these lands freely before 1066.

[in HIGHAM Hundred]

39 he also holds 2 hides, less 1 virgate, in BOZEAT. Land for 4 ploughs.
In lordship 1; 2 slaves.
6 villagers with 2 smallholders have 3 ploughs.
Meadow, 10 acres; woodland 2 furlongs long and 1 furlong wide.
The value was and is 40s.
Sihtric held it from Earl Waltheof.

in MAWSLEY Hundred

40 Fulchere holds 3 hides and 3 virgates of land in WALGRAVE.
Land for 7 ploughs. In lordship 2.
14 villagers with 9 smallholders have 4 ploughs. 4 Freemen with 8 smallholders have 1½ ploughs.
Meadow, 12 acres.
The value was and is £3.
The Countess has the jurisdiction. Alfsi held it, with full jurisdiction.

228 d

Hugo ten̄ de . Co . II . hid̄ 7 unā v̄ træ in *SCALDESWELLE*.
Tra . ē . IIII . car̄ . Has hn̄t ibi . VII . sochi 7 IIII . bord̄.
Valuit 7 uat . XXI . sot 7 IIII . den̄.
Idē . H . ten̄ de . Co . I . hid̄ 7 unā v̄ træ in *HOHTONE* . Tra . ē
II . car̄ . Has hn̄t ibi . VI . sochi cū . IIII . bord̄.
Valuit 7 uat . XIII . sot 7 IIII . den̄.
Idē ten̄ de . Co . I . hid̄ 7 unā v̄ træ 7 dim̄ in *HOLECOTE*.
Tra . ē . II . car̄ . Has hn̄t ibi . V . sochi cū . III . bord̄ . Vat . XX.
Idē ten̄ unā v̄ træ in *MVLETONE* . Ibi . I . sochs solid̄.
ht̄ dim̄ car̄ . 7 redd̄ XXXIII . den̄.
Idē ten̄ de . Co . in *ASEBI* . II . hid̄ una v̄ min̄ . 7 p̄ tanto
se defend̄ . T.R.E. Tra . ē . V . car̄ . In dn̄io st̄ . II . 7 XII . uitti
cū . VI . bord̄ hn̄t . III . car̄ . Ibi molin̄ de . VI . sot . 7 VIII . den̄.
7 XII . ac̄ p̄ti . Silua . I . q̄z 7 XI . ptic̄ in lḡ . 7 in lat̄ . I . q̄z
VII . ptic̄ min̄ . Valuit . XX . sot . Modo . IIII . lib̄.
Huic m̄ ptin̄ in *GREDONE* una v̄ træ de soca . Ibi . IIII.
sochi hn̄t . I . car̄. *IN RODEWELLE HVND̄.*
Eustachī ten̄ de . Co . II . hid̄ 7 dim̄ . 7 tciā partē unī hidæ
in *RISETONE* . Tra . ē . V . car̄ . In dn̄io . ē . I . car̄ . 7 I . ancilla.

229 a

7 XIX . uitti cū . VIII . bord̄ hn̄t . IIII . car̄ . Ibi . ē . I . sochs.
7 molin̄ de . XXXII . den̄ . 7 IIII . ac̄ siluæ.
Valuit . X . sot . Modo . XL . sot. *IN ANDFERDESHO HD̄.*
Alan̄ ten̄ de . Co . I . hid̄ in *HERDEWICHE* . Tra . ē . II . car̄.
Ipse st̄ ibi cū . II . seruis . 7 III . uittis 7 I . bord̄ Valuit 7 uat
XX . solid̄ . Vlf tenuit cū saca 7 soca. *IN ORDINBARO HD̄.*
Idē ten̄ de . Co . I . hid̄ in *HARDEWICHE* . Tra . ē . II . car̄ . Ibi
VII . uitti cū . I . bord̄ hn̄t . III . car̄ . 7 VII . ac̄s p̄ti.

41 Hugh holds 2 hides and 1 virgate of land in SCALDWELL.
Land for 4 ploughs.
7 Freemen and 4 smallholders have them there.
The value was and is 21s 4d.

42 Hugh also holds 1 hide and 1 virgate of land in (Hanging) HOUGHTON.
Land for 2 ploughs.
6 Freemen with 4 smallholders have them there.
The value was and is 13s 4d.

43 he also holds 1 hide and 1½ virgates of land in HOLCOT.
Land for 2 ploughs.
5 Freemen with 3 smallholders have them there.
Value 20s.

[In SPELHOE Hundred]

44 He also holds 1 virgate of land in MOULTON.
1 Freeman has ½ plough; he pays 33d.

From the Countess
[in WYMERSLEY Hundred]

45 he also holds 2 hides, less 1 virgate, in (Castle) ASHBY. It answered for as much before 1066. Land for 5 ploughs. In lordship 2.
12 villagers with 6 smallholders have 3 ploughs.
A mill at 6s 8d; meadow, 12 acres; woodland 1 furlong and 11 perches in length and in width 1 furlong, less 7 perches.
The value was 20s; now £4.
To this manor belongs 1 virgate of land of the jurisdiction in GRENDON. 4 Freemen have 1 plough.

in ROTHWELL Hundred

6 Eustace holds 2½ hides and the third part of 1 hide in RUSHTON.
Land for 5 ploughs. In lordship 1 plough; 1 female slave.
19 villagers with 8 smallholders have 4 ploughs. 1 Freeman. 229 a
A mill at 32d; woodland, 4 acres.
The value was 10s; now 40s.

in HAMFORDSHOE Hundred

7 Alan holds 1 hide in HARDWICK. Land for 2 ploughs;
they are there, with 2 slaves and
3 villagers and 1 smallholder.
The value was and is 20s.
Ulf held it, with full jurisdiction.

in ORLINGBURY Hundred

8 he also holds 1 hide in HARDWICK. Land for 2 ploughs.
7 villagers with 1 smallholder have 3 ploughs and
meadow, 7 acres.

Valuit . xx . sol . Modo . xl . sol. *In Hocheslav hd.*

Walter⁹ ten de . Co . v . hid in *Lilleforde* . Tra . ē . xiiii . car̄ . In dn̄io sī . iii . 7 iiii . serui . 7 xx . uitti 7 xvi . bord hn̄t xii . car̄ . Ibi molin̄ de . xxiiii . sol . 7 l . ac p̄ti . Valuit 7 uat viii . lib . Turchil libe tenuit T.R.E.

Rohais ten de . Co . i . hid in *Sprotone* . Tra . ē . ii . car̄. In dn̄io . ē una . 7 i . uitts cū . viii . bord hn̄t . i . car̄ 7 dim. Ibi molin̄ de . lxiiii . den . Valuit . x . sol . Modo . xx . sol.

Corbelin⁹ ten de . Co . ii . hid in *Wilavestone*. Tra . ē . iii . car̄ 7 dim . In dn̄io . ē una . cū . i . seruo . 7 vi . uitti cū . i . bord hn̄t . ii . car 7 dim . Ibi molin̄ de . vi . sol 7 viii . den . 7 xii . ac p̄ti . Valuit . xvi . sol . Modo . xl . solid. Stric libe tenuit . Winemar de hanslepe calūniat.

Dodin⁹ ten de . Co . unā v tre in *Estone* . Tra . ē dim car. Ibi sī . ii . bord 7 i . ac p̄ti . Valuit . xii . den . Modo . iii . sol.

Gislebt⁹ ten de . Co . dimid v træ in *Wedlingeberie* . Tra est . i . bou . H tra ptin ad Dodintone . 7 ibi appciata . ē.

Winemar⁹ ten de . Co . unā v træ in *Bosiete* . Ibi sī . iiii . bord.

Idē ten de . Co . dimid hidā in *Dodintone*.

Tra . ē dim car . 7 tant ibi . ē.

Idē ten una v tre de soca in *Bragefelde* . Tra . ē dim car. Ibi sī . ii . bord cū . ii . bob⁹ arantes.

Idē ten de Soca *Gerdelai*. In *Hqhtone* . unā v træ. In *Prestone* . iii . v træ . 7 iii . acs p̄ti. In *Qvintone* . iii . v træ. 7 v . acs p̄ti . 7 In ead uilla dim hid. In *Witone* . i . hid.

The value was 20s; now 40s.

in HUXLOE Hundred

49 Walter holds 5 hides in LILFORD. Land for 14 ploughs.
In lordship 3; 4 slaves.
20 villagers and 16 smallholders have 12 ploughs.
A mill at 24s; meadow, 50 acres.
The value was and is £8.
Thorkell held it freely before 1066.

[in SPELHOE Hundred]

50 Rohais holds 1 hide in SPRATTON. Land for 2 ploughs. In lordship 1.
1 villager with 8 smallholders have 1½ ploughs.
A mill at 64d.
The value was 10s; now 20s.

[in HIGHAM Hundred]

51 Corbelin holds 2 hides in WOLLASTON. Land for 3½ ploughs.
In lordship 1, with 1 slave.
6 villagers with 1 smallholder have 2½ ploughs.
A mill at 6s 8d; meadow, 12 acres.
The value was 16s; now 40s.
Sihtric held it freely. Winemar of Hanslip claims it.

52 Dodin holds 1 virgate of land in EASTON (Maudit). Land for ½ plough.
2 smallholders.
Meadow, 1 acre.
The value was 12d; now 3s.

[in HAMFORDSHOE Hundred]

53 Gilbert holds ½ virgate of land in WELLINGBOROUGH. Land for 1 ox.
This land belongs to (Great) Doddington and it is assessed there.

[in HIGHAM Hundred]

54 Winemar holds 1 virgate of land in BOZEAT.
4 smallholders.

[in WYMERSLEY Hundred]

55 he also holds ½ hide in ?DENTON. Land for ½ plough;
as much there.

56 He also holds 1 virgate of land of the jurisdiction in
BRAFIELD (on the Green). Land for ½ plough.
2 smallholders who plough with 2 oxen.

57 a He also holds of the jurisdiction of YARDLEY (Hastings):-
b In HOUGHTON 1 virgate of land.
c In PRESTON (Deanery) 3 virgates of land and meadow, 3 acres.
d In QUINTON 3 virgates of land and meadow, 5 acres.
e In the same village ½ hide.
f In WOOTTON 1 hide.

In *HOHTONE* . unā v̄ træ . 7 v . acs p̄ti.

Int̄ om̄s . ē Tra . vi . car̄ . Ibi st̄ . v . sochi 7 ix . uitti 7 ii. bord . hn̄tes . iiii . car̄ . Tot̄ ualuit . xxx . sol . m̊ . liii . solid.

Norgiold ten̄ de . Co . iii . v̄ træ in *CVGENHO* . Tra . ē . i . car̄ 7 dimid . 7 tant . ē ibi cū . vi . sochis . 7 x . ac p̄ti.

Valuit . v . solid . Modo . x . solid.

Robt̄ ten̄ de . Co . iii . v̄ træ in *WIDETORP* . Tra . ē . i . car.

Hæc ibi . ē in dn̄io cū . iiii . uittis . 7 iiii . ac p̄ti.

Valuit . iiii . sol . Modo . x . solid.

Idē ten̄ de Comit̄ unā v̄ træ in *BVCHEDONE* . Tra . ē dim̄ car. quæ ibi . ē 7 ualet . iii . solid . Vlchet libe tenuit. *HVND.*

Ipsa comitissa ded S̄ Wandregisilo [IN BVCHEDONE] | c̄cessu *IN SPELEHOV* regis . iii . hid dim̄ v̄ min̄ . Tra . ē . vi . car̄ . In dn̄io st̄ . ii. car 7 dimid . 7 xiiii . uitti cū xii . bord hn̄t . iii . car̄ 7 dim. Ibi . x . ac p̄ti . Valuit . xx . sol . Modo . xl . sol . Duo taini libe tenuer̄. Ibi st̄ . ii . bord.

Girard ten̄ de . Co . dim̄ v̄ træ in *BVCHENHO* . 7 ual . iiii . solid.

Nigellus ten̄ de . Co . dimid v̄ tre de soca in *HOHTONE.*

Idē ten̄ in ead uilla . ii . hid de . co . 7 p tanto se desd.

Tra . ē . v . car̄ . In dn̄io . ē una . 7 viii . uitti cū . ii . bord hn̄t . ii . car̄ . Ibi molin̄ de . xiii . solid . 7 x . ac p̄ti . Silua . i . q̄z lḡ . 7 dim̄ q̄z lat̄ . Valuit . xl . sol . Modo . l . sol . Vlf tenuit.

g In HOUGHTON 1 virgate of land and meadow, 5 acres.

h Between them land for 6 ploughs.
5 Freemen, 9 villagers and 2 smallholders who have 4 ploughs.
The value of the whole was 30s; now 53s.

58 Norgiold holds from the Countess 3 virgates of land in COGENHOE.
Land for 1½ ploughs; as many there, with
6 Freemen.
Meadow, 10 acres.
The value was 5s; now 10s.

[In UPTON Hundred]

59 Robert holds from the Countess 3 virgates of land in ?WOTHORPE.
Land for 1 plough; it is there, in lordship, with
4 villagers.
Meadow, 4 acres.
The value was 4s; now 10s.

[In SPELHOE Hundred]

60 He also holds from the Countess 1 virgate of land in BOUGHTON.
Land for ½ plough, which is there.
Value 3s.
Ulfketel held it freely.

In SPELHOE Hundred

61 The Countess herself gave 3 hides, less ½ virgate, in BOUGHTON to St. Wandrille's with the King's assent. Land for 6 ploughs.
In lordship 2½ ploughs.
14 villagers with 12 smallholders have 3½ ploughs.
Meadow, 10 acres.
The value was 20s; now 40s.
Two thanes held it freely.

From the Countess

62 Gerard holds ½ virgate of land in BOUGHTON.
Value 4s.

[in WYMERSLEY Hundred]

63 Nigel holds ½ virgate of land of the jurisdiction in HOUGHTON.
2 smallholders.

64 he also holds 2 hides in the same village. It answers for as much.
Land for 5 ploughs. In lordship 1.
8 villagers with 2 smallholders have 2 ploughs.
A mill at 13s; meadow, 10 acres; woodland 1 furlong long and ½ furlong wide.
The value was 40s; now 50s.
Ulf held it.

Gisleb̃t ten de Comitissa.i.hid̃ 7 iii.v̄ træ in *PIDENTONE*.
Tra.ē.iiii.car.In dñio.ē una.cū.i.seruo.7 iiii.uitti cū.v.bord̃
7 pb̃ro hñt.ii.car 7 dimid̃.Ibi.xx.ac p̃ti.Silua.iiii.q̃z
lḡ.7 ii.q̃z lat.Valuit.xx.sot.Modo.xl.solid̃.
Duo hões Burredi tenuer̃.7 quo uolebant ire poterant.
Goisfrid eps̃ calūniat.7 Winemar de Anslepe.
Witts peurel ten de.co.i.hid̃ 7 q̃ntā partē.i.hidæ in *PIRIE*.
Tra.ē.iii.car.In dñio.ē una.7 ii.serui.7 vi.uitti cū.iii.
bord̃ hñt.ii.car.Ibi.v.ac p̃ti.Silua.iiii.q̃rent lḡ.
7 ii.q̃z lat.Valuit 7 uat.xxx.sot.Biscop libe tenuit.

.LVII. TERRA GISLEBERTI. *IN SPELEHOV HD̃.*

GISLEBERT cocus ten de rege.iiii.hid̃ in *BELLINGE*.Tra.ē.viii.
car.In dñio st̃.ii.car.7 v.serui 7 i.ancilla.7 x.uitti cū.vii.
bord̃ hñt.vi.car.Ibi molin̄ de.xx.solid̃.7 xxviii.ac
p̃ti.Valuit.xl.sot.Modo.c.solid̃.Thor libe tenuit T.R.E.
Idē ten.ii.hid̃ in *WATFORD*.Tra.ē *IN GISLEBVRG HD̃ 7 DIM̃.*
iiii.car.In dñio st̃.ii.cū.i.seruo 7 i.ancilla.7 xx.uitti
cū.v.bord̃ hñt.ii.car.Ibi molin̄ de.xii.den.7 vi.ac p̃ti.
Valuit.x.sot.Modo.xl.sot.Thor libe tenuit.Id̃.G.ten.ii.partes uni v̄ træ in HOLEWELLE. Tra.iii.bou̅. Vat xii.den.
Idē ten unā v̄ træ in *RAVENESTORP*.Tra.ē dim car.Hanc
hñt.i.uitts 7 i.bord̃.Valuit.iii.sot.Modo.v.sot.Normann
tenuit.

65 Gilbert holds 1 hide and 3 virgates of land in PIDDINGTON. 229 b
Land for 4 ploughs. In lordship 1, with 1 slave.
4 villagers with 5 smallholders and a priest have 2½ ploughs.
Meadow, 20 acres; woodland 4 furlongs long and 2 furlongs wide.
The value was 20s; now 40s.
Two men of Burgred's held it; they could go where they wished.
Bishop Geoffrey claims it, and Winemar of Hanslip too.

[in CLEYLEY Hundred]
66 William Peverel holds 1 hide and the fifth part of 1 hide in POTTERSPURY. Land for 3 ploughs. In lordship 1; 2 slaves.
6 villagers with 3 smallholders have 2 ploughs.
Meadow, 5 acres; woodland 4 furlongs long and 2 furlongs wide.
The value was and is 30s.
Bishop held it freely.

57 LAND OF GILBERT [COOK]

In SPELHOE Hundred
1 Gilbert Cook holds 4 hides from the King in BILLING. Land for 8 ploughs. In lordship 2 ploughs; 5 male slaves, 1 female.
10 villagers with 7 smallholders have 6 ploughs.
A mill at 20s; meadow, 28 acres.
The value was 40s; now 100s.
Thor held it freely before 1066.

In GUILSBOROUGH Hundred and a half
2 He also holds 2 hides in WATFORD. Land for 4 ploughs.
In lordship 2, with 1 male and 1 female slave.
20 villagers with 5 smallholders have 2 ploughs.
A mill at 12d; meadow, 6 acres.
The value was 10s; now 40s.
Thor held it freely.

3 Gilbert also holds 2 parts of 1 virgate of land in HOLLOWELL.
Land for 3 oxen.
Value 12d.

[In NOBOTTLE Hundred]
4 He also holds 1 virgate of land in RAVENSTHORPE.
Land for ½ plough.
1 villager and 1 smallholder have it.
The value was 3s; now 5s.
Norman held it.

.LVIII. TERRA DAVID.

DAVID teñ de rege.III.v̄ træ in *CASTRETONE*. Tra.ē.I.car 7 dimid. In dñio tam̄.ē una car̄.7 VI.uitti cū pbro 7 III.bord hnt.II.car̄. Ibi.II.serui.7 molin̄ de.XII.sot.7 V.ac̄ pti. Valet.XL.sot. Osgot tenuit cū saca 7 soca. *IN FOXLEV HD.*

Idē teñ.I.hid 7 IIII.partes dim hidæ in *BRADENE*. Tra.ē.III. car 7 dim. In dñio.ē una car̄.cū.I.uitto 7 I.bord.7 I.ac̄ pti. Valuit.V.sot. Modo.X.solid. Biscop libe tenuit T.R.E.

.LIX. TERRA RICARDI *IN OPTONE HVND.*

RICARD⁹ teñ de rege.II.hid in *STABINTONE*. Tra.ē.II.car. In dñio.ē una.7 III.uitti cū.V.bord hnt aliā.7 redd.V.sot. Ibi molin̄ de.VIII.sot.7 XII.ac̄ pti. Silua.L.pticas lḡ.7 XV. ptic lat. Valuit.II.sot. Modo.XX.sot. *IN HOCHESLAV HD.*

Idē teñ.III.v̄ træ in *BENEFELD*. Tra.ē.II.car̄. In dñio.ē una. 7 V.uitti hnt aliā. Ibi.V.ac̄ pti. Silua.I.leu lḡ.7 dim leu lat. Valuit.II.sot. Modo.X.solid. *IN SPELEHOV HD.*

Idē teñ.IIII.hid in *ABINTONE*. Tra.ē.VIII.car. In dñio.ē una.cū.I. seruo.7 XII.uitti cū.V.bord hnt.II.car̄. Ibi molin̄ de.XX.solid. 7 XX.ac̄ pti. Valuit.XL.sot. Modo.IIII.lib. *IN CORBEI HD.*

Idē teñ unā v̄ træ in *CHERCHEBERIE*. Tra.ē.II.car. Ipsa.ē in dñio 7 V.uitti cū.I.bord hnt aliā. Ibi.III.ac̄ pti. Silua.IIII. q̄rent lḡ.7 una q̄z 7 dim lat. Valuit.XII.den. Modo.VI.sot.

8 LAND OF DAVID

[In WITCHLEY Wapentake]

1 David holds 3 virgates of land from the King in CASTERTON.
Land for 1½ ploughs. In lordship, however, 1 plough.
6 villagers with a priest and 3 smallholders have 2 ploughs.
2 slaves; a mill at 12s; meadow, 5 acres.
Value 40s.
Osgot held it, with full jurisdiction.

In FOXLEY Hundred

2 He also holds 1 hide and 4 parts of ½ hide in BRADDEN.
Land for 3½ ploughs. In lordship 1 plough, with
1 villager and 1 smallholder.
Meadow, 1 acre.
The value was 5s; now 10s.
Bishop held it freely before 1066.

9 LAND OF RICHARD

In UPTON Hundred

1 Richard holds 2 hides from the King in STIBBINGTON.
Land for 2 ploughs. In lordship 1.
3 villagers with 5 smallholders have another; they pay 5s.
A mill at 8s; meadow, 12 acres; woodland 50 perches long and 15 perches wide.
The value was 2s; now 20s.

In HUXLOE Hundred

2 He also holds 3 virgates of land in BENEFIELD. Land for 2 ploughs.
In lordship 1.
5 villagers have another.
Meadow, 5 acres; woodland 1 league long and ½ league wide.
The value was 2s; now 10s.

In SPELHOE Hundred

3 He also holds 4 hides in ABINGTON. Land for 8 ploughs.
In lordship 1, with 1 slave.
12 villagers with 5 smallholders have 2 ploughs.
A mill at 20s; meadow, 20 acres.
The value was 40s; now £4.

In CORBY Hundred

4 He also holds 1 virgate of land in KIRBY. Land for 2 ploughs.
It is in lordship.
5 villagers with 1 smallholder have another.
Meadow, 3 acres; woodland 4 furlongs long and 1½ furlongs wide.
The value was 12d; now 6s.

.LX. TERRA WILLELMI. *IN ORDIBARO HVND.*

WILLELM' ten de rege.II.hid in *PITESLEA*.Tra.e.IIII.car. In dnio st.III.car.7 v.serui.7 VII.uitti cu.I.bord hnt.I.car. Ibi.VI.ac pti.Silua.III.qrent in lg 7 lat.Valuit.XI.solid. Val Modo.XL.solid.Has tras Ricardi 7 Willi tenuit Aluuin uenator T.R.E.

Ide.W.ten *LASTONE*.Ibi.e.I.hida 7 dim.Tra.e.IIII.car.In dnio e una.7 XII.uitti cu.I.socho hnt.II.car.Valuit.x.sol.M.xxx.solid. Turulf libe tenuit.T.R.E.

OLAF ten de rege una v trae in *WELEDONE*.Soca.e in *CORBEI* regis.Tra.e dimid car.H ibi.e cu.I.bord.Valuit.II.sol.m.III.sol.

DODIN ten de rege dim hid in *CODESBROC*.Tra.e.I.car.Ibi.e un uitts cu.I.seruo.Valuit.XII.den.Modo.II.solid. *IN STOTFALD HD.*

OSLAC ten de rege.III.v trae 7 tcia parte uni v in *FERENDONE*. Tra.e.I.car.Tam st ibi.II.car.cu.IIII.uittis 7 v.bord.Ibi molin de.XII.denar.Valuit 7 ual.XVI.solid.

0 LAND OF WILLIAM [AND OTHER THANES]

In ORLINGBURY Hundred

1 William holds 2 hides from the King in PYTCHLEY.
Land for 4 ploughs. In lordship 3 ploughs; 5 slaves.
7 villagers with 1 smallholder have 1 plough.
Meadow, 6 acres; woodland 3 furlongs in length and width.
The value was 11s; value now 40s.
Alwin Hunter held these lands of Richard and William before 1066.

[In CORBY Hundred]

2 William also holds LAXTON. 1½ hides. Land for 4 ploughs.
In lordship 1.
12 villagers with 1 Freeman have 2 ploughs.
The value was 10s; now 30s.
Thorwulf held it freely before 1066.

3 Olaf holds 1 virgate of land from the King in WELDON. The jurisdiction is in Corby, (a manor) of the King's. Land for ½ plough;
it is there, with
1 smallholder.
The value was 2s; now 3s.

[In GUILSBOROUGH Hundred and a half]

4 Dodin holds ½ hide from the King in COTTESBROOKE. Land for 1 plough.
1 villager with 1 slave.
The value was 12d; now 2s.

In STOTFOLD Hundred

5 Oslac holds 3 virgates of land and the third part of 1 virgate from the King in (East) FARNDON. Land for 1 plough.
2 ploughs there, however, with
4 villagers and 5 smallholders.
A mill at 12d.
The value was and is 16s.

229 b

NORTHAMPTONSHIRE HOLDINGS
ENTERED ELSEWHERE IN THE SURVEY

The Latin text of these entries is given in the county volumes concerned.

In BEDFORDSHIRE

3 **LAND OF THE BISHOP OF COUTANCES** 209 d

EB 9 In NEWTON (Bromswold) William, his Steward, holds 1 virgate from 210 a
1 the Bishop.
The value is and was 12d; before 1066, 16d.
Alwin, Burgred's man, held this land; he could not grant or sell without his permission.

EB 17 In RUSHDEN Alfwold holds ½ hide from the Bishop. Land for 6 210 b
2 oxen; ½ plough there.
Meadow for 6 oxen.
Value 5s; as much when acquired; before 1066, 10s.
Aelfric, Burgred's man, held this land; he could sell to whom he would.

7 **LAND OF ST. PETER'S OF PETERBOROUGH** 210 c

In STODDEN Hundred
EB 1 The Abbot of Peterborough holds STANWICK. It answers for 2½ hides.
3 Land for 2½ ploughs; 1 plough there; another 1½ possible.
2 villagers and 2 smallholders.
Meadow for 2 ploughs.
Value 30s; when acquired 50s; before 1066, 40s.
St. Peter's of Peterborough held this manor before 1066.

22 **LAND OF WILLIAM PEVEREL** 212 c

In WILLEY Hundred
EB 2 In RUSHDEN Malet holds 1 virgate of land from William Peverel. Land for
4 2 oxen; they are there. 212 d
The value is and was 16d; before 1066, 2s.
Saemer the priest, Countess Gytha's man, held this land; he could grant to whom he would.

In HUNTINGDONSHIRE

3 **LAND OF THE BISHOP OF COUTANCES** 204 a

[LEIGHTONSTONE Hundred]
EH 1 M. In HARGRAVE Saemer had 1 virgate of land taxable. Land for 2 oxen.
1 Jurisdiction in Leightonstone. Now he still holds it himself from the
Bishop of Coutances. He ploughs there with 2 oxen and has 2 acres of meadow.
Value before 1066, 5s; now the same.

5 **LAND OF CROWLAND ABBEY** 204 a

EH [LEIGHTONSTONE Hundred]
2 2 In THURNING 1½ hides of land taxable. Land for 1½ ploughs. Jurisdiction

in the King's manor of Alconbury. Eustace now holds from the Abbot of Crowland. He has 1 plough;
1 villager with ½ plough.
Meadow, 6 acres.
Value before 1066 and now 20s.

6 LAND OF ST. BENEDICT'S OF RAMSEY 204 b

NORMANCROSS Hundred........

EH 3 14 M. The Abbot of Ramsey had in LUTTON 2½ hides taxable. Land for 2 ploughs. Now in lordship ½ plough. 204 c
Edric holds from the Abbot.
Meadow, 12 acres.
Value before 1066, 40s; now 20s.

19 LAND OF EUSTACE THE SHERIFF 206 a

KIMBOLTON Hundred........

EH 4 13 M. In HARGRAVE Langfer had 1 virgate of land taxable. Land for 2 oxen. 206 b
Now Herbert, Eustace's man, ploughs it with ½ plough. He has
1 villager.
Meadow, 6 acres.
Value before 1066 and now 5s.
Tovi claims this land from Eustace, as unjustly taken from him.

EH 5 14 M. There also Young Alwin had 1 hide of land. Land for 1½ ploughs.
Now in lordship 1 plough.
Meadow, 7 acres; underwood, 2 acres.
Value before 1066 and now 20s.
Herbert and Edmer hold from Eustace.

EH 6 18 S. In THURNING 5 hides taxable. Land for 5 ploughs. Jurisdiction in Alconbury.
Now in lordship 1½ ploughs.
16 villagers and 1 smallholder have 2½ ploughs.
Meadow, 24 acres.
Value before 1066 and now 60s.
Alfred and Jocelyn hold from Eustace. Robert the Bursar claims 1 virgate and 1 hide.

EH 7 19 S. In LUDDINGTON (in the Brook) 2½ hides taxable. Land for 3 ploughs.
Jurisdiction in the King's manor of Alconbury. Now in lordship 1 plough;
1 villager and 6 smallholders with 1 plough.
Meadow, 4 acres.
Value before 1066, 60s; now 40s.
Ingelrann and Herlwin hold from Eustace.

In LEICESTERSHIRE

C The City of LEICESTER........ 230 a

ELe 1 12 In this Borough Hugh (of Grandmesnil) has 2 churches and 2 houses, and 4 unoccupied houses. Hugh of Gouville holds 5 houses from Hugh himself with full jurisdiction. They are from exchange with Watford.

E

23 LAND OF GUY OF RAIMBEAUCOURT 235 a

In GUTHLAXTON Wapentake

ELe 2 2 Abbot Benedict holds 9 carucates of land in 'STORMSWORTH' from Guy.
Land for 6 ploughs.
12 Freemen have 2 ploughs.
This land belongs to Stanford in Northamptonshire. 235 b
The value was 30s; now 60s.
Leofric held it before 1066.

3 The Abbot also holds 1 carucate of land in MISTERTON from Guy.
Land for 1½ ploughs. Waste.
Value however, 2s.

In GARTREE Wapentake

4 The Abbot also holds 2 carucates and 2 bovates of land in (Husbands) BOSWORTH from Guy. Land for 1 plough. However, 1 in lordship.
4 villagers with 3 smallholders have 1 plough.
Meadow, 8 acres.
The value was 6s; now 20s.
Abbot Benedict bought these lands from Guy.

5 Robert holds 2½ carucates of land from Guy in KILWORTH. Land for 1½ ploughs.
7 Freemen with 4 smallholders have 2 ploughs.
Meadow, 6 acres.
The value was 5s; now 10s.

6 He also holds 11½ carucates of land in (Husbands) BOSWORTH from Guy.
Land for 12 ploughs.
20 Freemen with 5 smallholders have 6 ploughs.
Meadow, 20 acres.
The value was 30s; now 20s.

These three lands belong to Stanford. Leofric held them.

In LINCOLNSHIRE

S STAMFORD, the King's Borough 336 d

ELc 1 1 gave tax before 1066 for 12½ Hundreds; for the army, in ship service, and in Danegeld. There were and are six wards, five in Lincolnshire, the sixth in Northamptonshire; it is across the bridge; however, it paid all customary dues with the others, except tribute and tolls, which the Abbot of Peterborough had and has.

WITCHLEY WAPENTAKE HOLDINGS ENTERED ELSEWHERE IN THE SURVEY

56 LAND OF COUNTESS JUDITH 366 d

[In NESS Wapentake]

ELc 2 4 In UFFINGTON Abbot Leofric of Peterborough had 60 acres of land without tax. Countess Judith has this land. She has no livestock on it, but cultivates it in the manor of Belmesthorpe.
Value 10s.

CK CLAIMS IN KESTEVEN 376 d

ELc 3 2 The Wapentake states that before 1066 (the Abbot of) Peterborough had 60 acres which Countess Judith has (in UFFINGTON) and cultivates with the Belmesthorpe ploughs. Of these 60 acres of land, and of 48 acres of meadow, the *Warnode* lies in (the lands of) Alfred of Lincoln's Uffington, but has been withheld by force.

ELc 4 10 Archbishop Aldred acquired LAVINGTON and SKILLINGTON, with the outlier, HARDWICK, from Ulf, Topi's son, with his own money, which he gave him in the sight of the Wapentake; and later they saw the King's seal, through which he was repossessed of these lands, because Ilbold had dispossessed him of them.

Notes on the Text and Translation

NOTES

ABBREVIATIONS used in the notes. ASC...*The Anglo-Saxon Chronicle* (translated G.N. Garmonsway) London 1960. Baker...G. Baker *History and Antiquities of the County of Northampton.* 2 vols. 1822-41. Baring...F.H. Baring *The Hidation of Northamptonshire in 1086* and *The pre-Domesday Hidation of Northamptonshire* in EHR (1902) pp.76-83; 470-9. Bridges...J. Bridges (ed. Whalley) *History and Antiquities of Northamptonshire* 2 vols. 1791. County Hidage...Abstracted in Maitland pp.525-7. CP...*Chronicon Petroburgense* (ed. Thomas Stapleton) London 1849. Dauzat...A. Dauzat *Dictionnaire Etymologique des noms de famille et prénoms de France,* revised edition by Marie-Thérèse Morlet, Larousse, Paris 1951. DB...Domesday Book. DEPN...E. Ekwall *The Concise Oxford Dictionary of English Placenames* 4th Edition, Oxford 1960. DG...H.C. Darby and G.R. Versey *Domesday Gazetteer* Cambridge 1975. DGM...H.C. Darby and I.B. Terrett *The Domesday Geography of Midland England* Cambridge, 2nd Edition, 1971. EcHR...Economic History Review. EHR... English Historical Review. Ellis...H. Ellis *General Introduction to Domesday Book* folio edition DB 4, i-cvii; quarto edition 1833 (reprint 1971). EPNS...English Place-Name Society Survey vol. x (1933) ed. J.E.B. Gover, A. Mawer and F.M. Stenton. FA...*Inquisitions and Assessments relating to Feudal Aids with other analogous Documents preserved in the Public Records Office AD 1284-1431* London 1899-1920 6 volumes. FE...J.H. Round *Feudal England* London 1895. Fees...*Book of Fees (Testa de Nevill)* London 1920-31 3 vols. Finberg...H.P.R. Finberg *Gloucestershire Studies* Leicester 1957. Forssner...T. Forssner *Continental-Germanic Personal Names in England in Old and Middle English Times* Uppsala 1916. Geld Roll...in A.J. Robertson *Anglo-Saxon Charters* (see below). Hart...C. Hart *The Hidation of Northamptonshire* Leicester 1970 (Department of English Local History Occasional Papers Second Series No. 3). LSR...R.E. Glasscock (ed.) *The Lay Subsidy of 1334* London 1975. Maitland...F.W. Maitland *Domesday Book and Beyond* Cambridge 1897. Mon. Ang...W. Dugdale *Monasticon Anglicanum* London 1846 6 vols. MS...Manuscript. OE...Old English. OEB...G. Tengvik *Old English Bynames* Uppsala 1938 (Nomina Germanica 4). OFr...Old French. OG...Old German. OS...Ordnance Survey. First Edition maps of Northamptonshire (early 19th Century) reprinted Newton Abbot 1970, sheets 43-44, 52-53, 61-62. PNDB...O.von Feilitzen *The Pre-Conquest Personal Names of Domesday Book* Uppsala 1937 (Nomina Germanica 3). RH...*Rotuli Hundredorum* Record Commission 1812-18 2 vols. Robertson...A.J. Robertson *Anglo-Saxon Charters* Cambridge 1939 pp.230-7; 481-4. (2nd Edition 1956). RMLWL...R.E. Latham *Revised Medieval Latin Wordlist* London 1965. Survey...12th Century Survey of Northamptonshire in VCH Northants.i pp.357-389. VCH...Victoria County History, Northamptonshire vol i 1902 (Introduction and translation by J.H. Round).

The editors are very grateful to Mr. J.D. Foy for reading the typescript and proofs and to Mr. P.I.King, Chief Archivist of Northamptonshire,for help with the County boundary.

The Manuscript is written on leaves, or folios, of parchment (sheepskin) measuring about 15 by 11 ins. (38 by 28 cm.), on both sides. On each side, or page, are two columns, making four to each folio. The folios were numbered in the 17th century, and the four columns of each are here lettered a,b,c,d. The Manuscript emphasises words and usually distinguishes chapters and sections by the use of red ink. Underlining here indicates deletion.

The Northamptonshire folios are less carefully compiled than those for some other counties. Chapters 15 and 16 in the list of landholders are in reverse order in the text which also misnumbers Chapter 23 (as 33) and 31-38 (as 30-37), thus giving two chapters numbered 30. A third Chapter 30 is found after the misnumbered 33 and is really Chapter 35. Chapter 6 is divided in the text between lands of Peterborough Abbey and lands of the Church's men, but the second heading is not in the landholders list. The last two entries of Chapter 19 appear at the foot of columns 224 a and b, across both, and Chapters 23 and 22 are found transposed on columns 224 c,d. Moreover Chapter 24 is written at the foot of 224c thus breaking into Chapter 23.

Land belonging to nearby counties, but remote from the Northants. border is found in Chapter 16, and at the ends of Chapters 4,19,23,36 and 46. In the case of Lapley (16,1) the correct Staffs. Hundred heading is included. Similar displacements are found in other DB counties, but the scale of the Northants. errors suggests a particularly careless sorting of the returns for individual fiefs,which probably spanned more than one county.

Marginal additions are found in columns 220b (Roade 2,9), 225a (Titchmarsh 25,2) and 229b (Hollowell 57,4); and cramped, possibly post-scriptural, entries are found at the foot of columns 220b (Ch.3), 222c (West Haddon 12,4), 223c (Creaton 18,53) and 227c (Crick 47,2). The term Wapentake is sometimes used for Hundred, and vice versa; Guilsborough is sometimes termed a Hundred, sometimes a Hundred and a half.

Hundred heads are entered only sporadically in the text and this causes difficulty in identifying places in a County where *Torp* can represent seven different places, *Stoche* four and *Estone* three. Some of the spellings are odd: *Mermeston* for Armston, *Arniworde* and *Narninworde* for Arthingworth, *Bellica* and *Belinge* for Billing, *Bracstone* for Draughton and *Dotone* for Clopton.

Fortunately these deficiencies can in part be made good by near-contemporary documents. A 'Geld Roll', probably dating from the early years of the Conqueror's reign and perhaps intended to explain the apparently low yield of tax from the County, survives in a MS (no.60) belonging to the Society of Antiquaries *(Certificatio Hundredorum in Comitatu Northampt'* folio 47 f.) and has been discussed by Round (FE pp. 147-156; VCH Introduction; Hart pp. 16-21) and published by Robertson (pp. 230-7;481-4). It lists hides held, Hundred by Hundred, but without placenames, though several holdings can be identified by comparison with DB.

More detailed is the 'Northamptonshire Survey' (British Library Cotton MS Vespasian E xxii folio 94 f.), a composite document dating from the reigns of Henry I and II, discussed by Round (FE pp. 215-224; VCH pp. 357-364) and transcribed in full by him in VCH pp. 365-389. Hundred by Hundred it lists landowners and the hidage of their holdings, in such detail that most DB holdings can be found there, often in the hands of the sons of the DB 1086 holder. It is cited below as the 'Survey' to support identifications. It should be noted that the term 'great virgate' represents the Domesday virgate, a quarter of a hide, while 'small virgate' refers to a tenth of a hide.

The descent of manors and the evolution of the forms of the DB placenames are outside the scope of this edition, but enough evidence is given in the notes below to identify places of the same or difficult names where there might otherwise be doubt. Northants. contains many places of the same basic name, now distinguished by East and West, St Mary and St Peter. Only Little Weldon (23,1) is so distinguished in the text, the separate existence of other adjacent villages such as Great and Little Billing being only evidenced later. No attempt is made to distinguish such places in the text and index, and only the larger is mapped, but the notes below discuss some of the later evidence. The only places with distinguishing names that are included in the text (e.g. East and West Haddon) are those that are in different areas of the County.

The text sometimes uses *alius* or *alter* to distinguish holdings, as at Addington (4,22), Harrowden (4,6) and Heyford (18,8), where separate villages are later found. But 'another' Courteenhall is also found, where there is no later evidence for two villages, and the evidence of other counties, e.g. Seaborough in Somerset (3,1) and Thistleton in Rutland (ELc 8), suggests that these terms refer often to different holdings in a single place rather than to different places.

The shire emerged from a part English, part Danish area in the late 9th Century. Watling Street had marked the North-East boundary of English territory from the time of Alfred's peace with Guthrum until the surrender of the Danish army, which was based on Northampton and stretched as far north as the Welland, to Edward the Elder about 918 (ASC Parker Chronicle years 920-1). The County was probably not formally organised around the town of Northampton until early in the eleventh century and it is likely that the County Hidage records the earliest organisation of the County (see Hart pp. 12-14; Finberg pp. 17-45; Stenton in EPNS Northants. p. xviii on.).

A notable feature of the Northants. Inquest is the small number of hides in the DB shire compared with earlier surveys and the relation of hides to ploughlands and ploughlands to ploughs. The hide is both a term of areal measurement and a term of tax assessment. In some counties, the two are identical, but in Northants. the tax liability of a hide was considerably reduced. The 'County Hidage' allots 3200 hides to Northants.; the 'Geld Roll' implies the existence of 3200, but accounts for 2663½, although at the time of DB and in the Pipe Roll of 1130, the shire contained 1244 and 1192¾ hides respectively. Cambridgeshire is similarly reduced. This successive reduction in hidage implies that many lands held by the King were not only not taxed, but not even hidated; it also implies a reduced assessment of the County as a whole, probably as a result of the devastation of the County by Morcar's army in 1065 (ASC). The 'Geld Roll' records 900 hides, about a third of the County, as waste. Between 1066 and 1086 most estates show an increase in values, but these are especially sharp in the areas through which Morcar and his supporters may be presumed to have passed on their way to Northampton. Even in 1086, however, the County contained much waste, some with a nominal value. This reduction in assessment was unequal and progressive: in the 'Geld Roll', while in the South and East of the County 15 Hundreds returned 100 hides each, in the centre and North, two Hundreds had been cut to 90 hides, six to 80. In the North and East, reductions were greater: a double Hundred cut to 108½ hides, four Hundreds to 62, one to 60, one to 47 and one to 40. In Domesday however, each of the Hundreds has been evenly reduced to about 40 hides apiece. (See Hart, and John Morris in DB Sussex Appendix).

Hides are fewer than ploughlands in the County, in some areas on a clear ratio of 2:5. The ploughlands themselves show traces of a decimal or a duodecimal system of assessment, depending whether they belong to the 'English' or the 'Danish' areas of the County. The ploughlands probably represent an earlier assessment of the County prior to the reduced hidation and may have been retained in the text of DB because obligations other than tax (such as roads, bridges, fortification) were based on them.(See Round in VCH p. 263, Baring and Hart).

Land in Northants. is predominately measured in hides and virgates, thus contrasting with the adjacent counties of Lincs. and Leics. where the 'Danish' carucate and bovate is the norm. Carucates are found sporadically in Northants, and bovates are mixed with hides and virgates mainly in the North and East of the County. A feature of Northants. measurements is the number of small divisions of the hide, such as the third part of half a hide, and (at 56,5) 3 parts of 2 parts of 1 hide.

Detailed changes in the County boundary are discussed at the end of the notes. The major difference in the 1086 county, however, was the inclusion of the Southern third of Rutland, Witchley Wapentake, in Northants. The remaining two Rutland wapentakes Alstoe and Martinsley, had a quasi-independent existence in 1086 as 'Roteland', attached to Notts. 'for the collection of the King's tax'. Rutland is given a separate section for its landholders on the Notts. landholders page (280d) and a separate schedule at the end of Notts. (folios 293c-294a). Witchley was clearly an integral part of Northants. in 1086: not only are entries for it scattered through the Northants. text like those of any other Hundred, but it is also measured mainly in hides and virgates, like Northants. itself, the only part of England north of the Welland to be so measured. East and West *Hwicceslea* are found as part of the County in the 'Geld Roll', but by the time of the 'Survey' Witchley was not included in Northants. The marginal *Rotel* entered in the MS against some Witchley entries is in a late 13th century hand, by which time the modern Rutland had been formed.

The pioneer works on the Northants. Domesday are those of Bridges and Baker, but the masterly VCH of Round (translation based on that of Stuart Moore) is the fundamental work, requiring only a few adjustments to identifications. The EPNS volume of 1933 put the names on a sounder base, and the whole county has recently been indexed and mapped in the Domesday Gazetteer. There is a useful bibliography in DGM pp. 419-20.

NORTHAMPTONSHIRE. *NORTHANT(ONE)SCIRE* in red across both columns on folios 219ab to 229ab. Folio 229cd was originally blank, but now contains part of an Edward I Inquisition in a later hand.

References to other DB counties are to the Chapter and Sections of the editions in this series.

B Persons who are major landholders are discussed below at the head of their own chapter.

B1 60 BURGESSES... AS MANY RESIDENCES. The detail amounts to 61.
IN THE NEW BOROUGH. Possibly a new quarter to replace buildings devastated by Morcar's army in 1065. Nottingham similarly consisted of an old and new Borough in 1086 (DB Notts B3; see DGM p. 415.)

B2 29s 4d. Old English currency lasted for a thousand years until 1971. The pound contained 20 shillings, each of 12 pence, abbreviated £(ibrae) s(olidi) and d(enarii). DB often expresses sums above a shilling in pence (e.g. 32d instead of 2s 8d) and above a pound in shillings, as here.

B8 ABBOT OF SELBY. Benedict of Auxerre, founder of the Abbey, see 41,3 note. Resigned and retired to Rochester in 1096/7.

B17 WILLIAM THE ARTIFICER. *Inganie* from OFr suggests both 'engineer' and 'ingenious', 'crafty', 'tricky'. See Ch. 60, also DB Hunts. 19,15 note; Bucks. ch. 42 note.

B30 ANSFRID OF VAUBADON. Near Bayeux, in Calvados, OEB 116.

B31 4d. *ii. den* , with superscript *ii* correcting the figure to *iiii*.

B36 THREE NIGHTS' REVENUE. Originally the amount of food needed to support the King and his household for three nights, though by the 11th century these food rents were generally commuted. See R.L. Poole, *The Exchequer in the 12th Century*, p. 29.
As £100 was the average 1086 payment for one night's revenue, the £30 here may be a mistake for £300, *xxx* and *ccc* being often similar in 11th century hands.
WHITE POUNDS. Or Blanched or Dealbated, *albas, candidas,* or *blancas* in DB. A sample of coin was melted as a test for the presence of alloy or baser metal. Money could also be said to be blanched when, without a test by fire, a standard deduction was made to allow for clipping or alloying. See *Dialogus de Scaccario* (ed. C. Johnson) 1950, p. 125,and next note.
AT 20 (PENCE) TO THE *ORA*. An *ora* was literally an ounce, a unit of currency still in use in Scandinavia. It was reckoned at either 16d. or 20d. 16d. was normal, the 20d payment being regarded as the equivalent of 16d in blanched or assayed coin. See S. Harvey in EcHR (2nd Series) xx (1967) pp. 221 ff.
QUEEN EDITH'S MANOR. She was wife of King Edward (the Confessor), and daughter of Earl Godwin and died in 1076. Her manor was Finedon 1,32.

B37 THE SHERIFF. William of Keynes whose holdings in the County are listed in Ch.34.

L10 THORNEY ABBEY. *Torniyg* in the MS is reproduced as *Tornyg* by Farley.

L15-16 The order does not correspond to the text, where the chapters are reversed. The List here is more correct, placing Church holdings before those of individuals as in other counties. Indices follow the order of the text.

1,1 7 HIDES. The Hide is a unit of land measurement, either of productivity, of extent or of tax liability, and contained four virgates. Administrators attempted to standardize the hide at 120 acres but incomplete revision and special local reductions left hides of widely differing extents in different areas. See introduction to the Notes and J. Morris in DB Sussex Appendix.

12 FREEMEN. See Technical Terms and Maitland pp. 66-79.

24 VILLAGERS. *vill'i* in the MS is incorrectly reproduced by Farley. The MS is rubbed here.

1,2b 1 BOVATE. A measure of land generally regarded as an eighth of a carucate.

4 ACRES. *ii āc* with superscript *ii* to correct to *iiii.*

1,2g 1 FURLONG. A Furlong is 220 yards or an eighth of a mile.

SPINNEY. *Spinetū vi q'* ... in the MS. Farley adds 7 in error.

1,3 LUFFENHAM AND 'SCULTHORP'. Sculthorp' lay about a quarter of a mile to the south-west of North Luffenham and is included with the latter in LSR p. 247. The Luffenham of 1,2f may thus represent the later South Luffenham.

HUGH OF PORT. From Port-en Bessin near Bayeux in Normandy, OEB 108. Sheriff of Hampshire, with Basing as head of his fief. Also Sherriff of Notts. and Derbys.; DB Notts. B3 note.

1,4 EARL MORCAR. The Northumbrians deposed Tosti their earl in 1065 and chose Morcar, son of Algar. He marched south and occupied and devastated Northamptonshire while, via Earl Harold, he negotiated his creation as Earl of Northumberland.

HUGH SON OF BALDRIC. Sheriff of Nottinghamshire and Derbyshire.

1,5 *PORTLAND*... BOROUGH. The name of the Borough is not given. Both Peterborough and Stamford have Churches to Saint Peter and All Saints, but the position of the entry after Casterton suggests a place in Witchley Wapentake adjacent to Stamford. *Portland* is not found as a name in Stamford, but may not be a place-name at all, being 'land of the Market town'. The bounds of Stamford field were probably different in 1086, with a detached portion of Rutland incorporating some of the town, and another part being in Witchley. See DB Rutland R21 and ELc 1 notes.

CARUCATE. A measure of land used in former Danish districts and presenting the same problems of definition as the hide. See Ellis i,149; Round FE p. 35 ff.

1,6 THE KING HOLDS. Repeated at the beginning of sections 1,7-20;24-27;30-32.

BLAKESLEY. Woodend (Grid Reference SP 61 49) was formerly Little Blakesley and represents the Peverel holding (35,24 note). The other DB holdings (here, 18,95 and 22,7) were probably at Blakesley itself.

LAND FOR... The number of ploughs is omitted.

4 LEAGUES. Generally reckoned as a mile and a half though the term may well have been used loosely in DB. See Round in VCH p. 280.

WHEN STOCKED. Probably with game; see 56,7 'when it is stocked and the King is hunting there'.

1,8 WHITFIELD. An outlier, in Alboldstow Hundred in the Survey (369a).

INLAND. The Lord's land, usually exempt from tax, comparable with *dominium,* 'Lordship'.

1,10 IN COLLINGTREE HUNDRED. DB *Coltrewestan* probably an alternative form of *Colentreu* and *Colestreu.*

1,13 BRIGSTOCK. Two of the members, Geddington and Stanion,were in Corby Hundred in the Survey (387 a,b); the third, Islip, if correctly identified must have been a remote outlier in Huxloe Hundred. The 1 hide 3 virgates here, added to the 1 hide 1 virgate at 4,27 correspond to the three hides at Islip in the Survey (365a) and support the identification.

1,14 GRETTON,ABOVE. See 1,11.

1,15 MEMBERS. The first five, (Loddington to Desborough) are later in Rothwell Hundred; Kelmarsh, Oxendon and Clipston are in Stotfold in the Survey and Cransley and Broughton later in Orlingbury. All are on the borders of Rothwell Hundred and may have been regarded as part of it in 1086. The rest of Kelmarsh was probably in Rothwell (35,13 note), the other parts of Oxendon and Clipston were certainly in Stotfold.

1,16 THE KING'S FOREST. Possibly Rockingham Forest which in the Middle Ages extended as far south as the River Nene. See DGM p.418.

HOLCOT. Later in Hamfordshoe Hundred, but perhaps in Mawsley in 1086; see 56,43 note.

1,17 IN LORDSHIP. Gall has been applied to the MS over the word *dn̄io,* but it is just legible.

WALDGRAVE AND OLD. The superscript *b* and *a* may be intended to correct the order, suggesting perhaps that Old came first in the original return. In the MS the *a* is written slightly further to the left than Farley has it.

1,18 KINGSTHORPE. A Hundred head, Spelhoe, may have been omitted. Geographically Kingsthorpe, like Moulton and Weston, falls in Spelhoe, but the same amount of land is included at Kingsthorpe in Mawsley Hundred in the Survey (381a). Moulton and Weston have parts in both Hundreds in the Survey. All three are mapped in Spelhoe in this edition.
THE KING HOLDS. *ten* in the MS and Farley, the facsimile not reproducing the rather faint abbreviation sign.

1,21-22 BARFORD AND RUSHTON. Later in Rothwell Hundred. Rothwell places held by the King have already been entered in Ch. 1 and it is possible that Barford and Rushton intruding between places in Willybrook Hundred are really outliers of Nassington, like Apethorpe.

1,23 APETHORPE. DB *Patorp,* EPNS 198, Survey 388a.

1,24 THE KING HOLDS. See 1,6 note above.

1,25 BARNWELL. Clearly in Huxloe Hundred in 9,5; but the text here implies an outlier of Tansor which is in Willybrook Hundred. There are later two villages, All Saints and St Andrew, though still apparently regarded as one in the Survey and in FA iv 13. See EPNS 178,210. The Royal Holding was Barnwell All Saints.

1,26 EARL ALGAR. Of Mercia, son of Earl Leofric and the Lady (Countess) Godiva; father of Earls Edwin and Morcar; died 1062.

1,27 A CASTLE. Still to be seen south of the village.

1,30 THE KING HOLDS. See note 1,6 above.
AT FACE VALUE. *Numer* in the MS and Farley, the facsimile not reproducing the faint abbreviation sign over the *r.*

1,32 FINEDON. DB *Tingdene, Thingdene.* See Survey 389a, EPNS 181.
QUEEN EDITH. See B 36 note.
27 HIDES. There is a gap of 2 letters in the MS between the *xx* and the *vii.* In the left hand margin is *rq hid num,* 'ask the number of hides'. In fact the figure seems to be nearly correct, the detail amounting to 26 hides, 3 virgates and 3 parts of a hide.
IN GRETTON HUNDRED. Lying between Huxloe and Rothwell Hundreds, *Geritone* is probably an alternative name for Corby, the lands of Finedon being listed anti-clockwise, and Gretton (EPNS 166), from which the name appears to be derived, lies in Corby Hundred

2 THE BISHOP OF BAYEUX. Odo, half-brother of King William. He was Earl of Kent and regent during some of William's absences.

2,1 WITH FULL JURISDICTION. See Technical Terms and Maitland pp. 80-107.

2,2 FROM THE HOLDING OF THE BISHOP. *De (ipso) episcopo* 'from the Bishop (himself)' would be expected. The unusual phrase is probably used because the Bishop was in prison and had forfeited his lands following his arrest in 1082. The treatment of his fief varies from county to county in DB.
HOUGHTON. Probably the Houghton where Simon holds 1 hide and 1 virgate in the Survey (375b), which is the same as the Houghton held of the fee of Peverel, which in FA iv.6 is Great Houghton. See 35,21 note.
COUNTESS JUDITH CLAIMS. In 56,63-64 Judith holds land in Houghton which had formerly been Ulf's.

2,3 FROM THE HOLDING... HOLDS. Repeated at the beginning of 2,3-9.
NIGEL CLAIMS IT. At 56,20h the same amount of land is held in Brafield by Countess Judith, though with different detail.

2,4 GREATWORTH. The same land is held in Warden Hundred in the Survey (370a). Greatworth and Sulgrave are later detachments of Warden and it is possible that in 1086 Greatworth was in Alboldstow, though Sulgrave was certainly in Warden (43,11).

2,6 ALNOTH OF CANTERBURY. Perhaps the same as Alnoth the Kentishman *(chenticus),* a thane of King Edward's in DB Bucks. 4,36.

2,7 HARTWELL. The holding re-appears exactly in the Survey in Cleyley Hundred (374b). Although the Cleyley Hundred head is beside the next entry, it may be intended to refer to Hartwell. Such postponements are found elsewhere in DB. See 4,17 note.

2,9 THIS ENTRY is written outside the righthand marginal rulings of col. 220b, beside the Puxley entry. There are no signs to indicate its correct position in the text. Gall has been applied to the whole entry which is now only just legible. The *.i.hid'* given by Farley may be *ii hid',* the dot before the figure appearing large in an otherwise very small script.

2,10 FROM THE HOLDING... BAYEUX. Repeated at the beginning of 2,10-12.

2,12 HEYFORD. Great or Nether Heyford, Survey 377b, FA iv. 8.

3 THE BISHOP OF DURHAM. William of St Carilef, or Calais, Bishop 1081-96. The Chapter is written in smaller script at the bottom of col. 220b.

3,1 PERCH. DB *Pertica* or *perca,* a measure of length, generally reckoned as 5½ yards, though a 20 foot perch was in use for measuring woodland until last century. See Ellis i, 158.
LANGFER. PNDB 308.

4 THE BISHOP OF COUTANCES. Geoffrey of Mowbray, a principal minister of King William. Many of his lands are later held by the Earls of Gloucester.

4,1 LAND FOR... The number of ploughs is omitted.
W(ILLIAM) CLAIMS. William Peverel, the disputed land being mentioned at 35,1j.

4,2 DENFORD. Later in Huxloe Hundred, but possibly in Higham in 1086, as in the Survey 377a. See Hart p. 62.
LAND FOR... The number of ploughs is omitted.

4,3 AUBREY. Aubrey de Vere, ancestor of the Earls of Oxford and a major landholder in Hunts. (ch. 22).

4,3-4 WADENHOE. Held by Aubrey de Vere, son of the DB holder in the Survey (366a). He also holds Old *(Walde)* in the Survey (380b) to which Scaldswell is adjacent. It is possible that there is some confusion here, see VCH p. 362.
SCALDWELL. In Mawsley Hundred, remote from Wadenhoe, the 3 virgates recurring as 3 great virgates in the Survey (380b).

4,5-6 HARROWDEN. The Bishop's holding seems to have included both Great and Little Harrowden, FA iv 1. *Alia* (another) does not necessarily imply a separate village, see Introduction to the Notes.

4,8 FROM THE BISHOP HIMSELF. Repeated at the beginning of 4,8-14;16-20.
ISHAM. See 41,5.

4,9 BURTON (LATIMER). Unless a Hundred head has been omitted, this portion of the land was in Orlingbury Hundred, in 1086, the rest (4,12 and 41,1) being in Navisland.

4,11 EDGCOTE. DB *Hocecote*. *Hochecote* in the Survey (370a), EPNS 34.
IN LORDSHIP... 3 PLOUGHS. Grammatically the Latin sentence has 2 verbs, *sunt* and *h(abe)nt; vill(an)is* is perhaps a mistake for *vill(an)i*, or *h(abe)nt* for *h(abe)ntibus* after *cum*. In 41,1. 46,5. 49,1 *etc.*, and in other counties, the singular is used after *xxi, xxxi etc.*, so *vill'is* may be a mistake for *vill's (villanus)*; but see 6,17. 11,5.
LIKE THE ABOVE (MANORS). *Superiores* is plural and thus probably refers to those sections where Burgred held *cum saca et soca,* 4,1;8-9. There is no TRE holder in 4,10.

4,14 ALWIN COBBOLD. OEB 216.
HANTONE. If this is Northampton, a Hundred head has been omitted in an otherwise well rubricated chapter. It is more likely to be an unidentified village on the River Nene, bordering Higham Hundred, another part of *Hantone* being in Higham Hundred in 40,3. The p.n. *Hantone* represents OE *(æt pœm) hēan-tūne* 'The high farm or estate' rather than OE *hām-tūn* 'manor farm' which would be represented *Hamtone.*

4,16 FROM THE BISHOP HIMSELF. See 4,8 note above.
PRESTON (DEANERY). Held in the Survey as 1 hide and 1 virgate (375b).

4,17 BARTON (SEAGRAVE). Held in the Survey (389b) from the fee of Gloucester. The omitted Hundred head (Navisland) is probably deferred to the end of the entry; see 2,7 note.

4,19 NORIGOT. From O.G. *Nor(i)gaud,* Forssner 193.

4,20 NEWTON (BROMSWOLD). This Newton corresponds to that in the Survey in Higham Hundred (376b). The Bishop holds part of the village in Bedfordshire; EB1= Beds. 3,9.

4,21-22 ADDINGTON. The Bishop's holding probably included both the later Little and Great Addington; see Survey 388b, 389a and 11,4. 6a,29 notes. *Parva Adington* was held from the Earl of Gloucester in FA iv 12 and *Magna* in FA iv 49. For *alia* see 4,6 note.

4,23 ALSO FROM THE BISHOP. Repeated at the beginning of 4,23-28.
WOODFORD. Accounted for in Navisland Hundred in the Survey 388b.

4,24 THRAPSTON. Held by Robert son of *Edelin'* in the Survey 365b in Navisford Hundred.

4,27 ISLIP. The value clause is omitted. See 1,13 note.

4,28 HORTON. In Wymersley Hundred, Survey 375b.

4,29 FROM THE BISHOP. Repeated at the beginning of 4,29-36.

4,30-36 Oxfordshire places. Although some are close to the border, others are remote, and it seems likely that a part of the return for the Bishop's fief was included in the wrong county, there being no schedule for the Bishop's lands in the Oxfordshire folios. The identification of Oxfordshire places is less secure than those of Northants; see Introduction to the Places Notes in the Oxford volume.

4,30 FINMERE. Held from the Earl of Gloucester in Fees 836 FA iv. 157. See DB Oxford 7,16.

4,31 HETHE. DB *Hedhā,* i.e. 'Heath ham', EPNS (Oxford) 217. Held from the Earl of Gloucester in Fees 836, FA iv 157.

4,32 SHELSWELL. EPNS (Oxford) 231; Fees 836; FA iv 157.

4,34 WOOTTON. DB *Oitone,* EPNS (Oxford) 245. See DB Oxford 1,4.

4,35 ? WORTON. DB *Hortone,* EPNS (Oxford) 295; see DB Oxford 7,52. 58,37.

4,36 HEYFORD. DB *Egford* and *Hegford,* EPNS (Oxford) 218. See DB Oxford 28,12 and 35,19. The three DB holdings together total 20 hides and will have involved both Upper and Lower Heyford.

5 THE BISHOP OF LINCOLN. Remigius of Fécamp, promised the bishopric of Dorchester (Oxon.) in 1066 in return for ships furnished to William; succeeded Bishop Wulfwin of Dorchester who died in 1067, and translated the see to Lincoln between 1072 and 1086 (Ellis i 474).

5,2 'SNELSTON' 1½ miles south-east of Stoke Dry, on Speed's map of 1610. *Snelleston* is found with Caldecott in LSR p.247.

6-6a CHAPTER 6a is not included in the List of Landholders. Entries in chs. 6 and 6a are frequently parts of a single village; Castor (6,4 and 6a,1), Ailsworth (6,5 and 6a,3), Werrington (6,8 and 6a,8), Warmington (6,11 and 6a,12), Irthlingborough (6,5 and 6a,31). With the exception of Ashton (6a,34) probably omitted earlier, places occuring in both chapters are entered in the same order. From this it appears that the Hundreds are entered in the order U, Wk, P, (Wt), Nf, O, Hu, Nb, with trifling exceptions, and this parallelism helps to restore Hundred heads and to identify places. Two of the headings in the text (6,1 and 6,10 notes) are probably errors.
Many of the tenants or their sons are found in MS 60 of the Society of Antiquaries, printed and discussed in E. King, *The Peterborough 'Descriptio Militum'* (English Historical Review, 1969), pp.84-101, and in CP pp.168-175, and discussed by Round FE pp.157-168, VCH pp.390-392.

6,1 IN STOKE HUNDRED. Probably inserted in error and belonging rightly with the next entry.
11 PLOUGHS. The MS has *xi car̃,* Farley *ii* in error.

6,2 THE CHURCH ITSELF HOLDS. Repeated at the beginning of sections 6,2-17.

6,3 THORPE. Thorpe Hall and Longthorpe in Peterborough (*Thorp juxta Burgh*) FA iv.49, beginning a list of Upton Hundred places.

6,9 ELTON. Now wholly in Hunts., but parts of the parish were in Northants.until the nineteenth century. See 9,3; Hunts. 6,13 and Survey 387b.

6,10-13 The value clauses record a great increase, possibly the result of recovery from devastation by Morcar's army (see Introduction).

6,10a VALUE WHEN STOCKED. See 1,6 note.

6,10b THURNING. Part of the village was transferred from Hunts. in 1888, the rest having always been part of Northants. See EH2;6.

6,10c STOKE (?DRY). The Hundred heading in the text is clear, but Stoke Dry in Rutland is very remote to be an outlier of Oundle, and there are no traces of a Peterborough holding here later. The men of Peterborough Abbey hold Stoke Doyle in 6a,19, and the land here is probably part of the same village, the Hundred head being an error.

6,11 WARMINGTON. *Werminne* has been corrected in the MS to *Wermintone.* In the lefthand margin is a red cross not reproduced by Farley. The position of this section suggests that Warmington is here regarded as part of Polebrook Hundred. The part of the village detailed in 6a,12 is in Willybrook. The village is similarly divided between hundreds in FA iv 23 and 28.

6,13 VALUE. The MS has *valb' (valebat)*;Farley prints *valuit.*

6,16 STANWICK. Lying across the River Nene, opposite Irthlingborough, it was probably surveyed with it, thus being listed between two Navisland Hundred places.
Part of the village is held by the Abbey in Bedfordshire, EB3 = Beds. 7,1.

6a,9 HE HAS. In the MS *hn̄t (habent* 'they have') probably an error for *ht̄* (*habet* 'he has'). But the line above there is a gap after *de abbate* which itself is written crooked. It may be that the compiler of DB thought that there were two 1086 holders, but was unsure of the second one, left a gap and used the plural *habent*. Later realising his mistake he partially filled the gap with the extended *de abbate (de abb'* or *de abb'e* being normal), but forgot to correct *habent.*

6a,11 LUTTON. DB *Lidintone,* EPNS 204. The Survey (387b) has the same 2½ hides at *Lodington'* in Willybrook Hundred. See 6a,16 note and VCH p.271.

6a,12 WARMINGTON. See 6,11 note.

6a,13 1 VIRGATE OF LAND. As there is no dot after the *t'rę* in the MS, the scribe may have intended to add the value of the virgate later.

6a,16 LUDDINGTON (IN THE BROOK). DB *Lullingtone,* EPNS 213. See 6a,11 note and EH7.

6a,17 WINWICK. See Hunts. 19,16-17. Part of the village was in Northants, until transferred to Hunts. in 1888.
2 FREEMEN WITH 2 VILLAGERS, Villagers normally precede freemen in the schedule.

6a,18 THEY BELONG. i.e. the hides.

6a,19 STOKE (DOYLE). *Stokes iuxta Undele,* CP 120; FA iv 48. It is later in Huxloe Hundred, but may have been in Polebrook in 1086; see 6,10c note.

6a,25 PYTCHLEY. Falls naturally in a group of Navisford places in the text, but it is clearly in Orlingbury Hundred in the Survey, 383 a.
HOUSEHOLD BUILDING. That is, belonging to the lordship.

6a,26 CATWORTH. Now in Hunts., but it was included in Navisford Hundred in the Survey, (366b) and scattered fields were a detached part of Northants.in the 19th Century. Most of the village was in Hunts, in 1086, see Hunts. DB 13,4. 19,12;32. 29,3. D,17.

6a,27 ALDWINCLE. Now two villages, St Peter and All Saints, but not distinguished in DB nor in the Survey nor in FA iv 13.

FERRON. 'Blacksmith', 'Ironmonger' from OFr *fer* 'iron' Dauzat p.253.

6a,28 THE WHOLE MANOR. Unless this refers only to the 3 virgates held by Roger, Hugh and Siward, then the 20s. former value of the main holding is the value at a time after its acquisition. See 11,5 for three values given for a manor.

6a,29 ADDINGTON. Probably both the later Great and Little Addington. 3½ hides are held of Peterborough in the Survey (388b) at one Addington, clearly Little Addington from FA iv 12; but a further Peterborough hide is at another Addington, Survey 389a. See 4,21-22 note; 11,4 note.

6a,32 FROM THE KING. Possibly an error for de *abb'e*, 'from the Abbot'. The gap in the MS of about thirteen letters immediately after may be for the insertion of a sub-tenant or tax,or for the hidage which has unusually been entered first.

6a,34 ASHTON. In Polebrook Hundred, Survey 367a.

8 ST EDMUND'S.The Abbey is at Bury (St Edmunds) in Suffolk.

8,1 BOUGHTON. It is later counted in Corby Hundred, part of the village being there in 1086 according to 48,1. See Survey 387a.

8,2 THE ABBEY HOLDS. Repeated in sections 8,2-12. The abbreviation *Abb'* can stand for *Abbas* (Abbot) and *Abbatia* (Abbey), also for *Abbatissa* (Abbess).

8,4 QUEEN MATILDA. Wife of King William, died November 1083.

8,4-6 SCALDWELL, (HANGING) HOUGHTON, LAMPORT. All are on the border of Rothwell Hundred, but are included in Mawsley in the Survey. St. Edmund's claims 2½ virgates of land in Hanging Houghton in 18,31.

8,9 HOTHORPE. DB *Udetorp*, EPNS 115.

8,11 *CALME*. Falling in a group of Stotfold Hundred places, it is perhaps part of Kelmarsh where St Edmund's holds ½ hide in the Survey (383b).

LAND FOR ½ PLOUGH. The *I* after *dim car* in the text is the beginning of *Ibi* begun afresh on the next line.

8,13 AELFEVA, MORCAR'S MOTHER, HELD IT. In the MS *tenuit* is interlined above *Morcari*, but an attempt was made to erase it, although it appears clearly in the facsimile. Farley does not reproduce it.

9,2 THE ABBEY HOLDS. Repeated in 9,2-6. See 8,2 note above for the abbreviation *abb'*.

LUTTON. Ramsey Abbey holds another portion of Lutton in Hunts. (EH3 = Hunts. 6,14).

9,3 ELTON. The Abbey holds a portion in Hunts. (DB Hunts. 6,13). See 6,9 note.

9,5 BARNWELL. Barnwell St Andrew, earlier *Le Moyne*, held from the Abbey by Reginald *Le Moyne*, Survey 365b. See 1,25 note.

IN LORDSHIP 2 PLOUGHS. The facsimile omits the abbreviation sign above *car*.

9,6 DENTON. DB *Dodintone*, later Doddington *Parva* to distinguish from Great Doddington (56,16). Held as *Dodington* by the Abbey in Wymersley Hundred, Survey 376a; see VCH p.272.

WOODLAND WITHOUT PASTURE. The entry is unusual, it being normal to mention when the wood contains pasture *(silva pastilis)* as in the adjacent Rutland.

COUNTESS JUDITH. She holds other portions of Brafield on the Green, 56,20h;56.

10,3 SAWBRIDGE. In Warwickshire, possibly included in Northants.in error, there being no schedule for Thorney Abbey in Warwicks. DB. The place is, however, close enough to the border to have been an outlier in 1086.

11,2 THE ABBEY HOLDS. Repeated in 11,2-6. See 8,2 note for the abbreviation *abb'*.

11,4 ADDINGTON. The Crowland holding seems to have included both Great and Little Addington. The Abbey holds Addington *Major* in FA iv 12 and 2 hides there in the Survey (389a); also in the Survey (388b) ½ virgate of its fee is held in the other Addington.

11,5 WELLINGBOROUGH. This holding is in Hamfordshoe Hundred in the Survey (382a), but may have been part of Navisland in 1086 (Hundred head at 11,4).

12,1 WINWICK. In Hunts. but some fields were in Northants. until the 19th century.

12,2-4 THE ABBEY HOLDS. Or perhaps 'the Abbot'. See 8,2 note above.

12,2 (COLD) ASHBY. *Esseby* in Guilsborough Hundred, Survey 380a.

12,4 (WEST) HADDON. Associated with Winwick; see Survey 379a. East Haddon is in Nobottle Hundred.

14 THE ABBEY of Grestain probably received its lands in Northants, as elsewhere, by gift from the Count of Mortain.

14,2 THE CHURCH ITSELF HOLDS. Repeated in sections 14,2-6.

14,6 WESTON (FAVELL). See Hart p.64.

15-16. THE ORDER of the chapters is the reverse of that given in the list of Landholders. Indices follow the numbering of the text.

16,1-2 LAPLEY, MARSTON. Deep in Staffordshire, apparently included in Northants. in error.

17 THE CHAPTER is '(Land of) Leofwin the priest and other clergy' in the list of Landholders.

17,1 ADSTONE. See 18,73 note.

17,3 (KINGS) SUTTON. The 3 virgates and the fifth of a virgate seem to correspond to the 8 small virgates at Sutton in Sutton Hundred, Survey 367b.

18 THE LANDS of the Count of Mortain, half-brother of King William, reappear in the Survey as held either by the Earl of Leicester, or of the fee of Berkhamsted. A 4 hide holding of the Count at Hellidon in Gravesend Hundred seems to have been omitted from DB (Survey 370b).

18,2 THE COUNT HOLDS. Repeated in 18,2-11.

BILLING. This part of the village might have been in Hamfordshoe Hundred (18,1 Hundred head), though the rest of the village is in Spelhoe (48,3. 57,1).

MEADOW, 10 ACRES. In the MS there is *x* with the partly erased remains of another figure, possibly another *x*, with a smudge above and to the right. Farley prints *xx*.

18,3 [VALUE...] The clause is omitted.

18,4 IN BILLING. The *In* is probably repeated from the entry above, the natural expression being *Bellica est soca huius manerii:* 'Billing is a jurisdiction of this manor'.

18,5 (EAST) HADDON. Survey 378b. West Haddon is in Guilsborough Hundred.

18,6 BOTH LANDS. i.e. (East) Haddon and Ravensthorpe.

18,8 HEYFORD. The Mortain lands included both Upper (Little) and Nether Heyford, FA iv 8-9; Survey 377b. The 'chief manor' is probably the Heyford of 18,83, or the Brampton of 18,7. Similar phrases occur elsewhere, usually of a dependency of a manor just mentioned, e.g. DB Worcs. 2,41 which however clarifies by beginning *ad supradictum maneriu[m] iacet....*

18,11 *CELVERDESCOTE.* Derived like *Celvertone* (Charwelton) from the river Cherwell. It lies in Gravesend Hundred in DB, but in the Survey ½ hide is in Alboldstow, 2 hides in Gravesend, and 1 hide and 2 small virgates in Alwardsley. The ½ hide in Alboldstow is probably an outlier or an error, and *Celverdescote* probably lay on the Cherwell at the boundary that in the 12th century divided Gravesend from Alwardsley (see note on Hundreds *infra*), between Catesby, Badby and Charwelton.

18,12 HE HOLDS. *Comes* or *idem* is probably omitted in the MS.

18,13 (EAST) CARLTON. 'East' to distinguish from Carlton Curlieu to the west in Leicestershire, EPNS 162.

18,17 HE ALSO HOLDS. Repeated at the beginning of sections 18,17-25.

18,18 (EAST) FARNDON. Survey 384a. West Farndon is in Warden Hundred.

3 VILLAGERS HAVE ANOTHER. The land is for 2 ploughs and 2 are mentioned, one in Lordship, one held by the villagers. The Latin, however, reads *aliam* (another) rather than *alteram* (the other), and this distinction has been maintained in translation, since ploughs and ploughlands are not always directly related. In other sections (e.g. 6a,32) the land is for 3 ploughs with one in Lordship and one held by the villagers. Here *aliam* is clearly right, no third plough being mentioned.

FREGIS. Also 18,20;26;90. From Old German *Fredegis.* Other forms of the same name in Northants. are *Fredgis* (18,31. 35,14) and *Fregist* (43,1). See PNDB 254.

18,19 (LITTLE) BOWDEN. EPNS 110. In Leicestershire since 1888, where Great Bowden has always been.

18,20 OXENDON. Little Oxendon, held as *Oxendon' Parva* of the fee of Berkhamsted, Survey 384a. See FA iv 10.

18,21 HASELBECH. DB *Esbece,* held in Stotfold Hundred in the Survey 383b.

18,24 UNDERWOOD, 2 FURLONGS. The furlong is used here as a square, not linear measure.

18,27 HE ALSO HOLDS. Repeated at the beginning of 18,27-30.

18,28 (COLD) HIGHAM. At Grimscot, a hamlet of Cold Higham in the Survey 373b.

18,29 WEEDON (BEC). In the Survey (370b) 4 hides are held at *Wedon'* in Gravesend Hundred of the fee of Leicester. These must have included the Count's holding and that of Hugh of Grandmesnil (23,3).

18,31 (HANGING) HOUGHTON. 1 hide and 3 virgates are held of the fee of Berkhamsted in the Survey 380a in Mawsley Hundred.

THE ABBOT OF ST EDMUND'S CLAIMS. His holding at Houghton is 8,5. See 8,2 note on *abb'.*

18,32 ARCHBISHOP STIGAND. Of Canterbury 1052-1070.

18,33 LEOFING. DB *Leuing,* to be distinguished from *Leuuin* (18,45 etc.) which is Leofwin. See PNDB 312,317.

18,36 HE ALSO HOLDS. Repeated at the beginning of 18,36-41.

18,38 CHARLTON. Held of the fee of Berkhamsted in Sutton Hundred in the Survey 368a.
WASTE. Exceptionally this has a value, as has the next entry.

18,41 HEYFORD. See 18,8 note.

18,42 WILLIAM. De Cahagnes.

18,43 HE ALSO HOLDS. Repeated in 18,43-52; 55-66.

18,44 BRINGTON. Probably Great Brington, not separately named in the Survey or in FA. But in the latter (p.8) *Brunton* has two separate entries, one held from the Earl of Leicester, the other held with Nobottle by William *Ferrers* (35,3c). The latter is no doubt Little Brington, adjacent to Nobottle, the former Great Brington.
(EAST) HADDON. See 18,5.

18,50 (COLD) ASHBY. *Esseby* is held by Hugh *de Kaynes* in Guilsborough Hundred in the Survey 380a, probably the son of the 1086 holder William de Cahagnes.

18,52 SILVERSTONE. In 1086, it must have been an isolated part of Foxley Hundred, cut off by Wappenham (43,4) which was in Towcester. See 43,3. 45,7.

18,53 THIS ENTRY is written in paler ink, some 6 letters into the lefthand margin of col. 223c below the marginal rulings; no sign indicates its correct position in the text.
CREATON. Little Creaton. Two Creatons are distinguished in the Survey (379a), ½ hide at the smaller being held of the fee of Ralph *de Gaynes*, William's successor.

18,54 THE FIFTH PART OF 1 HIDE. *v partē uni' hidae*. Possibly '5 parts...'. Although a horizontal line usually abbreviates *partem* and a vertical sign *partes*, the usage is not consistent.

18,55 HE ALSO HOLDS. See 18,43 note.

18,61 PURSTON. Buston Farm, (Burston, 1st edition OS map) Grid Reference SP 5038 is similarly derived from DB *Prestetone* EPNS 58.

18,62 WALTON (GROUNDS) See 18,35 note.

18,67 ? THRUPP (GROUNDS). DB *Torp*. The position in the schedule suits a Gravesend Hundred place. It is possibly the holding of the fee of Berkhamsted mentioned under Welton in the Survey 371b.

18,68 HE ALSO HOLDS. Repeated at the beginning of 18,68-71.
'CHILCOTES' is Chilcotes Cover on 1st edition OS map (EPNS 65). It is probably the same as *Cotes* held in the Survey (379b) by William son of Alfred.

18,73 THE FIFTH PART OF 1 VIRGATE. See 18,54 note.
ADSTONE. DB *Etenestone* as 17,1, also *Atenestone* 1,6; to be distinguished from *Estanestone*, Easton Neston 48,16. Adstone, *Atteneston*, is held in Norton (Foxley) Hundred in the Survey (373a) by Geoffrey *de Turvill'* who elsewhere holds from the Earl of Leicester.
MEADOW, 3 ACRES. This interlineation should follow *Quae ibi ē,* although it precedes in the text, perhaps because there are less tails to obstruct the interline at this point.

18,74 PRESTON. The several Mortain holdings (also 18,85;90) encompassed both Preston Capes (*alias* Magna) and Little (or Wood) Preston, Fees 495; 498.

18,76 THORPE (MALSOR) DB *Alidetorp,* EPNS 122. It is held in Rothwell Hundred in the Survey (385b) by *Fucher' Malesoures* as descendent of the 1086 holder.
The holding like 18,77-78 could have been in Orlingbury hundred in 1086.

18,77 EDWIN HELD THIS FREELY ALSO. *et hanc* could refer to the next entry, 'Edwin held it freely and this (next) also'.

18,79 WALGRAVE. In Mawsley Hundred, 56,40, but close to the Orlingbury border.

18,82 LOKKI, SCOTEL, STEINKELL, See PNDB 321, 356,373.

18,83 HEYFORD See 18,8 note.

18,85 PRESTON. See 18,74 note.
SAEWATA. DB *Sauuata* may represent an otherwise unrecorded feminine personal name, see Old Scandinavian *Sǽhuati* PNDB 351; or is perhaps an error for the known *Sauuara,* from OE *Sǣwaru.*

18,86 HOLDENBY. DB *Aldenesbi* EPNS 85, see 18,92 note.

18,88 SPRATTON. On the Nobottle-Spelhoe Hundred border. It seems to be in Spelhoe in 30,16, but it could end a Nobottle group here.

18,90 PRESTON. See 18,74 note.

18,92 ?HOLDENBY. DB *Aldenestone.* Possibly a variant of *Aldenesbi*,18,86. The two holdings form a 4 hide unit, had the same TRE holder and are both entered before Haddon. See Survey 378a, VCH p.328 note 1.

18,95 BLAKESLEY. See 1,6 note.

19 THE COUNT OF MEULAN. Roger of Beaumont, who inherited Meulan through his mother. Styled Earl of Leicester by 1107.

19,2-3 THESE ENTRIES are written across the bottom of cols. 224 a,b in two lines, the beginni of each being exdented in the Latin text. Transposition signs indicate their correct positio BERKSWELL, WHITACRE. Wrongly entered in Northants. Another 4 hides held by the Count at Berkswell are listed in Warwick. 16,27. For Whitacre see DB Warwicks. 17,14. 18 24,2.

19,2 WOODLAND 1 LEAGUE LONG. Possibly '2 leagues'; in the MS there is a blot or spot of gall, with a rim of very dark brown ink, after *silva* and as far as the *i,* which may conceal another *i* or just a dot.

20 COUNT ALAN. Of Brittany.

21 EARL AUBREY. Aubrey of Coucy; created Earl of Northumbria in 1080, but as he was 'of little use in difficult circumstances' he went home to Normandy. His lands were in the King's hands in 1086, and had not yet been granted afresh, see 21,1 *tenuit,* 21,6 end.

22 EARL HUGH. Hugh of Avranches; Earl of Chester and nephew of King William.

22,3 HE ALSO HOLDS. Repeated at the beginning of 22,3-8.
1 VIRGATE OF LAND. In the MS a large *In* follows, evidently the beginning of a Hundre head. But Trafford was in Warden Hundred (heading at 22,1), so no rubrication was needed. An attempt was made to erase it.

22,4 MARSTON (ST LAWRENCE). 4 hides are held here in Alboldstow Hundred in the Survey 369a.

22,7 BLAKESLEY. See 1,6 note.

23 THE CHAPTER is misnumbered XXXIII in the text and entered before ch.22, the order being restored by transposition signs.
HUGH OF GRANDMESNIL. Sheriff of Leics. His lands passed to his son Ivo and were acquired from him by the Count of Meulan. See DB Leics. ch.9 note.

23,1 (WEST) FARNDON. Held by the Earl of Leicester in the Survey (369b) in Warden Hundred.

23,2 HUGH. Of Gouville, see next note.

23,3 WEEDON (BEC). Held by the Earl of Leicester in Gravesend Hundred, Survey 370b.
WATFORD. Held by Gilbert Cook, 57,2. Also acquired in the exchange were 5 houses held by Hugh of Gouville from Hugh in Leicester (Leicester C12 = ELe 1).

23,4 ASHBY (ST LEDGERS). This Ashby was held by the Earl of Leicester in Alwardsley Hundred, Survey 371b.

23,7 THRUPP (GROUNDS). DB *Torp,* ending a Gravesend Hundred Group. See Survey 371a, a holding of the Earl of Leicester.

23,10 MIDDLETON (CHENEY). In Sutton Hundred, Survey 368b.

23,13 WOODFORD (HALSE). Held from the Earl of Leicester in Warden Hundred, Survey 370a

23,16-19 THE ENTRIES ARE interrupted by Chapter 24, written at the foot of col. 224c; these lands are all in Oxfordshire. The later descent of the holdings proves that they are part of the fief of Hugh of Grandmesnil, rather than additional ch. 24 entries; see ch. 24 note. There is no schedule for Hugh in Oxford and it is likely that his small fief there was attached to Northants. in error.

23,16 ROGER OF IVRY. Married to Azelina, daughter of Hugh of Grandmesnil.

23,17 CHARLTON (ON OTMOOR). Held from the Earl of Leicester, Fees 831.
4 HIDES ARE IN LORDSHIP. Apparently an afterthought. Lordship hides are not given generally in Northants. though the practice is common in some other counties.

23,18 SHIPTON (ON CHERWELL). Held in Fees 834, from the Earl of Winchester who inherited from Hugh. See also DB Oxford 7,26.

23,19 SIBFORD. EPNS (Oxford) 404. Held from the Earl of Winchester, Fees 834. It is Sibford Gower, Fees 823. See also DB Oxford 24,3; Staffs. 12,30.

24 THIS CHAPTER is written some 6 letters into the left margin at the foot of col. 224c, the last line being below the marginal rulings. It is in thinner ink and smaller script.

25 HENRY OF FERRERS. His heirs were the Earls of Derby and Nottingham.

25,1 POTTERSPURY. This *Perie* is distinguished from Paulerspury (35,22 note) by the Survey (374a), where it is held by Robert *de Ferrar.* See FA iv 4 and 56,66 note.
VALUE. *Val'i* in the MS is presumably a mistake for *val' (valet).*
EARL TOSTI. Brother of King Harold and Earl of Northumbria; killed 1066.

25,2 TITCHMARSH. The placename is added in the left hand margin.

26,1 ROBERT...(HOLDS). *Tenet* is omitted in the MS.
STOKE (ALBANY). Survey 386a, in Stoke Hundred.

26,5 WELDON. In the adjacent Corby Hundred.

26,8 HILDWIN. DB *Ildvin,* from OE *Hildwine.*
BRAMPTON (ASH). In Stoke Hundred, Survey 386a.

27 ROBERT OF STAFFORD. Younger son of Roger of Tosny.

27,1 STONETON. DB *Stantone*. EPNS (Warwicks.) 273. Formerly in Northants, transferred to Warwicks. in 1896. It is held in Fees 936 from the Earl of Stafford.

28 ROBERT D'OILLY. Sheriff of Warwick, Oxford and perhaps Berkshire. See OEB 103.

28,3 ROBERT...HOLDS. Farley's *en'* is an error for *ten'* in the MS.

30,1 6 FREEMEN HAVE IT THERE. i.e. the plough.

30,2 HE ALSO HOLDS. Repeated at the beginning of sections 30,2-6.

30,2-3 WESTON, SUTTON. They fall in a group of Stoke Hundred places, and are thus probably Weston by Welland and Sutton Bassett. They share the same holder in the Survey, 386a. See 56,3-4.

30,4 IN THE LEFTHAND margin of the MS is an *r* for *require* 'enquire', omitted by Farley. It is not clear what additional information might be needed, unless meadow, pasture etc., but these are also missing from other entries in this chapter. There is no obvious later addition.

30,6-7 WELDON. Later held by the Bassett family with Sutton and Weston as Great Weldon, FA iv 18.

30,7 THE KING CLAIMS IT. The King holds Corby (1,12), which is adjacent and from which much land had been appropriated.

30,9 NORMAN HELD IT. Possibly referring to the entry above and not to the hide in Brampton Ash.

30,15 4 SMALLHOLDERS HAVE 1 THERE . *(ve)l una est...cu(m)* is interlined with the meaning 'or "there is 1 (plough) with 4 smallholders" '. There is no underlining for deletion,possibly in error, but the *vel* indicates that the scribe was unsure of the ownership of the plough.

30,19 KENRIC HELD BRADDEN. An explanatory addition to 30,17; see 41,2.

31-38 DB MISNUMBERS these chapters 30-33, 30, 35-37, but the numbering of the list of Landholders is correct.

31,1 THE UNNAMED HOLDING in Stoke Hundred is perhaps East Carlton, Survey 386a.

32,1 EARL MORCAR. See 1,4 note.

33,1 ROBERT BLUNT. He is called *Albus, Blancardus,* 'white', as well as *Flavus* 'yellow, fair' and *Blundus* 'blonde', the origin of the modern surname.

34 WILLIAM OF KEYNES. From Cahagnes, probably the place near Vire in Calvados (OEB 79) anglicised as Keynes.

35 WILLIAM PEVEREL. Sheriff of Notts. and Derbys. See Notts. B3 note.

35,1b RUSHDEN. William also holds part of the village in Bedfordshire, see EB4 = Beds. 22,2.

35,1f FARNDISH. See also Beds. 42,1. 43,1.

35,1g PODINGTON. See Beds. 32,5. 34,1.

35,1j GYTHA. William Peverel's predecessor in several counties. In this Chapter she is probably Gytha, wife of Earl Ralph of Hereford, nephew of Edward the Confessor; she should be distinguished from the better known Gytha, wife of Earl Godwin who also named her son Harold.

BISHOP GEOFFREY. Burgred's lands had passed to Geoffrey, Bishop of Coutances (ch.4). Here he claims homage from men who had been Burgred's. Raunds was held by the Bishop (4,1).

35,2 CLIPSTON. The place-name is interlined.

NASEBY. Just over the border in Guilsborough Hundred; see 35,5 and Survey 380a.

35,3a NOBOTTLE. The next five entries are clearly dependencies: (a) the wording and layout are similar to other such entries (e.g. 35,1); (b) the value is given at the end; (c) all places are adjacent to Nobottle.

35,3b 3 FREEMEN HAVE IT THERE. i.e. the plough.

35,3c BRINGTON. See 18,44 note.

35,9 WITCHLEY HUNDRED. *Wap* lined through in red, for Wapentake, the normal term for Witchley, is written in the left hand margin of the MS.

35,11 *ACESHILLE*. 'Oak-tree hill'. The identification with Ashton (40,4) is rejected by Round in VCH p.338 note 3, but accepted by DG.

35,13 KELMARSH. Included in Stotfold Hundred in the Survey but it is a border place, and the Hundred head at 35,12 and the mention of Arthingworth suggest that it was in Rothwell in 1086. See 1,15 note.

35,15 HARGRAVE. See EH1.

35,19a COTON. DB *Cota* can be Coton or Claycoton (EPNS 66-67) but the latter is probably accounted for in Lilborne; see Survey 379b.

35,19c WINWICK. See 12,1 note.

35,19d (WEST) HADDON. William Peverel holds 1½ great virgates in the Survey (379a) at West Haddon in Guilsborough Hundred.

35,19e (COLD) ASHBY. See Fees 944.

35,21 HOUGHTON. 1 hide and ½ great virgate are held of the fee of Peverel in the Survey (375b in *Houcton'* which from RH ii 8a and FA iv 6 appears to be Great Houghton.

35,22 PAULERSPURY. *West pyria* in the Survey (374a). See FA iv 5 and 25,1. 56,66 notes.

35,23 THEY ARE THERE. The Latin *Ibi est ipsa* refers back to 'one plough and a half' *(i car 7 dim̄)* and so is singular.

35,24 BLAKESLEY. The Peverel holding was Little Blakesley (Grid Reference SP 61 49) which is now Woodend. See Survey 372a; 1,6 note.

35,25 COURTEENHALL. 'Another Courteenhall' is 35,6. Two villages are not found in later times. This holding may have been at Somershale, part of Roade, listed as 6 small virgates of the fee of Peverel in the Survey 374b.

35,26 MOLLINGTON. Parts of the village are entered in Warwicks. (37,9) and Oxfordshire (17,7 in 1086, and a portion was a detached part of Warwickshire into the 19th century. It is possible that the Northants. boundary was the river Cherwell in 1086, with some of Mollington on its east bank.

36 WILLIAM SON OF ANSCULF. William of *Pinkeni* (Picquigny) in Wilts. 24,19. 68,22-23. Ansculf of *Pinchengi* in Bucks. 17,2. Lord of Dudley Castle and an important figure in the midland counties.

36,1 IN LORDSHIP 1 (PLOUGH). The meaning is made less clear by the intrusion of *Rex inde hī socā.*

36,2 UPTON WAPENTAKE. Upton Hundred elsewhere. It lies in a 'Danish' area, but may have been influenced by Witchley Wapentake above, (36,1).

36,3-4 (WEST) BROMWICH. OVER. A Stafford, and a Warwicks. place, probably scheduled in Northants. in error.

36,4 AS DID OTHERS. Implying that Wulfwin was not the only TRE holder. Possibly it means 'as did the others' suggesting that other TRE holders in the chapter also held freely.

37 WILLIAM LOVETT. From O Fr *Lovet,* 'wolf-cub', diminutive of *lou, leu* 'wolf' from Latin *Lupus.* OEB 363. He holds lands in Berkshire, Bedford and Leicester.

39 WALTER THE FLEMING. Lord of the Honour of Wahill, now Odell in Bedfordshire.

39,2 A PRIEST. Interlined in the left hand margin.

39,3 (HANGING) HOUGHTON. Like Lamport (39,4) it is close to the border of Mawsley Hundred and could have been in Guilsborough in 1086.

39,7 HORTON. 2 hides and 1 virgate are held in *Horton* of the Honour of Wahill in Wymersley Hundred, Survey 375b.

39,8 EVENLEY. Lying on the boundary of Sutton and Alboldstow Hundreds, it is listed in bot in DB; in Alboldstow at 18,65. 39,10 and in Sutton in 21,5. Part of the village was also a detachment of Towcester Hundred both here and in the Survey, 373b.

39,9 (CANONS) ASHBY. Held in Norton (Foxley) Hundred from the lord of Wahill in the Survey 372a.

39,11 THE UNNAMED LAND is Astwick in Evenley, VCH p.341 note 1.

39,12 OF PATTISHALL CHURCH. *ad ecclesiam* should mean that two hides in Cold Higham were adjacent to Pattishall church. But Pattishall church is at the far end of the village away from the Cold Higham boundary (Watling Street in 1086 as now), and the land appears in the Survey 373b to have been at Grimscote (GR SP 6553). *Pertinentes* 'belonging' is perhaps to be understood with *ad.*

39,13 1 HIDE. There follows a gap of about 5 letters in the MS due to an erasure. The erasure is more likely to be of *7 dim'* as the same holding is 1½ hides in the Survey (372a), than of the place-name, despite its being interlined.

39,14 THE UNNAMED ESTATE may be at Preston where 3 hides, less 2 small virgates, were hel of the fee of Simon de Wahill in the Survey 370b.

39,15 GELDER. DB *Gildre,* presumably Old Danish *Gildaer, Gelder* (O. Nielsen *Olddanske Personnaune* Copenhagen 1883, p.31), Old Icelandic *Gellir,* originally a byname from *gialla* 'to yell', E.H. Lind *Norsk-Isländsks Personbinamn,* Uppsala 1921, column 107.
ASTCOTE. DB *Aviescote* EPNS 92, held by John de Wahill in FA iv 44.

39,18 PATTISHALL. 7 hides of this holding were in Towcester Hundred in the Survey, part in Foxley (372b, 373a).

40 WINEMAR. Winemar the Fleming, Lord of *Anslepe, Hanslip,* now Hanslope in Buckinghamshire, which adjoins Cosgrove (40,1), Grid reference SP 8046. See Bucks 46,1.

40,2 THE UNNAMED land is at Easton Maudit and Strixton, Survey 376b.
COUNTESS JUDITH CLAIMS. She holds Easton Maudit, 56,52.

40,3 *HANTONE.* See 4,14 note.

40,6 THE UNNAMED land is at Easton Neston, Survey 374b; Baker ii 139.

41 GUY OF RAIMBEAUCOURT. OEB 109 doubts the identification.

41,1 21 VILLAGERS. *xxi vill's* in the MS and Farley, (for *villanus);* the facsimile does not reproduce the *s* which, though faint, is not erased. For the singular see 4,11 note.

41,2 EARL RALPH. An explanatory addition to 41,1 (see 30,19). Ralph, nephew of King Edward, was Earl of Hereford from 1053 or earlier to 1057.

41,3 STANFORD (ON AVON). EPNS 74, also Stanford Abbatis. Though described as a purchase, Stanford was granted to Benedict, Abbot of Selby (Mon. Ang iii 499). The purchase included land in Leicestershire, see ELe 2 (DB Leics.23,2-6.)
17 VILLAGERS... WHO HAVE. *Habentes* refers only to the villagers.

41,4 HARROWDEN. Probably Great Harrowden. The 1 hide held by Guy in 1086 is held by Nicolas *de Cugeho* in the Survey (383a). A descendent, William *de Cokeho* holds *Magna Haruedon* in FA iv 1. Cogenhoe is also held by Guy in DB (41,9).

41,5 THE BISHOP OF COUTANCES CLAIMS. He holds another part of Isham 4,8.

41,6 ALDWINCLE. See 6a,27 note.

41,8 CRANFORD. Richard Fitz Guy holds 1 hide in Cranford in North Navisland Hundred in the Survey (389a), though from Peterborough Abbey.

41,10 SMALLHOLDERS WHO PLOUGH. *Arantes* could govern 'ploughs': '4 smallholders have them ploughing', as in Wilts. 28,10 'land for 6 oxen, which are there, ploughing'. In 56,56 however *'ibi sunt ii bordarii cum ii bobus arantes',* 'ploughing' clearly describes 'smallholders'.

42,1 EUDO. Elsewhere Eudo *dapifer* (the steward), son of Hubert de Rye(s).

42,2-3 EASTON (ON THE HILL). The village was divided between Upton and Willybrook Hundreds in 1086, as in the Survey (388a, 367b). See 46,6.

42,2 THIS LAND IS (PART) OF ST. PETER'S (CHURCH). The circumstances are given in the Peterborough 'Descriptio Militum' (see above note 6-6a), "King William the Elder gave Eudo the Steward 1½ hides in Easton; and from Normandy he sent his writs to the Bishop of Coutances and Robert d'Oilli in England ordering them to give the Abbot in exchange an estate of equal value in whichever of the three neighbouring counties he chose. But the Abbot refused.", King, op.cit., 97.

42,3 THROND. DB *Drond,* PNDB 397.

43 GILES BROTHER OF ANSCULF. Elsewhere Giles *de Pinkeni* (Picquigny)., see ch.36 note.

43,1 WEEDON (LOIS). The *caput* of Giles' barony, earlier *Wedune Pynkeny,* EPNS 45.

43,2 MORETON (PINKNEY). EPNS 41.

43,3 SILVERSTONE. See 18,52 note.

43,5 IN SUTTON HUNDRED. Apparently written as if it were a normal Hundred heading, but the scribe has incorporated it in his sentence. The first four letters, though capitals, are smaller than in usual Hundred heads, and there is no lining through in red.

43,6 *BRIME.* Probably in Culworth, the 2 hides and 4 parts of ½ hide reappearing in the Survey (369a) as 2 hides and 4 small virgates in Culworth itself.

43,7 THORPE (MANDEVILLE). This *Torp* falls in an Alboldstow Hundred group, and is found there in the Survey (369a).

43,11 SULGRAVE. See 2,4 note.

44 GEOFFREY ALSELIN. OEB 213.

45 GEOFFREY DE MANDEVILLE. Lord of Pleshey; ancestor of the Earls of Essex. He received Asgar the Constable's extensive lands throughout England.

45,1 OF THIS LAND. The MS has *de hac trā* (i.e. *terram)* in error.

45,2 SWARTLING. PNDB 379.

45,4 HINTON. These two hides recur in the Survey of Warden Hundred (369b) held from Earl William (de Mandeville).
WIHTBERT. DB *Vltbert.* So Dr. John Morris, citing *Vltret* for Wihtred in Devon (Exon. Domesday 402b3; 457b3); but PNDB 398, 402 equates *Vltret* with *Uhtræd* so *Vltbert* could be a scribal error for **Uhtbert, Wihtbert* or perhaps *Wulfbert.*

45,5 ASTON (LE WALLS). The land at this Aston is held in the Survey 369b with *Apeltreya* (Appletree, a hamlet of Aston, EPNS 32).

45,7 SILVERSTONE. See 18,52 note.

45,8 HINTON (IN THE HEDGES). Geographically in Alboldstow, and it is possible to take the Alboldstow Hundred head in 45,9 as referring back to it. But like its neighbour Evenley it was a detachment of Towcester Hundred in the Survey (373a) where 2 hides are held from William (de Mandeville). It was probably a part of Towcester or Foxley Hundreds in 1086.

45,9 ALL THESE LANDS. That is 45,4-9.

46,2 HEYFORD. Nether or Great Heyford held from Gilbert *de Gaunt* in FA iv. 8.

46,5 OF RUTLAND. In 1086 only the northern two-thirds of the later county, consisting of Alstoe and Martinsley wapentakes formed Rutland. The nearest royal holding to Empingham is Hambleton, Rutland R19.

46,6 SAINT-PIERRE-SUR-DIVES. In Calvados, south-east of Caen.
ALL THESE LANDS. That is 46,1-6.

46,7 WHICHFORD. In Warwickshire, entered among Northants. lands in error. The church was given to Bridlington priory, founded by Gilbert's son Walter, VCH p.346 note 5.

47,1a 1 FEMALE. The MS has *ancila* for the normal *ancilla.*

47,2 CRICK. In Guilsborough Hundred, governed by the Hundred head at 47,1a; the Stotfold Hundred head refers only to Sulby.
The entry is written across the foot of col. 227c in a smaller hand, and occupies part of the left-hand margin.

48 GUNFRID'S LANDS are later known as the Barony of 'Chokes'.

48,2 AZOR HELD THESE TWO LANDS. That is Boughton and Newton. For Azor see ch. 50 note.

48,3 HE ALSO HOLDS. Repeated at the beginning of 48,3-11.
SWEIN. See ch. 50 note.

48,6 THE UNNAMED LAND is probably Buckby, 2½ hides and 1 great virgate being held there from the fee of Chokes in the Survey 379a.

48,7 (WEST) HADDON. Survey 379a.

48,8 CREATON. Great Creaton, the larger Creaton being distinguished from the smaller (18,53 note) in the Survey 379a, held by Aunsel *de Chokes.*

48,9 ROTHERSTHORPE. *Trop'* is held by Ascelin *de Chokes* in Wymersley Hundred in the Survey 375a.

48,10 THRUPP (GROUNDS). DB *Westhorp* is identified by DG with Westhorp in Byfield, and is misplaced on the DG map. Westhorp must have been in Warden Hundred in 1086 whereas *Westhorp* is clearly in Gravesend, being probably the west end of Thrupp Grounds (EPNS [illegible] The holding appears in the Survey held by Stephen *de Turs* who was an undertenant of [illegible] *'e Choques* (Survey 371a).

48,11 GRIMSBURY. Transferred to Oxfordshire in 1889.
3 LORDSHIPS. The MS *dnioꝝ (dominiorum)* is faint and has probably been corrected to *dnoꝝ* for *dominorum* 'lords'. A similar phrase occurs in 48,16 'two lords hold it'.

48,12 KNUSTON. Survey 377a.
EUSTACE CLAIMS IT. His nearest holding is Hargrave 35,15 which like Knuston was regarded as an outlying part of Higham Ferrers.

48,14 WULFBALD. PNDB 418.

48,16 EASTON NESTON. DB *Adestanestone* i.e. *Ad Estanes-tone* in which the *ad* represents OE *æt* 'at'. See 18,73 note.

49,1 THE UNNAMED LAND appears in the Survey as Gayton held by the advocate of Bēthune. (373a).

50 SWEIN. Son of Azor in B29, Gunfrid's predecessor in Northants. and elsewhere.

52 OGER. The *caput* of his fief was at Bourne in Lincolnshire.

53,1 EARL WALTHEOF. Of Huntingdon and the Middle Angles 1065, of (Northern) Northumbria 1072-75. Son of Earl Siward (of Northern Northumbria) who died 1055. Married Countess Judith. Executed 1076.
COUNTESS JUDITH CLAIMS IT. She inherited some of Waltheof's lands. Chadstone had possibly been part of his large composite manor of Yardley (Hastings) which Judith held in 1086 (56,20).

54 MAINOU. The head of his Barony was Woolverton in Buckinghamshire.

54,3 ASSESSED. The MS has *ap̄pciat᷑ (appreciatur),* Farley *ap̄picat᷑* in error.

55 EUSTACE. Sheriff of Huntingdon.

55,2 (WOOD)NEWTON. This *Niwetone* occurs in Willybrook Hundred in the Survey (388a).
NORMAN HELD THESE TWO LANDS. That is, Isham and Woodnewton.

55,6 CLOPTON. The MS *Dotone* probably represents *d* - by error for *cl-,* since the holding re-appears as *Clopton* in the Survey, 366a. Cf. *Leoclai* for *Leofdai* in DB Wilts. 37,5.

56 COUNTESS JUDITH. Daughter of King William's half-sister Adelaide and of Lambert, Count of Lens; widow and heiress of Earl Waltheof. In the Survey many of her lands are held by King David of Scotland (acceded 1124).

56,1 4 SLAVES. So the MS and Farley; the facsimile has reproduced the dot after the *iiii* as a further *i,* as if there were 5 slaves.
BELMESTHORPE. Part of Uffington was cultivated by the Countess with this manor's ploughs, see ELc3 (Lincs. 56,4).

56,3-4 SUTTON (BASSETT), WESTON (BY WELLAND). See 30,2-3 note.

56,6 EARL WALTHEOF. See 53,1 note.

56,7 VALUE WHEN STOCKED. See 1,6 note.

56,11 DRAUGHTON. DB *Bracstone,* probably an error. The holding recurs in the Survey 385b.

56,15 (EARLS) BARTON. The *Bartone* of the text has been corrected to *Burtone,* but the *a* has not been underlined for deletion. The same place occurs in 56,18 as *Burtone.* It is nonetheless Barton to which Doddington and Mears Ashby are adjacent. The four hides are of the fee of King David in the Survey 382b. The scribe has perhaps been misled by the *Burtone* (Broughton) of 56,12. In some insular hands *a* and *u* are rather similar and the confusion may have arisen from an original draft.

56,16 (GREAT) DODDINGTON. Distinguished in later times from Doddington Parva which became Denton. It can be identified by its proximity to Earl's Barton and Mears Ashby. See Survey 382a, and the notes to 9,6. 56,20d;55.

56,18 (MEARS) ASHBY. The 4 hides in Hamfordshoe reappear held of the fee of King David in the Survey 382a.

56,20a MEMBERS. All appear to be in Wymersley Hundred except Wollaston, just in Higham, and Hardingstone which in 1,10 is in Collingtree, although on the border.

56,20d DENTON. DB *Dodintone* reappears in the Survey as 1 hide at *Dodington* in Wymersley Hundred (376a). See 56,16 note.

56,20e HACKLETON. DB *Bachelinton,* an error for *Hachelintone* (EPNS 146) through similarity of *b, h* in a minuscule script.

56,23 FROM THE COUNTESS. Repeated in 56,23-43;45-55; 62-66.

56,24 *WALETONE.* Its position in the schedule suggests a part of Wellingborough, rather than Walton Grounds, or Walton in Peterborough.

56,26 ALSO. See 18,77 note.

56,32 OXENDON. Great Oxendon, 1 hide being held there of the fee of King David in the Survey p.384a.

56,36 RESOURCES. Elsewhere in DB *pecunia* means 'livestock' or 'goods' (RMLWL s.v. *pecunia)*; here however, it seems to replace a value clause. No livestock is mentioned in 1,2 to which this entry refers. DGM p.361 prefers to see this as an example of incomplete revision, since the original returns, where they survive, contained livestock.

56,38 OAKLEY. Great Oakley, Survey 387a.

56,42 (HANGING) HOUGHTON. The land recurs in the Survey 380a in Mawsley Hundred.

56,43 HOLCOT. In Hamfordshoe in the Survey 382a, but it is a border land, perhaps in Mawsley here. See 1,16 note.

56,45 FROM THE COUNTESS. See 56,23 note.
(CASTLE) ASHBY. Survey 376b.

56,47 ALAN. Possibly the steward, *dapifer,* who holds from the Countess in Hunts.

56,50 1 VILLAGER... HAVE. Grammatically, a singular *habet,* should follow, rather than *hn̄t (habent).*

56,51 WINEMAR OF HANSLIP CLAIMS IT. He holds the adjacent Bozeat from the Countess, 56,54. See ch.40.

56,52 EASTON (MAUDIT). See 40,2 note.

56,53 WELLINGBOROUGH. Possibly a portion in Higham Hundred since it falls among Higham places.

56,55 ?DENTON. DB *Dodinton.* Judith holds at both Great Doddington and Denton (56,16;20) and the two holdings are accounted for in the Survey. The order of entries here favours Denton (so also Hart p.60, but see VCH p.272). The land is possibly that held at Denton by Walter *fitz Wynem(er)* in the Survey, 376a.

56,56 1 VIRGATE. In the MS *una* in error for *unā,* accusative after *ten(et).*

56,57b HOUGHTON. The holding (also 56,57g;63-64) encompassed both Great and Little Houghton, Survey 375b; Fees 494, 501.

56,59 ?WOTHORPE. DB *Widetorp,* possibly an error for *Wridtorp* (as 11,1) (Wothorpe EPNS 247), rather than an alternative form of Thorpe (Dowthorpe) in Earl's Barton (VCH p.354, see EPNS 138) Neither seems represented by a holding of Judith in the Survey.

56,61 ST WANDRILLE'S. In Seine Maritime, between Rouen and Le Havre on the north bank of the Seine.

56,63-64 HOUGHTON. See 56,57b, and 2,2 note.

56,65 BISHOP GEOFFREY..AND WINEMAR. Winemar holds the neighbouring Hackleton and Preston under Geoffrey, Bishop of Coutances, 4,15-16. Geoffrey had been granted the lands of Burgred, 35,1j note.

56,66 POTTERSPURY. *Pyria* in the Survey (374b) held by King David. The place is distinguished in the Survey from *West Pyria* (Paulerspury) held by William Peverel in chief. See 35,22 and 25,1 notes.

57,3 HOLLOWELL. This entry was originally omitted in error and is written in the right margin of col.229b, beginning at the end of 57,2 and extending down beside 57,4. The letters, apart from those in the place-name, are all of the same size, not as Farley prints them.

59 RICHARD. The Artificer, B21. 2½ hides paying no tax are held by Richard *Engayne* in the 'Geld Roll' for Upton Hundred, probably Stibbington below.

59,1 STIBBINGTON. In Hunts. See Hunts 7,7. 9,4. DB includes it in Upton Hundred.

59,4 IT IS IN LORDSHIP. *Ipsa* perhaps mistakenly for *una* '1 (plough)'.
60 WILLIAM. The Artificer, B17. See Round, FE p.155.
ELe 1 WATFORD. The exchange is mentioned at 23,3.
ELe 2 STANFORD (ON AVON).See 41,3 note.
ELc 1 STAMFORD. The ward in Northants. was no doubt south of the Welland, lying in Upton Hundred, the Bishop's soke; later known as Stamford Baron.
ELc 2-3 UFFINGTON. The land had been alienated from the Church, hence the unusual arrangements for cultivation.
LIVESTOCK. See 56,36 note.
BELMESTHORPE. In Witchley Wapentake, see 56,1.
WARNODE.See Rutland ELc 9 note.
ALFRED OF LINCOLN'S UFFINGTON. Lincs. 27,34-36.
ELc 4 HARDWICK. Probably the place in Witchley; see C.W. Foster and T. Longley *The Lincolnshire Domesday and the Lindsey Survey* Lincs. Record Society 19 (1924, reprint 1976) pp.x1 and 227.

THE HUNDREDS

The names of 29 Hundreds occur in the text of Northants. One of them, *Geritone,* is probably identical with Corby (1,32 note). The remaining 28 are evidenced in more or less detail: Hundred heads are sporadic in the text, Higham Hundred being entered only once as a rubrication, although the DB Hundred probably contained 16 places. Apart from scribal lack of care, other reasons are that Hundred heads are rarely entered for outlying parts of a manor, nor at the beginning of chapters, nor, it seems, when the place names the Hundred.

The relation of the Domesday Hundreds to those given in the 'Geld Roll', the Survey, the *Nomina Villarum* of 1316 (FA iv 19-30) and in the 1841 Census (the last to group parishes by Hundreds) is set out below. Only major variants of the DB name are given.

Geld Roll	*Domesday*		*Survey*	*Nomina Villarum*	*1841 Census*
Eadboldesstowe	Edboldeston Holeboldest Alboldestou Otboldestou	(Ab)	Albodestowe	[part of Sutton]	–
Egelweardesle	Aluratleu Aluuardeslea	(Aw)	Aylwoldesle	[part of Fawsley]	–
Klegele	Clailei Claueslea Claislund	(Cy)	Cleyle	Cleyle	Cleyley
–	Coltrewestan Colestreu Colentreu	(Ct)	[part of Wymersley]	–	–
Corebi	Corbei	(Cb)	Coreby	Corby	Corby
Uoxle	Foxle Foxeslau	(F)	Norton	Norton	(Green's) Norton
Gravesende	Gravesende	(Gr)	Graveshende Falewesle	Falewesle	Fawsley
Gildesburh (150)	Gisleburg	(Gu)	Gildesboru	Gildesburgh	Guilsborough
Anduerðeshoh	Hanuerdesho Andferdesho	(Ha)	Andfordesho	Aunfordesho	Hamfordshoe
Hehham (150)	Hechã	(Hm)	Hecham	Hegham	Higham (Ferrers)
Hocheshlauua	Hocheslau	(Hu)	Hokeslawe	Hokeslowe	Huxloe
Malesle	Maleslea	(M)	Mallesl[ea]	[part of Orlingbury]	–
Neresforda	Narresford	(Nf)	Navesford	Nauesford	Navisford
Nauereslund (200)	Neueslund	(Nn)	Suthnaveslunt Northnaveslunt	[part of Huxloe]	–
Newbotle grave (150)	Niuuebote Niuuebold Neubotlagraue	(Nb)	Neubotlegrave	Neubotlegrove	Nobottle (Grove)
Ordlingbære	Ordinbaro	(O)	Orlingberge	Orlyngbere	Orlingbury
Pocabroc	Pochebroc	(P)	Pokebroc	Polebroke	Polebrook

Geld Roll	Domesday		Survey	Nomina Villarum	1841 Census
Rodewelle	Rodeuuelle	(R)	Rowell	Rothewell	Rothwell
Spelhoh	Spelehou Spereholt	(Sp)	Speleho	Spelho	Spelhoe
Stoce	Stoche Stoc	(St)	Stokes	[part of Corby]	—
Stotfalde	Stodfalde Stofald	(Sf)	Stotfolde	[part of Rothwell]	—
Suttunes	Sutone Sudtune	(Su)	Sutton	Sutton	(King's) Sutton
Uyceste	Touecestre	(T)	Toucestr(e)	Toucestre	Towcester
Uptune (200)	Optone Optonegrave Optonegren	(U)	(missing)	Nasso Burgi	Nassaburgh (Double Hundred)
Werdunes	Waredone	(Wa)	Wardon	Wardon	(Chipping) Warden
Wilebroc	Wilebroc	(Wk)	Wylebroke	Welybrok	Willybrook
Hwicceslea west Hwicceslea east	Wiceslea	(Wt)	[part of RUTLAND]	—	—
Wimereslea (150)	Wimeresle Wimerleu	(Wy)	Wymeresle	Wymeresle	Wymersley

The 'Geld Roll' states that some Hundreds are double and some one and a half (marked 200 and 150 in above table). Domesday sometimes calls Guilsborough and Wymersley 'a hundred and a half'.

Amalgamations in the centuries following the compilation of Domesday removed Alboldstow, Alwardesley, Mawsley, Navisland, Stoke and Stotfold. Collingtree Hundred occurs only in Domesday, containing about 6 places, and was soon amalgamated with Wymersley where it was probably included in the 'Geld Roll'. Although a Hundred is named after Foxley in DB, the village itself was in Towcester Hundred in 1086, possibly a recent transfer.

Although Alwardesley Hundred occurs in the Survey, it appears at that time to have formed a much larger area to the north of the correspondingly reduced Gravesend Hundred, Staverton Badby and Dodford being on its southern edge. The Geld Roll Hundred of Alwardsley was similarly larger than the 1086 one which seems to have contained only Barby and Kilsby, since the other places that are included in the Hundred in the Survey are either beneath a Gravesend Hundred head in the text of DB, or among Gravesend places.

Two of the Domesday Hundreds were later divided: in the Survey South Navisland included Finedon, Irthlingborough, Addington and Woodford, the other 1086 Navisland places being in North Navisland in the Survey. Witchley, later in Rutland, became divided into two Hundreds, East and Wrangditch. East contained Ketton, Tinwell,Empingham and places to the east; Wrangditch consisted of Luffenham, Tixover and places west. Witchley is also divided in the 'Geld Roll'.

Apart from these major differences between the DB and later Hundreds, there were a number of variations in the 1086 Hundred boundaries. Some villages were split between Hundreds: Boughton being both in Rothwell and in Corby; Easton on the Hill in Upton and Willybrook. Evenley was both in Alboldstow and Sutton, with another part of the village an outlier of Towcester. Hardwick was both in Hamfordshoe and Orlingbury, Steane in Sutton and Alboldstow, and Warmington was probably in Polebrook and Willybrook.

Detached parts of Hundreds are unusual in 1086, but Evenley and Silverstone were certainly separated from Towcester and Foxley Hundreds respectively, and it is probable that Hinton in the Hedges and Kingsthorpe (with the dependent Moulton and Weston) were detachments of Towcester and Mawsley Hundreds respectively.

Hundred heads in the text or the order of entries suggest that some places were in different Hundreds in 1086 from those where they later lay: thus Cleyley contained Grafton Regis, placed by the Survey in Towcester; Denford was in Higham Ferrers (later Huxloe). Huxloe Hundred contained Benefield; Mawsley probably Holcot. Part of Wellingborough was probably in Navisland and part of Spratton in Nobottle. Orlingbury contained part of Burton Latimer; Stoke Doyle and Thurning were in Polebrook (later Navisford) and Kelmarsh and Pipewell were in Rothwell. Kelmarsh, included in the Survey in Stotfold,was later amalgamated with its Hundred with Rothwell; the latter was later part of Wilbarston parish and so in Corby. Other possibilities are explored in the notes.

In this edition, places have been indexed and mapped in their 1086 Hundred where this is known; others have been restored from the Survey, from later evidence or from probability, the Hundred abbreviations of these latter being bracketed in the index. Places split between two Hundreds are mapped and indexed in one for convenience, and outliers (except Silverstone) are mapped in geographically appropriate Hundreds.

THE COUNTY BOUNDARY

This edition ignores the major boundary changes of 1st April 1974 and the fact that the area around Peterborough, corresponding to Upton Wapentake, has long been regarded as a Soke, and even before 1974 as part of Huntingdonshire.

Even without these changes, the modern county differed in a number of ways from the 1086 shire. Apart from the early transfer of Witchley Wapentake to Rutland, most of the changes date from the nineteenth century. These changes are set out below. Until the last century Northants. along its south-eastern boundary was much interlaced with Huntingdon and Bedfordshire, with some villages divided by the County boundary, and some parts of Northants. being entirely detached. The 1086 bounds are complicated by the fact that some lords, the Bishop of Coutances, the Abbots of Ramsey and Peterborough and William Peverel, held adjacent ground on both sides of the boundary. Moreover it is not always possible from the Domesday evidence to determine if a piece of land was an outlying part of Northants. in another county in 1086, or if it was an integral part of the County but later isolated from it by an unrecorded boundary change. Domesday place-names are those of areas, often of a large number of hides, only a marginal portion of which could be in another county.

West and North	*1086*	*Later times*	*19thC. Changes*	*31.3.74*
Grimsbury	Northants.	Northants.	to Oxford 1889	Oxford.
Mollington	part Northants. part Warks. part Oxon.	part Warks. part Oxon.	rest to Oxford 1895	Oxford.
Stoneton	Northants.	Northants.	to Warks. 1896	Warks.
Sawbridge	Northants.	Warks.	–	Warks.
Little Bowden	Northants.	Northants.	to Leics. 1888	Leics.
South East				
Stibbington	part Northants. part Hunts.	Hunts.	–	Hunts.
Elton	part Northants. part Hunts.	part Northants. part Hunts.**	rest to Hunts. c 1890	Hunts.
Lutton	part Northants. part Hunts.	part Northants. part Hunts.	rest to Northants. 1888	Northants.
Luddington	part Northants. part Hunts.	part Northants. part Hunts.	rest to Northants. 1888	Northants.
Thurning	part Northants. part Hunts.	part Northants. part Hunts.	rest to Northants. 1888	Northants.
Winwick	part Northants. part Hunts.	part Northants. (detached) part Hunts.	rest to Hunts. 1888	Hunts.
Catworth	part Northants. part Hunts.	part Northants. (detached)** part Hunts.	rest to Hunts. c 1890	Hunts.
Hargrave	part Northants. part Hunts.	Northants.	–	Northants.
Stanwick	part Northants. part Beds.	Northants.	–	Northants.
Newton (Bromswold)	part Northants. part Beds.	Northants.	–	Northants.
Rushden	part Northants. part Beds.	Northants.	–	Northants.
Podington	part Northants. part Beds.	Beds.	–	Beds.
Farndish	part Northants. part Beds.	part Northants. part Beds.	rest to Beds. 1883-4	Beds.

** a few fields only were involved.

Index of Persons

Index of Places

Maps and Map Keys

Systems of Reference

Technical Terms

INDEX OF PERSONS

Familiar modern spellings are given where they exist. Unfamiliar names are usually given in an approximate late 11th century form, avoiding variants that were already obsolescent or pedantic. Spellings that mislead the modern eye are avoided where possible. Two, however, cannot be avoided: they are combined in the name of 'Leofgeat', pronounced 'Leffyet', or 'Levyet'. The definite article is omitted before bynames, except where there is reason to suppose that they described the individual. The chapter numbers of listed handholders are printed in italics.

Churches and Clergy. **Abbey of ...** St Edmund (Bury St Edmunds) *8*. Coventry *12*. Crowland *11*. Evesham *13*. St Benedict, Ramsey *9*. St Mary, Grestain *14*. St Peter, Peterboroug *6*; EB 3. St Peter, Westminster *7*. Thorney *10*. **Abbot ...** see Benedict, Leofric. **Abbot of ...** St Edmund's (Bury St Edmunds) B 3; 18,31. Coventry B 6. Crowland EH 2. Evesham B 7. Peterborough B 4; ELc 1-2, see Geoffrey. Ramsey B 5; EH 3. Selby B 8. **Archbishop ...** see Aldred, Stigand. **Bishop ...** see Geoffrey. **Bishop of ...** Bayeux *2*; B 16;30. Coutances *4*; B 2; 41, 5; EB 1-2; EH 1, see William the Steward. Durham *3*. Lincoln *5*. **Church of ...** Peterborough 42, 2. Ramsey 55,1. St Rémy (Rheims) *16*. Saint-Pierre-sur-Dives 46,6. St Wandrille 56,61. All Saints (?Stamford) 1,5. St Peter, (?Stamford) 1,5. **Chaplain ...** see Ansger. **Cleric ...** see Ansger. **Priest ...** see Godwin, Leofwin, Saemer.

Secular Titles and Occupational Names. **Artificer** (*inganie*) ... Richard, William. **Cook**(?) (*cocus*) ... Gilbert. **Count** (*comes*) ... Alan, of Meulan, of Mortain. **Countess** (*comitissa*) ... Gytha, Judith. **Earl** (*comes*) ... Algar, Aubrey, Hugh, Morcar, Ralph, Tosti, Waltheof. **Hunter** (*venator*) ... Alwin. **Queen** (*regina*) ... Edith, Matilda. **Reeve** (*prepositus*) ... Durand. **Sheriff** (*vicecomes*) ... B 37, Eustace. **Steward** (*dapifer*) ... Ralph, William.

INDEX OF PLACES

The name of each place is followed by (i) the initial of its Hundred and its location on the map in this volume; (ii) its National Grid reference; (iii) the chapter and section reference in DB. Bracketed figures denote mention in sections dealing with a different place. Unless otherwise stated in the notes, the identifications of EPNS and the spellings of the Ordnance Survey are followed for places in England, of OEB for places abroad. Inverted commas mark lost places with known modern spelling; unidentifiable places are given in DB spelling, in italics. The National Grid reference system is explained on all Ordnance Survey maps, and in the Automobile Association Handbooks; the figures reading from left to right are given before those reading from bottom to top of the map. Places are in the 100 kilometre grid square SP except those with Grid References beginning with F (in TF), K (in SK) or L (in TL). Places with bracketed Grid References do not appear on the current 1:50,000 maps. Places starred are not in Northamptonshire, those marked B being in Bedfordshire, H in Huntingdon, Lc in Lincolnshire, Le in Leicestershire, O in Oxfordshire, R in Rutland, S in Staffordshire and W in Warwickshire. All places in Witchley Wapentake were in Rutland. Places belonging to nearby counties but thought to have been included in the Northamptonshire folios in error are indexed below but not mapped: for these the relevant county volumes of this series should be consulted. Places within Northants.in 1086 or dependencies of it just over the border are mapped and indexed. Within the county, remote dependencies of other places are mapped in geographically appropriate Hundreds, not as detachments. The Northants.Hundreds are Alboldstow (Ab); Alwardsley (Aw); Cleyley (Cy); Collingtree (Ct); Corby (Cb); Foxley (F); Gravesend (Gr); Guilsborough (Gu); Hamfordshoe (Ha); Higham Ferrers (Hm); Huxloe (Hu); Mawsley (M); Navisford (Nf); Navisland (Nn); Nobottle (Nb); Orlingbury (O); Polebrook (P); Rothwell (R); Spelhoe (Sp); Stoke (St); Stotfold (Sf); Sutton (Su); Towcester (T); Upton (U); Warden (Wa); Willybrook (Wk); Witchley (Wt); and Wymersley (Wy). The Hundred initials of places that do not appear beside a Hundred heading in the text of DB are bracketed. The evidence from which their Hundreds have been identified is explained at the end of the notes. S in the Hundreds' Column stands for the Borough of Stamford.

	Map	*Grid*	*Text*
Abington	Sp 1	77 61	59,3
Aceshille	Cy -	- -	35,11
Achurch	(Nf 1)	L02 83	6a,22
Addington	Nn 1	95 75	4,21-22. 6a,29. 11,4
Adstone	F 1	59 51	1,6. 17,1. 18,73
Ailsworth	(U 1)	L11 99	6,5. 6a,3
Alderton	Cy 1	74 46	18,9;91
Aldwincle	Hu 1	L00 81	6a,27. 41,6
Althorp	(Nb 1)	68 65	18,23. 35,3b
Apethorpe	(Wk 1)	L02 95	1,23
Armston	(P 1)	L05 85	6a,14
Arthingworth	(R 1)	75 81	1,15e. 8,3. 18,15. (35,13)
Ashby St. Ledgers	(Gr 1)	57 68	23,4
Canons Ashby	(F 2)	57 50	39,9
Castle Ashby	(Wy 1)	86 59	56,45
Cold Ashby	(Gu 1)	65 76	12,2. 18, 50-51. 35,19e. 47,1b
Mears Ashby	(Ha 1)	83 66	56,18
Ashley	St 1	79 90	26,10-11. 30,1;8. 56,2

	Map	*Grid*	*Text*
Ashton (Polebrook)	(P 2)	L05 88	6,12. 6a,34
Ashton (Towcester)	Cy 2	76 49	40,4-5
Astcote	(T 1)	67 53	39,15
Aston le Walls	(Wa 1)	49 50	45,5
Astwell	(Ab 1)	60 44	43,9
Aynho	Su 1	51 33	45,1
Badby	Gr 2	55 58	11,6
Barby	Aw1	54 70	35,8
Barford	(R 2)	85 82	1,21;(22)
Barnack	U 2	F07 05	36,2
Barnwell	Hu 2	L04 85	1,25. 9,5
*Barrowden(R)	(Wt 1)	K94 00	1,2a. 26,3
Barton Seagrave	(Nn 2)	88 77	4,17
Earls Barton	(Ha 2)	85 63	56,15
*Belmesthorpe (R)	(Wt 2)	F04 10	56,1. ELc2-3
Benefield	Hu 3	98 88	59,2
*Berkswell(W)	-	- -	19,2
Billing	Sp 2	81 62	18,2;(4). 48,3. 57,1
*Bisbrooke(R)	(Wt 3)	88 99	1,2e. 56,25
Blakesley	F 3	62 50	1,6. 18,95. 22,7. 35,24
Blatherwycke	(Cb 1)	97 95	30,10
Blisworth	(Ct 1)	72 53	35,7
Boddington	(Wa 2)	48 53	18,96. 22,2
Boughton (Northampton)	Sp 3	75 65	17,5. 30,15. 56,19;60-62

	Map	Grid	Text
Boughton (Weekley)	Cb 2	90 81	8,1. 48,1
*Little Bowden (Le)	(Sf 1)	74 87	18,19
Bozeat	(Hm1)	90 59	35,14. 56,39;54
Brackley	Ab 2	58 37	21,1-2
Bradden	F 4	64 48	30,17;19. 58,2
Brafield on the Green	(Wy 2)	82 58	2,3. (9,6). 56,20h;56
Brampton Ash	(St 2)	79 87	26,8. 30,5; 9. 56,6
Brampton	(Nb 2)	71 65	18,7;99
Braunston	Gr 3	53 66	2,5. 38,1
Braybrooke	R 3	76 84	8,7. 14,2. 29,1. 30, 11-12. 56,10;31
Brigstock	(Cb 3)	94 85	1,13a
Brime	(Ab -)	- -	43,6
Brington	(Nb 3)	66 65	18,44. 35,3c
Brixworth	M 1	74 70	1,16
Brockhall	(Nb 4)	63 62	18,45
*West Bromwich(S)	-	- -	36,3
Broughton	(O 1)	83 75	1,15k. 56,12
Long Buckby	(Gu 2)	62 67	18,72
Bugbrooke	Nb 5	67 57	18,3;(41; 83-84)
Burghley	(U 3)	F04 06	6a,5
Burton Latimer	Nn 3	90 74	4,9;12. 41,1;(2)
Byfield	Wa 3	51 53	22,1. 23,12
Caldecott	(Hm2)	98 68	35,1c
*Caldecott(R)	(Wt 4)	86 93	5,2
Calme	(Sf -)	- -	8,11
East Carlton	St 3	83 89	18,13
*Casterton(R)	(Wt 5)	F00 08	1,4. 58,1
Castor	(U 4)	L12 98	6,4. 6a,1
Catesby	Gr 4	52 59	35,10
*Catworth(H)	(Nf 2)	L08 73	6a,26
Celverdescote	Gr -	- -	18,11
Chacombe	Ab 3	49 43	5,4
Chadstone	Wy 3	85 58	53,1
Charlton	Su 2	52 35	2,11. 18,38
*Charlton on Otmoor(O)	-	- -	23,17
Charwelton	Gr 5	53 55	10,2. 18,36; 66. 23,15
Chelveston	(Hm3)	99 69	35,1c
'Chilcotes'	(Gu 3)	(65 74)	18,68
Kings Cliffe	(Wk 2)	L00 97	B3b. 1,26
Clipston	Sf 2	71 81	1,15i. 4,10. 8,10. 35,2
Clopton	Nf 3	L06 80	6a,24. 55,6
Cogenhoe	(Wy 4)	83 61	41,9. 56,58
Collyweston	Wk 3	K99 02	32,1
Collingtree	Ct 2	75 55	44,1b
Corby	(Cb 4)	89 88	1,12;(28. 60,3)
Cosgrove	Cy 3	79 42	18,12;24.40
Coton	(Gu 4)	67 71	35,19a;19h
Cotterstock	(Wk 4)	L04 90	6a,10
Cottesbrooke	Gu 5	71 73	39,2. 60,4
Cottingham	St 4	84 90	6,2
*Cottisford(O)	-	- -	23,16
Courteenhall	Ct 3	75 53	35,6;25
Cranford	Nn 4	92 77	4,18. 6a, 31-32. 41,8
Cransley	O 2	83 76	1,15j. 48,5. 56,13
Creaton	Gu 6	70 71	18,(7);53. 30,18. 48,8
Crick	(Gu 7)	58 72	47,2
Croughton	Su 3	54 33	4,29. 18,64. 45,2-3
Culworth	Ab 4	54 46	45,9
Dallington	(Nb 6)	73 61	6a,33
Daventry	(Gr 6)	57 62	56,21
Deene	Cb 5	95 92	7,1
Denford	(Hm4)	99 76	4,2
Denton	Wy 5	83 57	9,6. 56,20d;
Desborough	R 4	80 83	1,15f. 18,26 26,6. 35,12
Dingley	(St 5)	77 87	18,14. 26,9. 30,4. 56,5
Dodford	(Gr 7)	61 60	18,58
Gt. Doddington	(Ha 3)	88 64	56,16;(53)
Draughton	R 5	76 76	1,15d. 54,3. 56,11
Duddington	Wk 5	K98 00	1,14
Duston	(Nb 7)	72 61	35,4
Easton Maudit	(Hm5)	88 58	35,1h. 56,5
Easton Neston	(Cy 4)	70 49	18,59. 48,1
Easton on the Hill	Wk 6	F01 04	42,2-3. 46,6
Ecton	Ha 4	82 63	25,3
Edgcote	Wa 4	50 47	4,11
Elkington	Gu 8	62 76	18,69. 41,1 47,1b
Elmington	(Wk 7)	L06 89	11,2-3
*Elton (H)	(Wk 8)	L08 93	6,9. 9,3
*Empingham(R)	Wt 6	K95 08	35,9. 46,4-5
*Essendine(R)	(Wt 7)	F04 12	5,3
Evenley	Ab 5	58 34	18,(64);65. 21,5. 39,8; 10;(11)
Everdon	Gr 8	59 57	2,10
Eydon	(Wa 5)	54 50	23,14
*Farndish(B)	(Hm6)	92 63	35,1f
East Farndon	Sf 3	71 85	8,8. 18,18. 56,28. 60,5
West Farndon	Wa 6	52 51	18,32. 23,1
Farthinghoe	(Su 4)	53 39	21,6
Farthingstone	(Gr 9)	61 55	18,57;75
Fawsley	Gr 10	56 56	1,9. (2,5;10) 17,2. (18,30 57-58;75)
Faxton	(M 2)	78 75	1,17
Finedon	Nn 5	91 71	1,32. 4,13
*Finmere (O)	-	- -	4,30
Flore	Nb 8	64 60	18,47. 34,1. 3f.45,6.48,1

	Map	*Grid*	*Text*
Fotheringhay	Wk 9	L06 93	56,7
Foxley	T 2	64 51	18,39
Furtho	Cy 5	77 43	18,34;55-56
Geddington	(Cb 6)	89 83	1,13c. 8,2
Glassthorpehill	(Nb 9)	66 60	18,48. 35,3e
*Glaston (R)	(Wt 8)	K89 00	1,2e. 56,36
Glendon	(R 6)	84 81	1,15c. 14,3
Glinton	(U 5)	F15 05	6,7. 6a,7
*Glympton (O)	-	- -	4,33
Grafton Regis	Cy 6	75 46	18,89
Grafton Underwood	Nn 6	92 80	33,1. 55,5
Greatworth	(Wa 7)	55 42	2,4
Grendon	(Wy 6)	87 60	56,20b;45
Gretton	Cb 7	89 94	1,11;(14)
*Grimsbury (O)	Su 5	46 41	48,11
Guilsborough	(Gu 9)	67 72	18,80. 35,23
Hackleton	Wy 7	80 55	4,15. 56,20e
East Haddon	Nb 10	66 68	18,5;(7;44); 87;93
West Haddon	(Gu 10)	63 71	12,4. 35,19d. 48,7
Halefield	Wk 10	L02 93	9,1
Halse	Ab 6	56 40	21,1
Hannington	O 3	81 71	18,42.56,14
Hantone	-	- -	4,14. 40,3
Hardingstone	Ct 4	76 57	1,10. 56,20j
Hardwick	O 4	85 69	56,47-48
*Hardwick(R)	(Wt 9)	K96 12	ELc 4
Hargrave	(Hm7)	L03 70	35,15. EH1; 4-5
Harlestone	Nb 11	70 64	1,19. 18,22; 43. 35,3d
Harpole	(Nb 12)	69 60	35,16
Harrington	R 7	77 80	14,5
Harringworth	(Cb 8)	91 97	56,8
Harrowden	O 5	88 70	4,5-7;(19). 41,4
Hartwell	(Cy 7)	78 50	2,7
Haselbech	(Sf 4)	71 77	18,21
Helmdon	Ab 7	58 43	18,10
Hemington	P 3	L09 85	6a,15. 9,4
*Hethe (O)	-	- -	4,31
*Heyford (O)	-	- -	4,36
Heyford	Nb 13	65 58	2,12. 18,8; 41;83-84. 46,2
Cold Higham	T 3	66 53	18,28. 39,12
Higham Ferrers	(Hm8)	96 68	35,1a;(14-15)
Hinton (Woodford Halse)	Wa 8	53 52	45,4
Hinton in the Hedges	(Ab 8)	55 36	45,8
Holcot	(M 3)	79 69	1,16. 56,43
Holdenby	(Nb 14)	69 67	18,86;92
Hollowell	Gu 11	69 72	5,1. 18,80; 94. 35,19g. 57,3
*Horn (R)	Wt 10	K95 11	3,1. 56,27
Horton	(Wy8)	81 54	4,28. 39,7. 56,20f;34
Hothorpe	(Sf 5)	66 85	8,9
Houghton	Wy9	79 58	2,2. 35,21. 56,57b; 57g;63-64
Hanging Houghton	(M 4)	75 73	8,5. 18,31. 39,3. 56,42
Hulcote	Cy 8	70 49	2,1. 48,15
Irchester	(Hm9)	92 65	18,81. 35,1e;(1j)
Irthlingborough	(Nn 7)	94 70	6,15. 6a,30
Isham	(O 6)	88 73	4,8. 41,5. 55,1
Islip	(Hu 4)	98 78	1,13b;13e. 4,27
Kelmarsh	(R 8)	73 79	1,15g. 35,13
Kettering	(Nn8)	86 78	6,17
*Ketton (R)	Wt 11	K98 04	1,1
Kilsby	Aw2	56 71	12,3
Kingsthorpe (Northampton)	(Sp 4)	75 63	1,18
Kingsthorpe (Polebrook)	(P 4)	L08 85	6a,14
Kirby	Cb 9	92 92	59,4
Kislingbury	Nb 15	69 59	18,46. 46,1
Knuston	(Hm10)	94 66	35,1d. 48,12
Lamport	(M 5)	75 74	8,6. 39,4. 56,9
*Lapley (S)	-	- -	16,1
*Lavington (Lc)	-	- -	ELc 4
Laxton	(Cb10)	95 96	60,2
Lilbourne	(Gu12)	56 76	18,70. 21,3-4
Lilford	Hu 5	L03 84	56,49
Litchborough	Gr 11	63 54	13,1
Loddington	(R 9)	81 78	1,15b
Lowick	Hu 6	97 80	4,26. 51,1
Luddington in the Brook	(P 5)	L10 83	6a,16. EH7
*Luffenham (R)	(Wt 12)	K93 03	1,2f;3. (56,36)
Lutton	(Wk11)	L11 87	6a,11. 9,2. EH3
*Lyddington(R)	(Wt 13)	87 97	5,2
Maidford	F 5	61 52	23,8
Maidwell	Sf 6	74 76	8,12. 15,1. 54,3
*Marston (in Church Eaton(S)	-	- -	16,2
Marston St. Lawrence	Ab 9	53 42	22,4
Marston Trussell	Sf 7	69 85	23,2
Middleton Cheney	Su 6	49 42	18,37. 22,6. 23,10
Milton (Castor)	(U 6)	14 99	6a,2
Milton Malsor (Northampton)	Ct 5	73 55	44,1a;1c
*Mollington (O)	(Wa 9)	44 47	35,26
*Morcott (R)	(Wt 14)	K92 00	1,2d
Moreton Pinkney	(F 6)	57 49	43,2
Moulton	Sp 5	78 66	1,18. 30,14. 56,29;33;44

	Map	Grid	Text
Muscott	(Nb 16)	62 63	18,45
Naseby	(Gu 13)	68 78	35,(2);5;(25)
Nassington	(Wk 12)	L06 96	1,20;(23)
Newbottle (Brackley)	Su 7	51 36	23,9
Newbottle (Harrington)	(R 10)	78 81	14,1
Newton (Geddington)	Cb 11	88 83	48,2. 56,30; 37
Newton Bromswold	(Hm11)	99 65	4,20. EB1
Nobottle	(Nb 17)	67 63	35,3a;(3b)
Northampton	(Sp 6)	75 60	B1;37
Nortoft	(Gu 14)	67 73	18,80. 35,19f
Greens Norton	(F 7)	66 49	1,6. (18,95. 22,7)
Norton (Daventry)	Gr 12	60 63	19,1
Oakley	(Cb 12)	86 85	56,38
Old	(M 6)	78 73	1,17
Orlingbury	(O 7)	86 72	18,78
Orton	R 11	80 79	1,15a
Oundle	(P 6)	L03 88	6,10a. (6a, 11;15-17)
*Over (W)	-	- -	36,4
Oxendon	Sf 8	73 83	1,15h. 18,20. 56,32
Passenham	Cy 9	78 39	1,30. 17,4. (18,24)
Pattishall	(T 4)	67 54	39,(12);18
Paulerspury	Cy 10	71 45	35,22
Peterborough	(U 7)	L19 98	(4,23). 6,1. (6a,30. 42,2. ELc 2-3)
Piddington	(Wy 10)	80 54	56,65
Pilsgate	(U 8)	F06 05	6,6
Pilton	(Nf 4)	L02 84	6a,20
Pipewell	R 12	83 85	18,16. 26,7. 39,1
Pitsford	Sp 7	75 68	18,25. 39,6
Plumpton	(F 8)	59 48	39,13
*Podington (B)	(Hm12)	94 62	35,1g
Polebrook	(P 7)	L06 87	6a,13. 55,3
**Portland* (R)	(Wt -)	- -	1,5
Potterspury	Cy 11	76 43	25,1. 56,66
Preston	(Gr 13)	57 54	18,74;85;90
Preston Deanery	(Wy 11)	78 55	4,16. 56,57c
Purston	Su 8	51 39	18,61. 28,3
Puxley	Cy 12	75 42	1,30. 2,8
Pytchley	O 8	85 74	6a,25. 18,77. 60,1
Quinton	(Wy 12)	77 54	56,20i;57d-e
Radstone	(Ab 10)	58 40	22,5
Raunds	(Hm13)	99 72	4,1. 35,1i;(1j)
Ravensthorpe	(Nb 18)	66 70	18,6. 35,17. 57,4
Roade	(Cy 13)	75 51	2,9. 48,17
Rockingham	(St 6)	86 91	1,27
Rothersthorpe	Ct 6	71 56	44,1c;2. 48,9
Rothwell	R 13	81 81	1,15a;15l
Rushden	(Hm14)	95 66	35,1b;(1j). EB2;4
Rushton	R 14	84 82	1,22. 14,4. 26,5. 30,13. 56,46
*Ryhall (R)	Wt 15	F03 10	56,1
*Sawbridge (W)	(Gr 14)	50 65	10,3
Scaldwell	(M 7)	76 72	4,3. 8,4. 56,41
*'Sculthorp'(R)	(Wt 16)	(K93 02)	1,3
*Seaton (R)	Wt 17	90 98	1,2b;2g. 26,3. (56,36
Seawell	F 9	62 52	26,4
*Shelswell (O)	-	- -	4,32
*Shipton on Cherwell (O)	-	- -	23,18
Sibbertoft	Sf 9	68 82	18,17
*Sibford (O)	-	- -	23,19
Silverstone	F 10	66 44	18,52. 43,3. 45,7
*Skillington (Lc)	-	- -	ELc 4
Slapton	F 11	64 46	22,9
Slipton	(Hu 7)	95 79	6,14
*'Snelston' (R)	(Wt 18)	(86 95)	5,2
Snorscomb	Gr 15	59 56	18,60;97
Southorpe	(U 9)	F08 03	6a,6
Spratton	(Sp 8)	71 70	18,88. 30,16. 56,50
*Stamford (Lc)	S	F03 07	ELc 1
Stanford on Avon	Gu 15	58 78	41,3;(7). ELe 2
Stanion	(Cb 13)	91 86	1,13d. 4,25
Stanwick	(Hm15)	98 71	6,16. EB3
Staverton	(Gr 16)	54 61	18,30. 23,6
Steane	Ab 11	55 39	43,5
*Stibbington (H)	U 10	L08 98	59,1
Stoke Albany	(St 7)	80 87	1,28. 26,1
Stoke Bruerne	Cy 14	74 49	B29.50,1
Stoke Doyle	(P 8)	L02 86	(6a,19)
*Stoke Dry (R)	Wt 19	85 96	5,2. 6,10c
*Stoneton (W)	Wa 10	46 54	27,1
Stowe	Gr 17	63 57	46,3
Stuchbury	(Ab 12)	56 44	43,8
Sudborough	Hu 8	96 82	7,2
Sulby	Sf 10	66 82	41,7. 47,1c
Sulgrave	Wa 11	55 45	43,11
Sutton Bassett	(St 8)	77 90	30,3. 56,3
Kings Sutton	(Su 9)	49 36	1,8. (2,6; 11). 17,3. 18,(37;61-62);63. (22,6). 23,11
Syresham	Ab 13	63 41	18,40. 21,1. 43,10
Sywell	Ha 5	82 67	18,1
Tansor	(Wk13)	L05 90	1,24;(25)
Teeton	(Nb 19)	69 70	35,18
Thenford	Su 10	51 41	28,2. 54,1
Thornby	(Gu 16)	67 75	35,19b;20
Thorpe (Peterborough)	(U 11)	L16 98	6,3
*Thorpe by Water (R)	(Wt 20)	89 96	1,2c. (56,36)

	Map	Grid	Text
Thorpe Lubenham	Sf 11	70 86	23,2
Thorpe Malsor	(R 15)	83 79	18,76
Thorpe Mandeville	(Ab 14)	53 44	43,7
Thrapston	Nf 5	99 78	4,24. 52,1
Thrupp Grounds	Gr 18	60 65	18,67. 23,7.48,10. 56,35
Thurning	(P 9)	L08 82	6,10b. EH2;6
*Tickencote(R)	(Wt 21)	K99 09	56,26
Tiffield	(T 5)	69 51	18,33;54
*Tinwell (R)	Wt 22	F00 06	6,13
Titchmarsh	Nf 6	L02 79	6a,23. 25,2
*Tixover (R)	(Wt 23)	K97 00	1,1
*Tolethorpe(R)	Wt 24	F02 10	36,1
Towcester	(T 6)	69 48	1,7. (18,54)
Trafford	(Wa 12)	52 48	22,3
Twywell	Hu 9	95 78	10,1. 56,22
*Uffington (Lc)	(Wt 25)	F06 07	ELc 2-3
Upton	(Nb 20)	71 60	1,19
Wadenhoe	Nf 7	L01 83	4,3-4. 6a,21
Wakefield	Cy 15	73 42	20,1
Wakerley	Cb 14	95 99	42,1
Waletone	-	- -	56,24
Walgrave	M 8	80 72	1,17. 18,79. 56,40
Walton Grounds	(Su 11)	50 34	2,6. 18,35;62
Wappenham	T 7	62 45	43,4
Chipping Warden	(Wa 13)	49 48	(43,11)
Warkton	Nn 9	89 79	8,13
Warmington	(Wk 14)	L07 91	6,11. 6a,12;(18)
Watford	Gu 17	60 68	(23,3). 57,2. ELe 1
Weedon Bec	Gr 19	63 59	18,20. 23,3
Weedon Lois	F 12	60 46	43,1
Weekley	Cb 15	88 80	1,31
Weldon	Cb 16	93 89	(26,5).30,6-7; (8;13). 60,3
Little Weldon	Cb 17	(92 90)	24,1
Welford	Gu 18	64 80	47,1a
Wellingborough	Ha 6	89 67	4,19. 11,5. 56,23;53
Welton	(Gr 20)	58 65	18,98. 23,5. 56,35
Werrington	(U 12)	F16 03	6,8. 6a,8
Weston by Welland	(St 9)	77 91	30,2. 56,4
Weston Favell	Sp 9	78 61	1,18. 14,6. 18,4;82. 48,13
*Whichford (W)	-	- -	46,7
Whilton	(Nb 21)	63 64	18,27
Whiston	Wy 13	85 60	9,6. 56,20c
*Whitacre (W)	-	- -	19,3
Whitfield	(Ab 15)	60 39	1,8
Wicken	Cy 16	74 39	28,1. 54,2
Wilbarston	(St 10)	81 88	1,29. 26,2
Wilby	(Ha 7)	86 66	56,17
Winwick	Gu 19	62 73	12,1;(2;4). 35,19c
*Winwick (H)	(P 10)	L10 80	6a,17. 55,4
Wittering	(U 13)	F05 02	6a;4;(9)
Wollaston	(Hm16)	90 62	48,4. 56,20g;51
Woodford (Denford)	(Nn 10)	96 76	4,23. 6a,28
Woodford Halse	(Wa 14)	54 52	23,13
Woodnewton	(Wk 15)	L03 94	55,2
Wootton	Wy 14	76 56	39,16. 56,57f
*Wootton (O)	-	- -	4,34
*Worton (O)	-	- -	4,35
Wothorpe	U 14	F02 05	6a,9. 11,1. 56,59
Wythemail	(O 9)	84 71	39,5
Yardley Hastings	Wy 15	86 56	56,20a; 57a
Yelvertoft	Gu 20	59 75	18,49;71. 22,8

Places not named

In CLEYLEY Hundred 39,17. In GUILSBOROUGH Hundred 48,6. In GRAVESEND Hundred 39,14. In HIGHAM Hundred 40,2. In STOKE Hundred 31,1. In STOTFOLD Hundred 37,1. In SUTTON Hundred 39,11. In TOWCESTER Hundred 49,1. In WARDEN Hundred 41,2. Hundred not stated 6a,18. 40,6.

Places not in Northamptonshire

Places indexed above are starred; for others see Index of Persons.

Elsewhere in Britain

BEDFORDSHIRE ... Farndish.* Podington.* BUCKINGHAMSHIRE ... Hanslope (Hanslip), see Winemar. CAMBRIDGESHIRE ... Thorney, see Abbey. DURHAM ... Durham, see Bishop. HUNTINGDONSHIRE ... Catworth.* Elton.* Huntingdon, see Eustace. Ramsey, see Abbey, Abbot. Stibbington.* Winwick*. KENT ... Canterbury, see Alnoth. LEICESTERSHIRE ...

Little Bowden*. LINCOLNSHIRE ... Crowland, see Abbey, Abbot. Lavington*. Lincoln, see Bishop, Alfred. Skillington*. Stamford*. Uffington*. MIDDLESEX ... Westminster, see Abbey. OXFORDSHIRE ... Charlton on Otmoor*. Cottisford*. Finmere*. Glympton*. Grimsbury*. Hethe*. Heyford*. Mollington*. Shelswell*. Shipton on Cherwell*. Sibford*. Wootton*. Worton*. RUTLAND ... see Witchley in List of Hundreds. STAFFORDSHIRE ... West Bromwich*. Lapley*. Marston*. Stafford, see Robert. SUFFOLK ... (Bury) St. Edmunds, see Abbey, Abbot. WARWICKSHIRE ... Berkswell*. Coventry, see Abbey, Abbot. Over*. Sawbridge*. Stoneton*. Whichford*. Whitacre*. WORCESTERSHIRE ... Evesham, see Abbey, Abbot. YORKSHIRE ... Selby, see Abbot. York, see Aldred, Archbishop.

Outside Britain

Aincourt ... Walter. Auvers ... Robert. Bayeux ... Bishop. Beuvrière ... Drogo. Bois-Normand ... Roger. Bucy ... Robert. Cahagnes ... William (of Keynes). Chocques ... Gunfrid, Sigar. Coutances ... Bishop. Ferrers ... Henry. Ghent ... Gilbert. Gouville ... Hugh. Grandmesnil ... Hugh. Grestain ... Abbey. La Guerche ... Geoffrey. Ivry ... Hugh, Roger. Limesy ... Ralph. Mandeville ... Geoffrey. Meulan ... Count. Mortain ... Count. Oilly ... Robert. Port ... Hugh. Raimbeaucourt ... Guy. (Rheims) ... Church of St. Rémy. Saint-Pierre-sur-Dives ... Church. Saint Wandrille ... Church. Tosny ... Robert. Vaubadon ... Ansfrid. Vessey ... Robert.

MAPS AND MAP KEYS

The County Boundary is marked by thick lines, continuous for 1086, broken where uncertain, dotted for the modern boundary. Detached parts of Northamptonshire on the Huntingdonshire — Bedfordshire border are drawn from the first edition Ordnance Survey maps. Hundred boundaries (1086) are marked by thin lines, broken where uncertain. On the map of the Northern Hundreds 'S' marks the Lincolnshire borough of Stamford.

National Grid 10-kilometre squares are shown on the map border.

Each four-figure square covers one square kilometre, or 247 acres, approximately 2 hides at 120 acres to the hide.

NORTHAMPTONSHIRE NORTHERN HUNDREDS

A star beside a placename indicates that the place has a Hundred heading beside it in the text of DB. Other places are assigned to individual hundreds by later evidence (see end of notes).

Corby (Cb)
1 Blatherwycke
2 Boughton*
3 Brigstock
4 Corby
5 Deene*
6 Geddington
7 Gretton*
8 Harringworth
9 Kirby*
10 Laxton
11 Newton*
12 Oakley
13 Stanion
14 Wakerley*
15 Weekley*
16 Weldon*
17 Little Weldon*

Huxloe (Hu)
1 Aldwincle*
2 Barnwell*
3 Benefield*
4 Islip
5 Lilford*
6 Lowick*
7 Slipton
8 Sudborough*
9 Twywell*

Mawsley (M)
1 Brixworth*
2 Faxton
3 Holcot
4 Hanging Houghton
5 Lamport
6 Old
7 Scaldwell
8 Walgrave*

Navisford (Nf)
1 Achurch
2 Catworth (HUNTS)
3 Clopton*
4 Pilton
5 Thrapston*
6 Titchmarsh*
7 Wadenhoe*

Navisland (Nn)
1 Addington*
2 Barton Seagrave
3 Burton Latimer*
4 Cranford*
5 Finedon*
6 Grafton Underwood*
7 Irthlingborough
8 Kettering
9 Warkton*
10 Woodford

Orlingbury (O)
1 Broughton
2 Cransley*
3 Hannington*
4 Hardwick*
5 Harrowden*
6 Isham
7 Orlingbury
8 Pytchley*
9 Wythemail

Polebrook (P)
1 Armston
2 Ashton
3 Hemington*
4 Kingsthorpe
5 Luddington in the Brook
6 Oundle
7 Polebrook
8 Stoke Doyle
9 Thurning
10 Winwick (HUNTS)

Rothwell (R)
1 Arthingworth
2 Barford
3 Braybrooke*
4 Desborough*
5 Draughton*
6 Glendon
7 Harrington*
8 Kelmarsh
9 Loddington
10 Newbottle
11 Orton*
12 Pipewell*
13 Rothwell*
14 Rushton*
15 Thorpe Malsor

S Stamford (LINCS)

Stoke (St)
1 Ashley*
2 Brampton Ash
3 East Carlton*
4 Cottingham*
5 Dingley
6 Rockingham
7 Stoke Albany
8 Sutton Bassett
9 Weston by Welland
10 Wilbarston

Stotfold (Sf)
1 Little Bowden (LEICS)
Calme
2 Clipston*
3 East Farndon*
4 Haselbech
5 Hothorpe
6 Maidwell*
7 Marston Trussell*
8 Oxendon*
9 Sibbertoft*
10 Sulby*
11 Thorpe Lubenham*

Upton (U)
1 Ailsworth
2 Barnack*
3 Burghley
4 Castor
5 Glinton
6 Milton
7 Peterborough
8 Pilsgate
9 Southorpe
10 Stibbington* (HUNTS)
11 Thorpe
12 Werrington
13 Wittering
14 Wothorpe*

Willybrook (Wk)
1 Apethorpe
2 Kings Cliffe
3 Collyweston*
4 Cotterstock
5 Duddington*
6 Easton on the Hill*
7 Elmington
8 Elton (HUNTS)
9 Fotheringhay*
10 Halefield*
11 Lutton
12 Nassington
13 Tansor
14 Warmington
15 Woodnewton

Places not Mapped, Hundred Unknown
Hantone
Waletone

Witchley (Wt) (RUTLAND)
1 Barrowden
2 Belmesthorpe
3 Bisbrooke
4 Caldecott
5 Casterton
6 Empingham*
7 Essendine
8 Glaston
9 Hardwick
10 Horn*
11 Ketton*
12 Luffenham
13 Lyddington
14 Morcott
Portland
15 Ryhall*
16 'Sculthorp'
17 Seaton*
18 'Snelston'
19 Stoke Dry*
20 Thorpe by Water
21 Tickencote
22 Tinwell*
23 Tixover
24 Tolethorpe*
25 Uffington (LINCS)

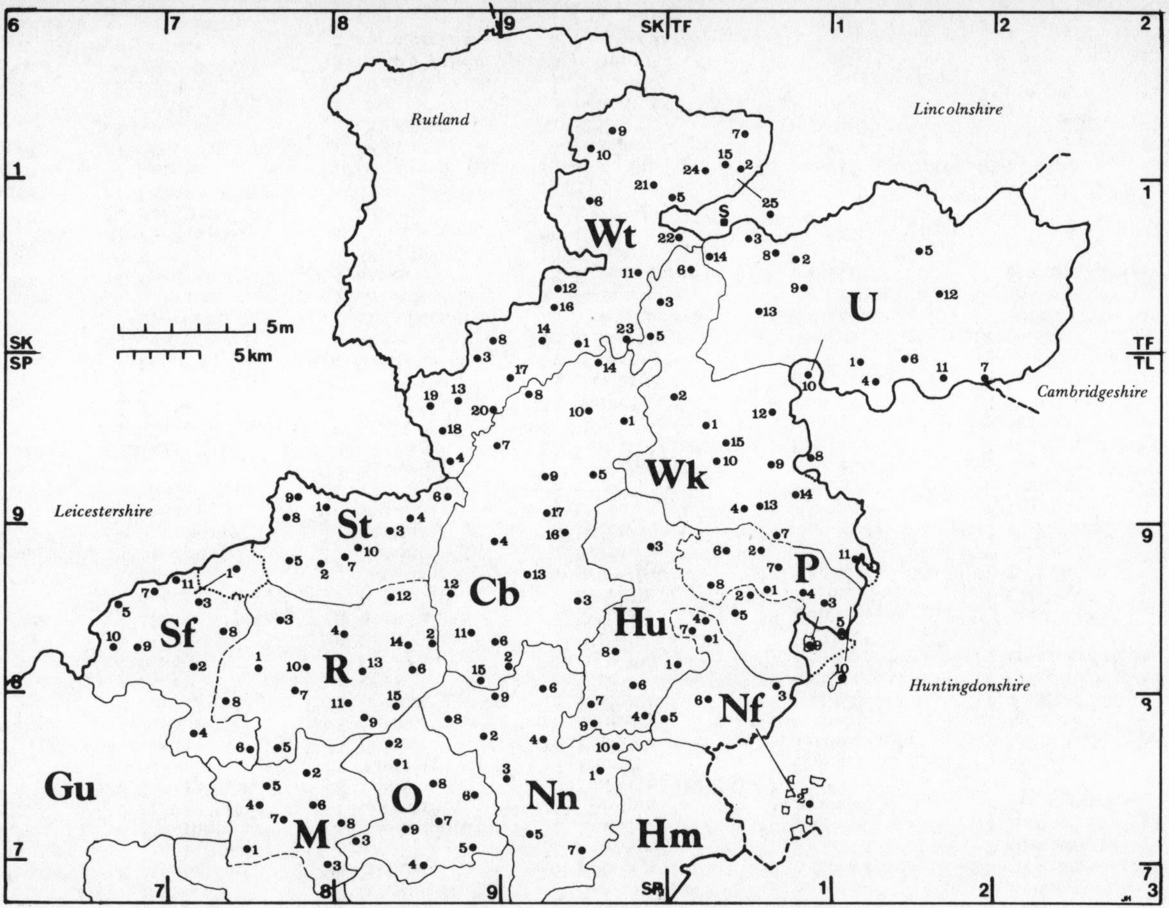

NORTHAMPTONSHIRE NORTHERN HUNDREDS

NORTHAMPTONSHIRE SOUTHERN HUNDREDS

A star beside a placename indicates that the place has a Hundred heading beside it in the text of DB. Other places are assigned to individual hundreds by later evidence (see end of notes).

Alboldstow (Ab)
1 Astwell
2 Brackley*
Brime
3 Chacombe*
4 Culworth*
5 Evenley*
6 Halse*
7 Helmdon*
8 Hinton in the Hedges
9 Marston St Lawrence*
10 Radstone
11 Steane*
12 Stuchbury
13 Syresham*
14 Thorpe Mandeville
15 Whitfield

Alwardsley (Aw)
1 Barby*
2 Kilsby*

Cleyley (Cy)
*Aceshille**
1 Alderton*
2 Ashton*
3 Cosgrove*
4 Easton Neston
5 Furtho*
6 Grafton Regis*
7 Hartwell*
8 Hulcote*
9 Passenham*
10 Paulerspury*
11 Potterspury*
12 Puxley*
13 Roade
14 Stoke Bruerne*
15 Wakefield*
16 Wicken*

Collingtree (Ct)
1 Blisworth
2 Collingtree*
3 Courteenhall*
4 Hardingstone*
5 Milton Malsor*
6 Rothersthorpe

Foxley (F)
1 Adstone*
2 Canons Ashby
3 Blakesley*
4 Bradden*
5 Maidford*
6 Moreton Pinkney
7 Greens Norton
8 Plumpton
9 Seawell*
10 Silverstone*
11 Slapton*
12 Weedon Lois*

Gravesend (Gr)
1 Ashby St Ledgers
2 Badby*
3 Braunston*
4 Catesby*
*Celverdescote**
5 Charwelton*
6 Daventry
7 Dodford
8 Everdon*
9 Farthingstone
10 Fawsley*
11 Litchborough*
12 Norton*
13 Preston
14 Sawbridge (WARKS)
15 Snorscomb*
16 Staverton
17 Stowe*
18 Thrupp Grounds*
19 Weedon Bec*
20 Welton

Guilsborough (Gu)
1 Cold Ashby
2 Long Buckby
3 'Chilcotes'
4 Coton
5 Cottesbrooke*
6 Creaton*
7 Crick
8 Elkington*
9 Guilsborough
10 West Haddon
11 Hollowell*
12 Lilbourne
13 Naseby
14 Nortoft
15 Stanford on Avon*
16 Thornby
17 Watford*
18 Welford*
19 Winwick*
20 Yelvertoft*

Hamfordshoe (Ha)
1 Mears Ashby
2 Earls Barton
3 Great Doddington
4 Ecton*
5 Sywell*
6 Wellingborough*
7 Wilby

Higham Ferrers (Hm)
1 Bozeat
2 Caldecott
3 Chelveston
4 Denford
5 Easton Maudit
6 Farndish (BEDS)
7 Hargrave
8 Higham Ferrers
9 Irchester
10 Knuston
11 Newton Bromswold
12 Podington (BEDS)
13 Raunds
14 Rushden
15 Stanwick
16 Wollaston

Nobottle (Nb)
1 Althorp
2 Brampton
3 Brington
4 Brockhall
5 Bugbrooke*
6 Dallington
7 Duston
8 Flore*
9 Glassthorpehill
10 East Haddon*
11 Harlestone*
12 Harpole
13 Heyford*
14 Holdenby
15 Kislingbury*
16 Muscott
17 Nobottle
18 Ravensthorpe
19 Teeton
20 Upton
21 Whilton

Spelhoe (Sp)
1 Abington*
2 Billing*
3 Boughton*
4 Kingsthorpe
5 Moulton*
6 Northampton
7 Pitsford*
8 Spratton
9 Weston Favell*

Sutton (Su)
1 Aynho*
2 Charlton*
3 Croughton*
4 Farthinghoe
5 Grimsbury* (OXON)
6 Middleton Cheney*
7 Newbottle*
8 Purston*
9 Kings Sutton
10 Thenford*
11 Walton Grounds

Towcester (T)
1 Astcote
2 Foxley*
3 Cold Higham*
4 Pattishall
5 Tiffield
6 Towcester
7 Wappenham*

Warden (Wa)
1 Aston le Walls
2 Boddington
3 Byfield*
4 Edgcote*
5 Eydon
6 West Farndon*
7 Greatworth
8 Hinton*
9 Mollington (OXON)
10 Stoneton* (WARKS)
11 Sulgrave*
12 Trafford
13 Chipping Warden
14 Woodford Halse

Wymersley (Wy)
1 Castle Ashby
2 Brafield on the Green
3 Chadstone*
4 Cogenhoe
5 Denton*
6 Grendon
7 Hackleton*
8 Horton
9 Houghton*
10 Piddington
11 Preston Deanery
12 Quinton
13 Whiston*
14 Wootton*
15 Yardley Hastings*

Places not Mapped, Hundred Unknown
Hantone
Waletone

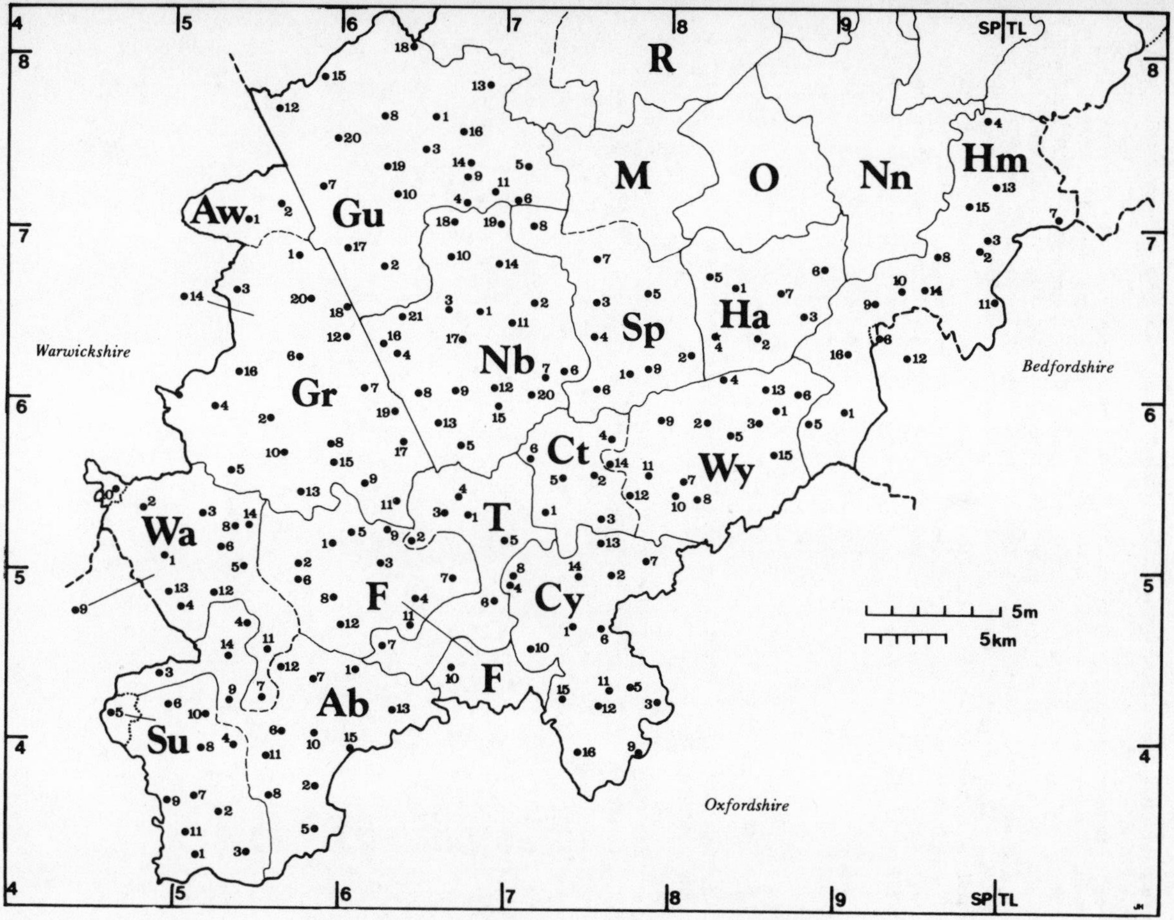

NORTHAMPTONSHIRE SOUTHERN HUNDREDS

SYSTEMS OF REFERENCE TO DOMESDAY BOOK

The manuscript is divided into numbered chapters, and the chapters into sections, usually marked by large initials and red ink. Farley, however, did not number the sections. References have therefore been inexact, by folio numbers, which cannot be closer than an entire page or column. Moreover, half a dozen different ways of referring to the same column have been devised. In 1816 Ellis used three separate systems in his indices; (i) on pages i - cvii; 435-518; 537-570; (ii) on pages 1-144; (iii) on pages 145-433 and 519-535. Other systems have since come into use, notably that used by Vinogradoff, here followed. This edition numbers the sections, the normal practicable form of close reference; but since all discussion of Domesday for three hundred years has been obliged to refer to page or column, a comparative table will help to locate references given. The five columns below give Vinogradoff's notation, Ellis' three systems, and that employed by Welldon Finn and others. Maitland, Stenton, Darby and others have usually followed Ellis (i).

Vinogradoff	*Ellis (i)*	*Ellis (ii)*	*Ellis (iii)*	
152 a	152	152 a	152	152 ai
152 b	152	152 a	152.2	152 a2
152 c	152 b	152 b	152 b	152 bi
152 d	152 b	152 b	152 b2	152 b2

In Northamptonshire, the relation between the Vinogradoff column notation, here followed, and the chapters and sections is

219a	Boroughs			223a	18,1	-	18,15	227a	41,6	-	43,5
b	Landholders. 1,1-3			b	18,15	-	18,34	b	43,5	-	45,5
c	1,4	-	1,13	c	18,34	-	18,53	c	45,5	-	47,2
d	1,13	-	1,20	d	18,54	-	18,71	d	48,1	-	48,17
220a	1,21	-	1,32	224a	18,72	-	18,89	228a	49,1	-	55,6
b	2,1	-	3,1	b	18,90-21,6. 19,2-3			b	56,1	-	56,20
c	4,1	-	4,11	c	23,1-15.		24,1	c	56,20	-	56,31
d	4,12	-	4,27	d	23,16-19.		22,1-9	d	56,32	-	56,46
221a	4,28	-	5,3	225a	25,1	-	26,9	229a	56,46	-	56,64
b	5,4	-	6,10	b	26,9	-	30,9	b	56,65	-	60,5
c	6,10	-	6a,6	c	30,10	-	[34],.1				
d	6a,7	-	6a,22	d	[35], 1	-	[35], 7				
222a	6a,23	-	6a,34	226a	[35], 8	-	[35],21				
b	7,1	-	9,6	b	[35], 22-		[38],1				
c	9,6	-	12,4	c	39,1	-	39,17				
d	13,1	-	17,5	d	39,18	-	41,5				

TECHNICAL TERMS

Many words meaning measurements have to be transliterated. But translation may not dodge other problems by the use of obsolete or made-up words which do not exist in modern English. The translations here used are given in italics. They cannot be exact; they aim at the nearest modern equivalent.

B. Marginal abbreviation for *Berewica*. *B.*

BEREWICA. An outlying place, attached to a manor. *outlier*

BORDARIUS. Cultivator of inferior status, usually with a little land. *smallholder*

BOVATA. A measure of land, usually an eighth of a *carucate*. *bovate*

CARUCA. A plough, with the oxen that pulled it, usually reckoned as 8. *plough*

CARUCATA. Normally the equivalent of the hide in former Danish areas (see 1,5 note). *carucate*

DOMINIUM. The mastery or dominion of a lord (*dominus*); including ploughs, land, men, villagers etc., reserved for the lord's use; often concentrated in a *home farm* or *demesne*, a 'Manor Farm' or 'Lordship Farm'. *Lordship*

FEUDUM. Continental variant of *feuum* not used in England before 1066; either a landholder's total holding, or land held by special grant. *Holding*

FIRMA. Old English *feorm*, provisions due to the King or lord, or a sum paid in place of these and other miscellaneous dues. *revenue*

GELDUM. The principal royal tax, originally levied during the Danish wars, normally at an equal number of pence on each *hide* of land. *tax*

HIDA. A unit of land measurement, generally reckoned at 120 acres but often different in practice; a measure of tax liability, often differing in number from the hides actually cultivated (see 1,1 note). *hide*

HUNDRED. A district within a Shire, whose assembly of notables and village representatives usually met about once a month. *Hundred*

INLAND. Old English lord's land, usually exempt from tax, comparable with *dominium*. *inland*

LEUGA. A measure of length, probably about a mile and a half (see 1,6 note). *league*

M. Marginal abbreviation for *manerium*, manor. *M.*

PERCA, PERTICA. A measure of length, 5½ yards, a 40th of a furlong (3,1 note). *perch*

PRAEPOSITUS, PRAEFECTUS. Old English *gerefa*, a royal officer. *reeve*

S. Marginal abbreviation for *Soca*. *S*

SACA. German *sache*, English *sake*, Latin *causa*, 'affair', 'lawsuit'; the fullest authority normally exercised by a lord, (2,1 note). *full jurisdiction*

SOCA. 'Soke', from *socn* 'to seek', comparable with Latin *quaestio*; jurisdiction with the right to receive fines and a multiplicity of other dues; district in which such *soca* is exercised; a place in a *soca*. *jurisdiction*

SOCMANNUS, SOCHEMAN. 'Soke man', exercising or subject to jurisdiction; free from many villagers' burdens; before 1066 often with more land and status than villagers (see Bedfordshire, Middlesex Appendices); bracketed in the Commissioners' brief with the *liber homo* (free man). *Freeman*

TAINUS, TEGNUS. Person holding land from the King by special grant, formerly used of the King's ministers and military companions. *thane*

T.R.E. *tempore regis Edwardi*, in King Edward's time. *before 1066*

VILLA. Translating Old English *tun*, town. The later distinction between a small *village* and a large *town* was not yet in use in 1086. *village* or *town*

VILLANUS. Member of a *villa*, usually with more land than a *bordarius*. *villager*

VIRGATA. A fraction of a *hide*, usually a quarter, notionally 30 acres. *virgate*

WAPENTAC. Equivalent of the English *Hundred* in Danish areas. *Wapentake*